MARY H in journal newspaper desire to travel took her first to London where she produced in-house business magazines and later to Holland, where she edited a global company newspaper. This was followed by relocation to Africa and then the Middle East. She moved to Spain in the late 1980s and enjoyed some 20 years there as a radio broadcaster. In 2006 she was awarded the "Communicator of the Year Award" for her series of programmes The Tsunami – One Year On, charting the reconstruction process in Sri Lanka.

It was in Marbella – after meeting Jenny Gucci – that Mary became interested in the real story behind the world's biggest fashion house and *Gucci Wars* was first published in 2008. Three years later she returned to the UK to produce website content for two Harley Street eye clinics. She also retrained as a Celebrant, creating bespoke ceremonies, including weddings, funerals and naming celebrations. With two adult children, and recently re-married, Mary has now returned to her roots in the beautiful Norfolk countryside where she's currently writing her first novel.

For more information please visit www.maryharboe.com

GUCCI WARS

JENNY GUCCI'S STORY

MARY HARBOE

Best wishes
M Harboe

SilverWood

Published in 2021 by SilverWood Books

SilverWood Books Ltd
14 Small Street, Bristol, BS1 1DE, United Kingdom
www.silverwoodbooks.co.uk

ISBN 978-1-80042-156-1 (paperback)
ISBN 978-1-80042-157-8 (ebook)

British Library Cataloguing in Publication Data
A CIP catalogue record for this book is
available from the British Library

Page design and typesetting by SilverWood Books

GUCCI WARS
JENNY GUCCI'S STORY

Dedication

Over the years many people have suggested that I should write a book about my life as a Gucci, but somehow, until I got to know my good friend Mary Harboe (in Marbella, in the early 2000s), the time never seemed quite right. Then, over countless cups of tea, I told her about the reality of life at the heart of the world's most iconic fashion house.

More recently, in 2021, we have got together again to update *Gucci Wars*. Back in 2007, I said there was more to come…and I was not wrong! Mary has listened patiently to it all and now, through her, I can share the full story.

With special thanks to

My dear, dear friend, Francis Butler, thank you from the bottom of my heart. You are one of the kindest, most generous hearted people…and certainly the naughtiest!

My 'New York Boys' – Joseph, Mario and Joe DeLeo and others who know who they are – I couldn't have made it without you.

Vicky McKenzie, for her spiritual help, wine and chorizo.

Peter Black and Phillip Kremmen for all their advice and guidance.

Sue Puddefoot – who is always there for me and makes me laugh… what a sister!

And not forgetting my dear niece Lucy who insists on a mention!

And, of course, my darling Gemma for her unstinting love. She has always been – and will always be – my everything…my world.

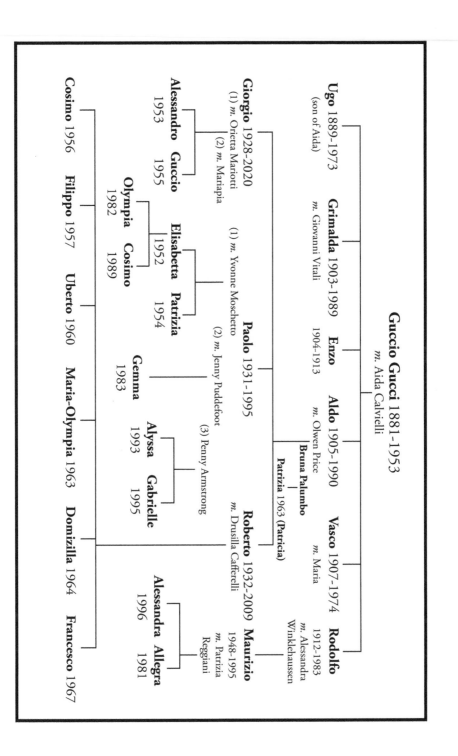

Contents

Foreword

West London, April 2021

"So, husband, you're late! What time do you call this?"

He grinned and then we both burst out laughing. After the explanation for the slightly delayed start (someone had written down an incorrect digit for my phone number), Jared Leto and I greeted each other properly, and then chatted about Rome where he was filming at the time. He was utterly delightful, gorgeous and very LA.

Jared Leto might not have been an obvious choice to play my husband, Paolo Gucci, in the upcoming Ridley Scott film "House of Gucci". He looks nothing like Paolo, but Jared is a master of disguise as anyone who has followed his career will know. More importantly, he is one of that rare breed of actors who doesn't just mimic the character he plays – he has the ability to morph into them, almost becoming another person – unrecognisable in every respect. This is achieved not just with the help of prosthetics and skilful make up artists, but also by adopting the small gestures and detailed characteristics of the part he is portraying. No doubt, he takes his craft seriously which includes scrupulous research, and I was only too happy to help him discover more about the personality of the man I had fallen in love with and married in 1977.

Apart from spending some quality virtual time with a good-looking Hollywood star, what was my motivation for doing the interview? This was a no-brainer. Since I had first heard that a film was to be made about the Gucci family of this period, I was worried as to how Paolo would be portrayed.

"I just couldn't bear it if they make him out to be a horrible person," I told my friend, writer Mary Harboe, when she announced that Jared Leto's office had been in touch.

Whatever cruel things he had done against me, Paolo still deserved to be recognised for his tremendous design skills and the great contribution he made to the Gucci brand – without him, there might never have been a ready-to-wear range.

Jared and I chatted away, for over an hour. We covered Paolo's habits – his gestures – the way he walked as well as the difficulties he had faced working within the family business. Jared wanted to know that Paolo was not a 'bad' person; and I was able to confirm that he had been a loving and devoted husband right up until the day that he sold his shares – it was then, when he had come into unlimited wealth, that his personality had radically changed and the rot had set in.

Having read the measures that Jared was prepared to take for authenticity in a role, I wanted to know if he had shaved off his iconic, long flowing hair. I told him that I was quite envious of his hair and he removed the baseball cap he was wearing backwards to show me that it had only been trimmed to shoulder length. As he stood up to also show me the spectacular knitted jacket – decorated with daffodils and lily-of-the-valley – that he was wearing, it struck me how calm and together he was.

It felt strange to be talking to the man who would portray my husband on film. I couldn't help but realise that only I would notice the tiny details that would give the seal of approval to the authenticity of his performance. As we became acquainted, I knew he would do a wonderful job of playing Paolo – the real person who had loved and been loved – as a son, a brother, and a husband…and yet someone who had also been disliked in equal measure. There are very few of us left who, like me, remember the Gucci dynasty in its heyday.

The current Gucci management are collaborating with the film and have granted the production company "total creative freedom". However, while back catalogues and archives showing the designs and fabrics of the day have been made available, only I could answer this actor's questions regarding Paolo's gait, his voice or the gestures he made with his hands. I was extremely grateful that Jared had made the effort to get to know the complicated character of Paolo. We made each other laugh – but, more importantly, he allayed my concerns. I felt reassured putting Paolo's memory in Jared Leto's hands.

That said, I am not sure that Paolo's daughter, the extremely vocal Patrizia, would agree. After seeing photos of the film shooting in Italy she hit out against the "horrible, horrible and ugly" casting. She claimed to be "offended" after seeing pictures of Jared Leto in character and the "shameful" representation of her tall and striking grandfather, Aldo, by the somewhat shorter and stouter Al Pacino.

Maybe, she's not wrong. In reality the Gucci men had all appeared classy and Aldo, especially, was incredibly charismatic…they didn't behave classily; but they looked it. However, putting the casting aesthetics aside, it is the *inside* story of the Gucci family that is at times shameful and embarrassing and this film will once again shine the spotlight on a deeply damaged family torn apart by dishonesty, jealousy, betrayal and greed… to say nothing of cruelty and murder. This was the family that I married into. It had been *my* family too.

Later, when I mentally replayed the conversation with Jared, there was one question that he had asked me that kept repeating in my head: "Jenny, do you miss, being a Gucci and all that life had to offer?"

At the time I had made a flippant reply about no longer fitting into Gucci clothes – which favour size zero models – then I confided to him that I had sometimes missed being husband and wife – part of a couple – who had loved each other very much. But I don't miss that life now.

To further complicate the story, there are three Patrizias in the Gucci family. Recently a documentary researcher from the German television company RTL, asked me a question I had never been asked before: "Why so many Patrizias?" My answer was a somewhat dismissive "Go figure," but, on reflection, it was a rather good question. Actually there is no answer – even within the family at the time, it had caused countless misunderstandings and confusions.

The original and first Patrizia (my outspoken step-daughter) is the second daughter of Paolo and his first wife Yvonne Moschetto. She was born in 1954 and for as long as I can remember, she has had a reputation for being somewhat difficult. Certainly she has made it clear in various press outbursts that she is not a fan of the new film. In addition to grumbling about the cast being too ugly to portray the Guccis, she has also complained that the producers "are stealing the identity of a family to make profit, to increase the income of the Hollywood system". I happen to disagree. There is massive global interest in all things Gucci, and I am certain that, as a businessman, Aldo would have approved…he would have loved the attention.

Why, Aldo, (Paolo's father) should give his love child the same name as his then nine year old granddaughter is not known and frankly unfathomable. Even with the English version of the name, Patricia, it was bound to create further complications to an already distinctly awkward situation when at the age of ten she and her mother – the love of Aldo's life – Bruna Palumbo, moved from London back to Rome.

Patricia Gucci had been born in the UK and, for the first year of her life, was hidden away so that no-one outside her immediate family knew of her existence and she was brought up with no idea that her father had another family. When Patricia and her mother set up home with Aldo in the US, she would frequently accompany her father to charity and society events. In New York we were neighbours and Bruna liked to keep a low profile – she lived almost as a recluse – preferring that her daughter take the spotlight beside Aldo. I remember Patricia as a tall and striking teenager – intelligent, sharp and extremely good looking. She was also likeable, despite always speaking her mind. I admired her for not being afraid of criticising the Gucci hierarchy. Back in Italy, Patricia would attend business meetings with her father and, at the age of 19, she broke what had always been considered to be the impenetrable Gucci glass celling by becoming the first woman to sit on the board of directors. She also became Aldo's sole heir.

You can't choose the name of the person you fall in love with and marry – even if you are the notable playboy Maurizio Gucci. Which brings us to the third Patrizia in the family – the infamous Patrizia Reggiani – later to be known as "The Black Widow". Unsurprisingly, this Patrizia prefers the epithet "Lady Gucci", and has publicly criticised Lady Gaga – who is to portray her in The House of Gucci film. She is reported as having told the Italian Press: "I am rather annoyed at the fact that Lady Gaga is playing me in the new Ridley Scott film without having had the consideration and sensibility to come and meet me. It is a question of good sense and respect."

Is it just me, or wouldn't you be more concerned about reliving the trauma of murdering your husband in a Hollywood blockbuster than the social niceties, or otherwise, of the film's leading lady. If I had been Lady Gaga, I wouldn't have paid her a visit either.

Since her early release from prison in 2014, Patrizia has never shown remorse or regret. On the contrary, she has maintained her audacious facade and still has the knack of coming out with inappropriate statements. Famously she turned down the first offer of early release (in 2011) on discovering that finding a job was a condition of her parole.

"I've never worked a day in my life," she told her shocked lawyer, "and I don't intend to start now."

Three years later, after taking the post of "design consultant" at a Milanese costume jewellery firm, she would celebrate her freedom by shopping in the city's *Via Monte Napoleone* (the equivalent of London's Bond Street) with a large tame macaw perched on her shoulder. Clearly, Lady Gucci had no intention of keeping a low profile. Although – even by her standards – an Italian TV crew couldn't believe their luck when they caught on camera the following exchange:

"Patrizia, why did you hire a hit man to kill Maurizio Gucci? Why didn't you kill him yourself?" the reporter demanded.

"My eyesight is not so good – I didn't want to miss," was her reckless reply.

What Patrizia Reggiani lacks in the conscience department she more than makes up for with *chutzpah*. Despite everything that has happened, in a recent interview she claimed to still be an asset to the Gucci brand. "They need me, I still feel like a Gucci – in fact I am the most Gucci of them all." This particular quote got me thinking. 'What *did* it feel like to be a Gucci – let alone – the most Gucci of them all?'

'Gucci' is – second only to *Coca-Cola* – the most recognised brand name in the world. No other name, which is also a brand, carries the same universal spark of recognition. There are no parallels – the word 'Gucci', and all that it conjures up, is totally international, global and unique.

Even after 44 years it still happens. I introduce myself and then wait a moment as my surname registers. This is usually followed by a simple request: "May I ask you something…?" and I know what's coming next…

"Yes," I reply, "I was married to the designer".

On hearing my surname is 'Gucci' sometimes people will joke, "Oh that's a nice name…can you get me any handbags or shoes free?" Depending on my mood, my response to "that's a nice name" might be a curt "you think?"

But what is it *really* like to be a Gucci? Here's my story which I hope will go some way to explain.

Prologue

Connecticut, March 1993

He looked the same. I don't know why, but I had somehow expected his appearance to have changed and was surprised to note that it hadn't. Several months had elapsed since I had last seen him and, although his sparse grey hair was possibly a bit longer, for the rest he looked like the man I had fallen in love with and married. He was still dressed in his classic, understated style with perfectly-cut, grey flannel trousers and a cashmere jacket. It was a look that might, to the casual observer, appear effortless but, in fact, costs a small fortune to achieve. It was a look that Paolo Gucci had down to perfection. It was slightly shocking that someone could change their personality so drastically but still appear the same on the outside.

My lawyer Peter Bronstein and I had been waiting in a car across the street for about half an hour. There wasn't much happening in this quiet corner of the town of Darien, Connecticut, where I had been told that my husband was in cahoots with a group of dubious cronies. My lawyer was there to take notes of where and with whom Paolo was doing business and present them later that day to the court.

Although the Supreme Court in Manhattan had become like a second home to me over the preceding months, this would be our first appearance out of New York State. While I wasn't sure of the legal significance, I welcomed the fact that at least something was happening and that Paolo would be legally obliged to pay maintenance money for our daughter Gemma. It felt like a stake-out in some television detective drama – the sort of programme that, in a previous life, Paolo and I had loved to watch curled up on the sofa together.

I saw him first. He paused briefly at the top of the steps to put on his sunglasses before walking briskly down, his Gucci briefcase in his hand. He looked tanned, fit and vibrant and was clearly heading towards his car when three plain-clothes Caribinieri [members of the Italian federal police force] blocked his path. Up until then, I hadn't realised that we were not the only ones waiting on this quiet city street for Paolo Gucci to emerge from the red-brick office block.

I could hear voices being raised as Paolo demanded to speak to his lawyer as his rights were read out to him and his wrists handcuffed firmly behind his back. His briefcase was taken from him as he was unceremoniously bundled into the back of the unmarked car between the two officers. As they drove away, Paolo turned round and looked out the back window. I can't be sure, but I think he saw me staring open-mouthed in surprise. He also looked shocked as if he, too, couldn't believe what had just happened.

For a few seconds, I felt sorry for him. I knew he had been vile to me but I wondered if he had fully understood the consequences of what he had got himself into. This was the man I had travelled the world with, my lover and companion who rubbed my back during childbirth, who held my hand when I crossed the road, who taught me about taste and elegance, and introduced me to the Gucci fashion dynasty. He had been loving and caring to my family and had often surprised me with spontaneous gifts of exquisite jewellery. We had been such a great team.

Memories tumbled over each other…we were together in the Tuscan countryside waiting for the pigeons to come home; me swathed in furs enjoying our favourite Swiss lunch of *bratwurst* in a crispy roll on a chilly terrace in Lugano; modelling the first Gucci swimwear line in Palm Beach; dressed up to the nines at glittering charity galas in New York; our heads together poring over fashion designs and sample swatches; him laughing uncontrollably as I sang 'I could have danced all night…' for the seventh time at a geisha house in Kyoto; cups of tea and slices of cake shared comfortingly in the middle of the night when he couldn't sleep. It was all too much.

It seemed incredible that it could have come to this – Paolo Gucci being arrested and sent to prison for the violation of a court order to pay child maintenance. Why wouldn't he give me my freedom and accept a settlement? Why was he being so cruel and prepared to go to such lengths to hurt me?

It was then that I lost it. I sobbed uncontrollably, my face in my hands, as hot tears spilled through my fingers and onto my trousers. Peter Bronstein put a comforting arm around my shoulders. 'This is as bad as it gets, Jen,' he said softly. 'You just have to get through this, and then it will be sorted. You'll see, he'll come to his senses after a night in the cells.'

But my lawyer was wrong. He had underestimated the determination of Paolo Gucci, who had vowed to leave me destitute and sworn that he would never give me a penny.

There was much, much worse to come.

I

Ballet Shoes and Bullies

The sound of the bell marking the end of another school day as usual brought mixed emotions. Although I longed to be out of the place and back home, I hated the thought of getting there.

I pushed back my chair and sorted the books needed for homework into my satchel. Maybe this evening would be different. Maybe I would open them and read the marked pages to prepare for tomorrow's classes. Maybe I would...but most probably they would remain untouched, as usual. It was not that I was a lazy pupil, more that I was completely de-motivated. Somehow I felt oddly disconnected and disinterested. Tomorrow I would muddle through another academic day just as I had muddled through this one.

Actually, today hadn't been too bad. The afternoon needlework session was almost enjoyable and the skirt that I had designed with the quirky patch pockets was taking shape nicely. From its unlikely beginnings as a lime-green swatch of sailcloth, it was emerging as a rather chic fashion statement. I noticed some of the other girls had looked at it rather enviously. If only I had a few more womanly curves to hang it on, but my figure remained stubbornly straight up and down – my breasts were still virtually non-existent and my hips positively boyish. Oh God, talking of boys…they'd all been whispering in an ominous huddle before leaving the classroom. It didn't bode well for the walk home.

Sure enough, the gang was there again – one bright spark decided to distract me. 'Well, if it isn't that posh cow, Puddy Foot…' he drawled, and while I turned to face the yob in question, another stuck out his foot to trip me up. Balance had never been my strong suit and I stumbled in an undignified way.

Insults and cruel name-calling were the norm. Why couldn't I have had a nice normal name? Why hadn't my mother – with the relatively acceptable maiden name of Nora New – have fallen in love with someone other than Toby Puddefoot? And here I was, their second daughter, not only burdened with such a surname but also taller and thinner than everyone else and somehow completely different. Even the way I speak is different, not that I speak with an upper-class accent. I just – according to my mother, anyway – speak 'properly', which also includes being grammatically correct. Not that you'd ever notice it from my marks in English. Anyway, I had decided to opt for an easier life and, in a pathetic attempt to blend in, to drop into the same north London accent as my classmates. But even at 11, I knew that it was a futile exercise as the true differences ran far deeper than just my vowel sounds and throwing in the odd swear word.

How many other 11-year-olds in a secondary modern school liked to sing excerpts from the operettas *Die Fledermaus* or *The Gypsy Baron* by Johann Strauss the Younger? Was there anyone else out there who dreamed of singing classical soprano roles? Possibly wearing a stunning green skirt with stylish patch pockets – albeit the evening silk version – with matching top, bowing her head graciously at the end of a spectacular performance at Covent Garden to rapturous applause? It would seem unlikely. But my daydream was shattered by the very unmelodious, menacing catcalls of my classmates. 'Duck face! Let's get her!' shouted Kevin the gang leader, encouraging the rest of his mates into action.

'F*****g Puddy Foot,' snarled Graham, who was always the first to swear.

'Lanky pants – just 'cos you sing in the choir you think you're soooooo special,' snarled Laura, who had the dubious honour of being the only female bully in the gang.

And so it went on…my blazer was the wrong shade of blue, my hair was ridiculous, my legs too long and spindly. Their cruel jibes echoed on and on.

A quiet, inner voice told me to keep my head down and not to react, but it was quickly drowned out by a gasp and scream from me as my hair was tugged…this horrible, burly, sweaty, spotty bully was hanging on to a fistful of my hair in his none-too-clean hand. I was close enough to see his bitten nails and ink-stained fingers. Suddenly, I was fighting back. I bit his wrist and, quick as a flash, felt the searing pain in my other arm which was held in a vice-like grip as the skin was pushed and pulled agonisingly in a crippling Chinese burn.

How dare they attack me like this? Pain and humiliation were replaced by anger as I fought back, kicking wildly, as a volley of blows hammered into my back.

Ouch…it really hurt that day, even more than usual. After what seemed like an hour – but was probably no more than ten minutes – I finally made my escape with the sneers and hateful jibes still ringing in my ears and my eyes smarting. One against three certainly isn't fair and there's no doubt that I had come off worse. The logical voice inside my head wondered if they would leave me alone if I didn't fight back or react to the name-calling. But it makes me feel so angry, frustrated and unhappy. I cannot believe that school days are meant to be the happiest of your life. I hate school – absolutely everything about it. I have nothing in common with my classmates who are horrible, and the academic lessons – with the possible exception of geography – are boring and irrelevant. Needlework and music don't count and only make up about an hour a week of the overall timetable.

All I remember about secondary school is the incessant bullying and cruel taunts in the school corridors, playground and surrounding streets and, in between, there were the dreaded lessons to be endured. I don't know why I never told anyone or reported the bullying attacks to a teacher. I imagine I was afraid it would make it worse. My parents never commented on the bruises or the fact that one of their children hated school with a passion that she normally reserved only for her love of classical music. Meanwhile, my sister Sue was blazing a successful trail through the same school with what seemed like a nice friendly group of chums two years ahead of me.

When we were young, my sister and I weren't exactly close. We didn't argue or fight; we just didn't really get on. It wasn't until much later, when I was 18 or 19, that we became close but, as children, we were completely different: I was noisy; she was quiet. I was bossy but definitely not academic; she was studious and brainy. In fact, when I was little, we were so different that I convinced myself she was an alien.

She had been very ill with a serious heart condition for the first five years of her life and it must have been terribly worrying for my parents. I suppose although we loved each other as members of the same family, I would never have felt able to confide in her.

Sometimes, I thought about sharing my misery with my mother, but somehow, as the words started to form reluctantly in my brain, something would stop me. I would look into her loving face and notice how tired she looked and how worried about the lack of money.

My mother was an ingenious housekeeper. Although money was always really tight, we ate well with home-grown vegetables from the back garden and the cake tins were always full of fresh and delicious home baking. She was of the generation who believed that a woman's place was in the home and so, as my father's business plummeted, she would always find a way of bringing in extra money to stretch the housekeeping. For many years, we took in a lodger and that really helped a lot.

Some nights, after my sister and I were tucked up in bed, we would hear them arguing. It would always be my mother's voice that would carry through the walls.

'How *could* you, Toby? How will we manage if we have to sell the house? Where will we go?' As her voice became shriller with frustration,

27

my father's responses remained muted and calmly quiet. Whether or not it was planned, this had the effect of infuriating her even more.

Sue and I feared that one or both of them would leave or that we would lose our house and end up living homeless on the street. It was a shame that we didn't share our fears until many years later and both suffered these night-time arguments alone – each in our own bedroom burying our heads in our pillows.

Usually, the mood had lifted by the morning – or our parents were good at putting on an act. Things would usually appear back to normal around the Puddefoot breakfast table and my fears and unhappiness would remain unsaid. How could I add to my poor mother's burdens by telling her of my unhappiness at school? In fact, I became increasingly adept at blocking it out as I retreated further into a fantasy world of pink, floaty dresses, operatic performances and boys who would fall in love with me.

Outside the school gates, things were different and I had several girlfriends in the neighbourhood – friends with whom I played in the streets around Hendon and shared adventures. I was especially close to Christine. On Saturday afternoons, we would sneak into the back of John Keeble Church in Edgware where we would watch the weddings and imagine how our own would be. It was a really girlie thing to dream of one day being a beautiful bride in a gorgeous dress marrying my own Prince Charming.

My parents had had me quite late in life. My mother was 42 when I was born on 16 January 1948. I was a big baby – over 9lb and my poor mother, at a mere 7st, was a tiny woman. It had been a long, cold labour, most of which my mother, for some unknown reason, was forced to spend on a chilled marble surface in Harrow Hospital (later Northwick Park) that left her with a lingering back problem that lasted a lifetime.

As I look back on my childhood, I cannot remember a time before there was music. Beethoven and Chopin were my father's favourites and, in my memory, they were always playing in the background whenever he was around. My mother had a pleasant singing voice and she'd often sing for pleasure around the house but would never have dreamed of taking her talent and developing it further. It would not have occurred to her to do so.

I adored ballet music – Tchaikovsky's *Sugar Plum Fairy* and *Swan Lake* would go round and round in my head as I skipped about my room. In the privacy of my bedroom, I became a prima ballerina, gracefully pirouetting, extending a leg behind in a neat *arabesque* and my *chassés* almost literally brought the house down.

I must have been about 5 years old when – after what felt like a lifetime of wheedling and pleading – my parents finally consented and let me join the local ballet school which met at the John Keeble Church Hall on Wednesday afternoons for classes with Miss Neep who wore golden ballet slippers. Children came from throughout north London to practice for dance festivals with Miss Neep and no one was remotely bothered that she looked more like the TV comedienne Hattie Jacques than dancing legend Margot Fonteyn.

I was in seventh heaven to be almost within touching distance of the magical world of dance. I had my own ballet shoes and the regulation red-and-black outfit and knew that it was only a matter of time before I, too, would own a net skirt and be allowed to go up on my points like the big girls.

But sadly, my career as a dancer was destined never to be. At first, everything was fine and I was able to keep up with the barre work and basic ballet positions. I limbered up, stretched and '*plié-ed*' with the others while gracefully extending my arms, hands and fingers positioned as instructed. Ballet class was everything I had ever dreamed of – I loved the music and hummed away happily as my muscles were extended and stretched.

The problems began when I left the comfort of the wall. In the middle of the room, I was a complete disaster. Miss Neep was quick to spot my inabilities and moved me to the centre of the class so that I might follow the better students at the front, but that didn't work. Then she moved me to the front to give me some extra attention, but I kept losing my balance and falling over, which seemed to distract the whole class. So then I was dispatched to the back of the room. But when it became horribly obvious to everyone – except me – that I clearly lacked the co-ordination to be a dancer and that enthusiasm alone was not going to be enough to get me through the Grade 1 exams, my mother was called in.

Mummy broke it to me as tactfully as she could: 'Darling, you have to be a bit older to do this type of ballet.' But it didn't help for I knew that there were other girls in the class who were the same age as me. I was heartbroken and still feel sad to this day as I recall my first huge disappointment and taste of failure.

I would have loved to go to the ballet at Covent Garden, but my parents couldn't afford the tickets and it wasn't really my father's favourite type of music. But it wasn't all doom and gloom as my sister and I were taken to concerts and the annual audio festival in Russell Square, where we would listen to different hi-fi systems. My father had a wonderful ear – music was at the core of his soul – and I learned to tune mine at an early age. I might not have had the balance or poise required for ballet, but my voice was coming on a treat.

Sadly, any skill I had vocally was lost on the thugs at school. The bullying happened on a regular basis, about twice a week, throughout my time at secondary school. It was destined to continue until I left three years later at the age of 14 – and I couldn't wait.

And finally – bliss, wonderful news, I was to leave school! It was on the advice of the headmaster who had admitted to my mother that I was somehow 'in with a very rough crowd' and, by his own admission, 'the worst class in the school'.

With hindsight, I think I was depressed – I knew that, although everyone at school seemed to hate me, there was nothing really wrong with me. I was just somehow different, all-round unpopular girl who simply didn't fit in at the Mill Hill Moat Mount Secondary Modern.

Whatever problems I had growing up, I always felt loved at home. Although in the dark, night-time hours I might have doubted that my parents loved each other, I never once doubted that they both loved me. My father was a man working in the wrong profession. He should never have been a 'businessman'. Maybe he would have been more successful in a more nuts-and-bolts profession like electronic engineering, something that would have given him satisfaction and the sense of something achieved at the end of the day. Instead, he had – completely inappropriately – inherited his brother's bookmaking business in Hendon and, from almost day one, it became horribly apparent that he wasn't any good at it. His judgement was flawed and his handling of money – his own, as well as other people's – was pretty disastrous However, despite the late-night arguments, I had a very happy and secure early childhood, especially before the horrors of my secondary school.

When I look back and relive the childhood disappointments and the misery of being a victim of bullies, I realize that it all helped to make me become a strong and independent fighter. Obviously, a skinny adolescent would be no match physically for a determined gang of bullies, but the attacks built within me not only an inner core strength that would last a lifetime, but also the determination to fight back – even when the odds were stacked against me. Never again would I be daunted by insults. I might not have achieved much in the way of academic success during my school days, but I had learned how to be strong and survive whatever life would throw at me. I also became aware, during those afternoon pavement scuffles, that you cannot rely on anyone else to fight your battles...I would always have to fight mine alone.

2

Dreams and Ambitions

It was one of those wonderful London afternoons when you know anything is possible. There was a real buzz of anticipation in the air and I didn't need the appreciative wolf whistles of workmen to tell me that I looked pretty good in my new, black-velvet hot pants. The purple, knitted waistcoat was also a success over a chiffon blouse with its 'pussycat' bow tied tastefully at the neck, tassel ends flapping in the spring breeze. The whole outfit – not forgetting the new, black, shiny boots – had set me back almost a week's wages, but it was most definitely worth every penny. At 17, being tall and slender was a distinct advantage. My long legs were no longer the butt of jokes more the object of envy among my peers. Ha, this ugly duckling was blossoming into a rather splendid swan.

The day I left school was one of the happiest of my life. At last, I could enter the sophisticated world of adulthood. Although I had wanted to go to stage school, my parents thought a secretarial course would be far more useful and so I was enrolled into a Pitman Training College, where, for the next two years, my life consisted of spiral-bound note books and pencil squiggles on, above and through the line. I took to shorthand, typing, bookkeeping and general office skills like a duck to water and landed a job as a part-time dental assistant. This later evolved into a trainee dental nurse and, after some more studying at the Eastman Dental Hospital, led to my earning the RDSA qualification (Registered Dental Surgical Assistant). I loved the medical side of my work and actually assisted in dental operations such as wisdom teeth extractions.

Thursdays were my favourite day – they always felt especially full of promise. There was a bounce in my step and a crisp, new copy of *The Stage* newspaper in my shoulder bag as I headed towards Hanover Street, W1, for one of my bi-weekly singing lessons with the maestro Harold Miller.

It had been difficult to be accepted as one of his pupils. Harold did not need to take just anybody – he concentrated on the really big names and possible up-and-coming new talent. Luckily, after an audition, I learned that I fell into the latter category. I loved being there, soaking up the atmosphere and absorbing the advice of such a great teacher. While singing, I am always at my happiest and it was so exciting to be surrounded by so much talent. You never knew who you'd meet on the stairs.

Some days, my lessons were scheduled between Barbra Streisand – who liked to warm up with Harold before performing in *Funny Girl* – and Anna Neagle, before she became a Dame. I couldn't understand why Anna Neagle, who must have been a very busy lady, was always early for her appointment until, one day, I was stunned when she told me that she liked to come early so that she could listen to my 'gorgeous' voice. I was embarrassed, but glowing with pleasure inside as well. Harold also taught Shirley Bassey, Juliet Prowse and even coached the young Sean Connery for his role in *South Pacific*. I couldn't have been in better company.

One day, I caught myself listening to the most amazing rendition of Tosca's *Vissi D'Arte*. The singer was young, like me, but she could manage the entire finale phrase in one breath. I was later introduced to Elaine Paige and she really tried to help me by singing this special sequence right in front of me, but I still found it impossible without taking a breath. It would be several years before I would manage to match her technical excellence, but I was secretly quite pleased with the sound I was now able to make. Others, who must have known, seemed similarly impressed.

On this particular afternoon, I was feeling pretty confident as I flipped through the new copy of my favourite magazine…and there was the announcement that auditions would be held for a new West End musical, *Pickwick*, starring Harry Secombe.

My voice coach Harold was full of encouragement, 'Absolutely, you should go for it, Jenny. There's an *ingénue* soprano role that would be perfect for you.'

And that's how, a few days later, I found myself on the stage in front of a panel of the producers for the first of what would be four auditions. I sang 'Waltz of My Heart' from Ivor Novello's *The Dancing Years* and Noel Coward's 'I'll See You Again'. They thought it was wonderful as all the other hopefuls had chosen pop songs.

After the fourth call-back, the director, the late Peter Coe (who then lived with Jenny Seagrove), took me aside and told me the part was mine. Then he asked the dreaded question: 'Have you got an Equity card?'

In those days, it was crucially important. The show's directors tried for six weeks to get me one. They tried everything, but Equity just said 'No' again and again. Apparently, I had to have done at least 40 weeks in the provinces, or have successfully completed an accredited course at a stage school and, of course, I fulfilled none of the criteria.

Eventually, the show's director gave up, and who could blame him? Peter Coe said he was heartbroken as I was perfect for the part, but they couldn't find a way out of the Union card problem. If I had had that crucial piece of paper, I would have been in the hit musical *Pickwick*; I would have had two solos and I would have sung with Harry Secombe… but it was not to be.

Life is full of 'ifs' and it's odd looking back to how differently my life might have been. Perhaps it's even odder to recall how I felt at the time. I thought of it merely as a minor setback. I wasn't heartbroken at all. I was thrilled to know how strong my voice was to have been selected for such an important role and so I took the Equity card problem in my stride. Not performing every night in the West End (which wasn't actually my dream, anyway) would leave me free to concentrate on auditions for

Glyndebourne Opera House or Covent Garden, which was what I really wanted. It didn't concern me that I would also still need an Equity card to realise my dream of becoming a classical performer...but I was young, apparently precociously talented, according to other professionals, and optimistic.

My parents were incredibly supportive and easygoing. 'Whatever you want, darling,' my mother would say fondly. She was not at all your typical, pushy, show business mother.

So, meanwhile, I studied and studied, and in between, gained experience by doing bits of concert work here and there. In 1969, the Mill Hill-Hendon area of London was full of excellent amateur dramatic and operatic societies. One of the local geniuses, a teacher by the name of Rex Walford, thought that he would like to get all these groups together and put on a production of *West Side Story*. It was an absolutely revolutionary idea and it created loads of publicity. The auditions were incredibly well attended as hopefuls turned up from all over the county. In fact, it became so massively successful that they were asked to take it over to the Westminster Hall. Of course, I auditioned and was chosen to play Maria, no doubt because I could reach the top notes – and I must have looked the part as well.

It was during this hugely successful production that I got the taste for being a real prima donna and my inner diva was born. It was all tremendously exciting, even the preparations. I loved every minute of it, from putting on the black wig and very dark make-up to having the photographs taken by the man who would later become my first husband. Despite feeling a bit sick before opening night, I knew I could do it – at least the singing. The dancing had been another matter and my lack of brain-to-feet co-ordination was still quite extraordinary. A double, wearing the same wig and dress, had to be brought in to do the famous dance scenes with Tony, while I took over the acting and singing part of the role.

It was a huge success and the tickets were sold out every night of the two-week run. It definitely gave me a taste of what real show business was all about. I adored being Maria because it was 'proper' music written by Leonard Bernstein. But afterwards, when the curtain fell for the last time, I knew with all certainty that I still really wanted to pursue a career in opera. I wasn't that madly in love with treading the boards and doing theatre work; it was only singing that was my true greatest love. I knew that clearly I would never be able to develop the dancing required for a West End Musical – my feet simply wouldn't move in the right direction.

I auditioned for Glyndebourne but was not accepted. However, I was selected for the student programme at Sadler's Wells in the days just before it was to become the English National Opera. Once again, it was the lack of an Equity card that stood in the way of my taking up the offer. This time, I was upset and terribly disappointed.

On 19 October 1968, at the tender age of just 20, I married my childhood friend Roger Garwood. We had begun dating properly when I was about 18, and it helped that our parents were also great friends. It would be difficult to pin-point the moment when we decided to take it further and make the commitment to marry. I think I just wanted to move out of my parents' home and to have lots of sex! It also meant that I could get rid of the Puddefoot surname once and for all – Jenny Garwood was a definite improvement.

I had the kind of wedding I had always dreamed of – a typical, English church wedding. I wore a beautiful white dress and had three bridesmaids – my sister, my friend Christine and one of Roger's nieces. For them, I chose something pretty unconventional – they wore chocolate-brown, satin dresses with deep-orange, petal hats and carried orange flowers. It was all very autumnal and we had a lovely time with our families and circle of friends, who included singers and photographers – all very arty. Then we left for our honeymoon in Wales.

I loved married life. We had a beautiful converted flat at the top of a Regency house in Little Venice, Maida Vale – I am still friendly with the neighbours to this day.

Roger was a freelance photographer working very odd hours – often, he'd come back late from covering a film première or something, bringing loads of other photographers and journalists with him and we'd sit around all night eating, talking and drinking. We knew that we didn't want children because we were far too young.

Although Roger was an extremely gifted photographer, money was very tight and things reached a crisis point when, one day, the bailiffs moved in and took away some of my wedding presents. Eventually, I felt that our hand-to-mouth existence had gone on for long enough and decided to do something about it. The British editor of *Paris Match* magazine lived just up the road from us and had became a friend. He suggested that Roger try Fleet Street for better-paid, more regular work. 'In the meantime,' he said, 'I've got a great job for Jenny.' It appeared that Gamma, one of the biggest photographic agencies in the world, was looking for a representative for Fleet Street. So I thought, why not?

Every day I took myself off to Fleet Street where I made the rounds of the editorial desks of the national newspapers. In my portfolio were the latest newsworthy photographs featuring a wide range of subjects from front line conflicts to French movie stars. Usually I took my two pet Pekingese dogs – Wellington and Boots – with me in a hand basket. Wearing hot pants or a mini skirt and Biba boots I always got a warm reception. Work place attitudes were very different in those pre-PC days. Although the pictures were top quality and taken by some of the best news photographers in the world, I am sure that the length of my legs and the cuteness of my dogs also helped open doors. I became friendly with many of the top journalists of the day including the columnist Nigel Dempster. 'I love your dogs', he would say as he gave them a treat. It didn't surprise me to learn that later he would go on to own seven Pekingese.

Although I was doing well with the international photographic agency, I was reaching the end of my tether with Roger's work and we were still struggling financially. One day, when things were particularly bad, a picture editor noticed that I had been crying and asked me what was wrong. I told him about Roger not being able to get work as a photographer and he made light of it.

'For heaven's sake! Phone him and tell him to bring in his portfolio.'

It was then that he got to work on the *Daily Sketch* and took brilliant pictures for them. Then he was snapped up by the *Daily Mail* and became their Royal Photographer. In those days, the papers wanted pictures of Princess Anne and Prince Charles with his girlfriends.

He was really a prototype paparazzo, together with fellow photographer Ray Bellasario. They'd do anything to get a great shot – climb up trees, hide in bushes or even do their speciality – the daddy and baby stunt. This was a particular favourite at polo matches where Roger would put on a baby's bonnet and climb into a pram while Ray would play the daddy role – that way they'd get up really close to the royals. All this was well paid and meant that we finally got out of debt.

I believe it was then that the *Daily Mail* changed its personnel and *Paris Match* offered Roger a job, and he became their London photographer. At the age of 24 or 25, this was a huge accolade because *Paris Match* and *Life* were *the* magazines to work on. So it was my hot pants that really launched his career.

I wasn't wearing hot pants but a silk tunic-top, trouser suit and high heels – very Seventies, and very fashionable now – when I was picked up by Sean Connery. Roger had a Press Pass for the *Sergeant Pepper* film launch party. A whole galaxy of stars was there – all the Beatles, of course (John was with Yoko Ono and Paul had Linda Eastman on his arm) – and all the Hollywood glamorous celebs of the day. I was sitting at the bar when Sean sidled up.

'Obviously I know who you are,' I said, 'but, in fact, we do have friends in common.' I was referring to my music teacher, Harold Miller, and his wife.

We got along really well and chatted away for some time when he suggested that we go out for dinner. Can you believe it? I turned him down. I told him that I was married and at the party with my husband. I must have been crazy to turn down a date with Sean Connery!

That's not to say that I remained faithful during my first marriage. Twenty is far too young to make such a commitment. You just don't know what might be around the next corner, and around mine was a gorgeous officer, a second-in-command of a cruise liner. I might have been able to resist the charms of the fabulous Mr Sean Connery, but I fell well and truly under the spell of this seafaring Adonis – hook, line and sinker! I was on board the Union Castle Cruise Line for an 11-day cruise accompanying a friend who was convalescing from a hysterectomy.

I really fell totally in love with this officer – he was the most beautiful man I'd ever seen, just like a movie star! The affair with Peter lasted on and off for a year – although I only slept with him once, the last night of the cruise. To this day, I regret not having left Roger to be with him. We would meet outside Safeway's on the Edgware Road and sit under 'our' tree in Hyde Park.

Of course, Roger found out that I'd being seeing this guy and he said that it had broken his heart. We got back together for a while to give our marriage another chance, but it was really over. He began to see someone else – who, incidentally, looked exactly like his mother, with big breasts, and decided to get as far away from me as possible, choosing to take up yachting photography in Australia.

Before he left with his new girlfriend, he called me up and invited me out for dinner to say goodbye. It would have been almost our seventh wedding anniversary and he had brought me a present. When I opened it, I couldn't believe my eyes. Roger was an artist and always had a great eye for craftsmanship but this was absolutely exquisite. It was a Gucci money wallet. I held it in my hands, smelled the soft-black leather and ran my fingers over the trademark red and green stripe and enamel clasp in the shape of a jockey's helmet. The label prophetically read: 'To Pudding, this is what you deserve for the rest of your life.'

3

La Dolce Vita

I might have had the most fabulous Gucci wallet, but it was almost empty.

At the time of my divorce, I had £25 in my bank account and not enough money to pay the rent on my flat in Belsize Park. I had to sort out my life and my finances.

Just up the road, about a five-minute walk away, was the new, state-of-the-art Royal Free Hospital and it was there that I applied for work as a medical secretary. The radiology department, specialising in thyroid and infertility problems, would be the centre of my working life for the next four years. I found the job fascinating but it wasn't totally fulfilling…my love of singing still needed to be satisfied.

Harold, my music coach, continued to be supportive and it was his idea that my night-life should take on an Austrian flavour. 'Would you like to earn some extra money?' he suggested.

What a question! I was a fashion-conscious young woman who loved clothes and had always an eye – if not the budget – for quality. Roger and I had mixed with a pretty racy crowd in London and a lot of the girls owned something with a Gucci label. I remember the first time I saw the Gucci store in Bond Street – the things were so gorgeous, I almost fainted! If it meant working a 16-hour day to own such beautiful things, it was definitely worth it.

And so that is how I found myself expanding my wardrobe – not, at first, with designer labels – but with a pseudo-Austrian outfit of 'dirndl' skirt, laced bodice, black seamed stockings and black patent stilettos. No wonder the men flocked in to The Old Vienna restaurant in Bond Street to hear me sing…as well as admire my legs.

Alongside an accordionist, I sang all the famous Viennese operettas and big show tunes, including my father's old favourites such as *Die Fledermaus* and *The Gypsy Baron*, as well as a popular selection from *The Merry Widow*.

I performed at the Old Vienna under the watchful eye of the 'old queen' who ran the place for three or four nights a week from 9.00pm–11.00pm before catching the 113 bus back home.

I also met the most fascinating people, such as Ava Gardner and the American mezzo-soprano Grace Bumbury. One night, I received a case of Möet as a gift from the King of Saudi Arabia. I am not sure if it was in appreciation of my music or my short skirt.

My love-life was also looking up, with safety definitely in numbers. It was here that my relationship with two men – one of them married – began. These complicated affairs would continue on and off for several years.

It was also thanks to this time at the Old Vienna that I finally got the crucial Equity card. One of the customers complimented me on my voice and suggested that I might pursue an operatic career. I told him about my previous experiences and he pointed out that, after four years of performing professionally at the restaurant, I was eligible to join Equity. So I got my card; but I had gone off the idea of auditioning for any more shows by then.

The two jobs and working a 16-hour day had definitely paid off and I had managed to save up enough money to buy my own piano. I bought a beautiful grand piano, and thanks to my early piano lessons, could play simple songs and arias that were not written in minor keys. I left my voice coach Harold Miller after seven years and, instead, worked with a teacher from the Royal Academy of Music. Mary Makower was German and lived in the next street from my Belsize Park flat, and, every Saturday morning, I would study German opera with her. I adore German opera and I found it quite easy to sing in the German language, but I didn't have any desire to go to Germany to study. Italy, however…now that was altogether a different story.

An idea and an ambition were taking shape. If I was really to progress as a singer, I should study in Italy. It was not that I had the ambition of being famous or becoming the next Maria Callas – her Greek, treacly sound didn't appeal to me. I wanted to sing beautifully like my idol, Joan Sutherland. Her voice was one that I could relate to.

Another reason for my plan was to escape my complicated love-life. I always had at least two men on the go at the same time. Remember, this was before AIDS, when sex was just fun. With contraception taken care of, it was all pretty much risk-free. I had never chosen conventional, 'suitable' boyfriends; I was, instead, attracted to rather unusual men, often considerably older than me, especially if they were intelligent and artistic. I always surrounded myself with interesting men and was falling in love – or lust – a lot of the time. Two boyfriends might sound like fun, but it had been going on for too long and demands were being made and things were becoming heavy and complicated, especially the affair with the married man. It was exhausting, and I felt I just had to get away.

But before making any long-term decisions, I would go on a holiday to Rome with my sister Sue in September 1976. We stayed with Christa, my friend from the Old Vienna. Christa's apartment was lovely, very central, but it was also horribly hot in the summer and she had the idea of visiting the hills above Florence to get us out of the city. She had a friend, Sergio, who had a home there with spare rooms, meaning we could save on hotel bills.

I asked what Sergio did for a living. 'He's the chief men's fashion boutique co-ordinator for Gucci,' Christa answered.

'Wow, that's interesting,' I said, perking up at the thought of such tasteful elegance.

'Hey, maybe we'll meet a Gucci,' said Christa, half joking.

On our third day in Florence, Sergio suggested that we all go for a drink at the Excelsior Hotel before dinner. I put my silver-blonde hair up on top of my head in a sort of bun, pulled on a navy-blue sweater with a silk scarf and a well-cut pair of very tight, expensive jeans and high heels completed my smart-casual look.

The Excelsior was very smart and Sergio said that one of the Guccis might join us for a drink. My first thought was, Oh my God, what am I going to do with my handbag? It was awful and cheap – I don't think it was even leather. I decided that if I met a member of the Gucci family, I would sit on it to save embarrassment.

In the Excelsior lounge, we were having a great time and the Bellinis – a cocktail of white wine and peach purée – were slipping down wonderfully; I was feeling relaxed and mellow with my friends.

Afterwards, I found out that the deal was a bit like a blind date – if Paolo Gucci liked the look of us, he'd ask us for a drink; if he didn't, he would ignore us and go on his merry way. Needless to say, I *did* have to sit on my handbag when he came over and Sergio made the introductions.

He was obviously somewhat older (I would discover later that he was 46 at the time) but incredibly charismatic. He was so chic and exceptionally well dressed in a camel cashmere jacket and beautiful blue Swiss cotton shirt that emphasised the colour of his eyes. His trousers were grey and perfectly-cut and he was, of course, wearing stunning Gucci shoes. He wasn't good-looking in the conventional sense but I was immediately attracted to him and I sensed that the attraction was absolutely mutual. His English was completely fluent but he spoke with a delightful Italian accent.

The pianist, who was playing opera, asked if anyone would like to sing. I hadn't realised that Christa – who was typically forceful in an Austrian kind of way – and very possessive about my singing talent, had spoken to him and was pointing her finger at me above my head and pushing me out of my seat.

Feeling a bit squiffy from all the cocktails, I wasn't too happy about performing, but it would have appeared churlish not to. So I sang 'O Mio Bambino Caro' from Puccini and Gershwin's *Summertime*.

After my performance, Paolo held out his arms to me and kissed me on the cheek – it was then that I felt the first spark. This wasn't lust – it was just a tremendous feeling of chemistry – a really heady sensation.

Afterwards, he took us all out to dinner and we had a great time. I sat next to him because it was obvious that we were getting on really well. We laughed and talked all evening. I don't think that the man had ever laughed so much in his life – he literally laughed until he cried. Christa is really funny in a Wagnerian kind of way and my sister is tremendously witty.

Someone came round the tables selling strange novelty souvenirs and Paolo bought us all a funny wind-up toy. Mine was a cat that bounced a ball, Christa got a dog and he bought my sister a rabbit that looked as if it was performing oral sex on a carrot, which we all thought was hilarious. Christa hissed, 'Don't laugh or you'll make Paolo feel uncomfortable...' – of course, we couldn't help ourselves and trying to suppress the giggles made it all much funnier. The wine flowed and I guess we all got pretty tight; he said that it was the best evening he had ever had. I don't think the poor man had had much fun in his life before. It had all been work, work, work and his home life can't have been happy either. He told me that his marriage was completely on the rocks, that his wife – Yvonne, who was Sicilian-Italian – had taken a lover and that he had had several girlfriends.

At the end of the evening, he said that he'd really like to see me again.

'Not easy,' I replied. 'I'm staying in Rome...and, besides, you are married.'

'I am in the process of separating,' he explained.

I suggested that he might give it another try but he said it had all gone beyond that, especially as his two girls, Elisabetta and Patrizia, were now grown up.

'Well, I don't know about that,' I replied, thinking of my own married lover from England whom I would be seeing in a few days.

44

But I really liked him a lot. We had shared a brilliant evening and I felt that spark again as he took hold of my hand and kissed it as we parted. I watched as he climbed into his chocolate-brown Porsche 911 Carrera – the latest model – and drove off. That was it. I was done for… completely and utterly under his spell.

But several months passed before I would hear from him again. I returned to Rome and wrote a thank-you note for the lovely evening. The wording had to be absolutely perfect and it took the three of us – I definitely needed Christa and Sue's help with the composition – ages to get it just right. I posted it to the address of the factory up in the suburbs of Florence, as that was his base as head of the Gucci design team. But I never got a reply.

He'd also given me his phone number in case I was ever in Florence again, and I tucked it away for safekeeping.

Back in England, I was more determined than ever to pursue my dream of studying music in Italy, but I would need a way to finance this venture. In the meantime, I went back to my medical and musical jobs and made plans.

I managed to sub-let my flat in Belsize Park to a very nice family and started to think seriously about the various options. It was difficult because I knew that, once in Italy, I would need free time for my music – this ruled out the offer of living with a family in Milan as an *au pair*, which was one suggestion on the table. To be honest, I wasn't very maternal and the thought of being a 'domestic' didn't really appeal.

And then an opportunity in Rome came up. It involved being an assistant to a photographer and, of course, with my Fleet Street experience, I was perfect…plus, I had the required shorthand and typing. I would also be able to stay with Christa in her apartment overlooking the Vatican. My parents had offered to help and, if I had done my sums right, I would have just about enough money to cover singing lessons and to eat. And so on my 29th birthday – 16 January 1977 – I left for Italy, planning to stay for at least two years.

Of course, I thought about Paolo and wondered if I'd see him again. But, in truth, I was having a great time in Rome and going through a bit of a celibate phase. Although there were men coming out of the woodwork, I had decided that Italian men were not for me – they were so completely different – not really my type at all. In fact, apart from visits from my British boyfriends, I wasn't seeing anyone else when Paolo came back into my life.

I was bumming around Rome looking like a student and trying for a place at the *conservatoire*. After a few weeks, things were getting a bit cramped at Christa's apartment so I decided to decamp for a month to Florence to learn Italian at the British Institute. Christa helped me get a wonderful deal on a room in a little hotel by the Florence train station. My room was tiny – about 9ft by 6ft – but it was clean and the owners were very good to me and would bring me tea each morning. I'd been there about two weeks when I pulled out the piece of paper with Paolo's number on it, took a deep breath and dialled.

He sounded thrilled to hear my voice and, yes, of course he remembered me. He said that he was busy in a meeting but would call me back. I doubted that he would, but true to his word, he called later that afternoon. It was an especially busy week, he explained, with the collections, but could we get together for dinner the following Monday?

It was our first proper date and I dressed as carefully as my limited wardrobe allowed. Brown trousers, a cardigan – it was cold and damp in Florence in February – and an expensive pair of shoes I could ill afford. My student budget didn't run to a new handbag, so my cheap one would, again, have to act as a cushion.

Paolo was a wonderful companion – everything and more than I had remembered from our previous meeting seven months ago. He was attentive and thoughtful, making suggestions from the menu and looking after my every need – he was completely and utterly charming. In fact, he was, without a doubt, the most 'gentlemanly' man I had ever met. His manners were impeccable.

He looked like a million dollars – it was his trademark always to look perfect. But I was a bit worried about the moustache. He had one of those shaggy, Seventies-style moustaches and I wondered what it would be like to kiss him. His baldness didn't bother me at all – I found him very attractive in every way…despite the moustache!

Later, I would discover that the moustache was, in fact, a sign of Paolo's rebellion against his family. His grandfather, Guccio, had apparently hated men's facial hair and banned any man with a beard or a moustache from working in his shops.

We were completely comfortable in each other's company and conversation flowed easily. I remember him speaking fondly of his Uncle Vasco who had died from lung cancer a couple of years previously. Paolo believed that he had inherited his artistic streak from his uncle. Certainly, Vasco had not had the hardened business head of his brother – Paolo's father, Aldo, who was running the company. Vasco was never happier than when he was out in the Tuscan countryside with his gun dog. Apparently, on one occasion, he had taken his young nephew with him and probably later regretted it because Paolo had accidentally shot him. Fortunately, the wounds, which were to his lower body, were not life-threatening. Nonetheless, Uncle Vasco bled profusely and had lost consciousness by the time he reached the hospital in Florence. Happily, he would later make a full recovery.

We also discussed our relationships and I learned that he was now in the process of legal separation from his wife. Music and fashion were other top topics.

'What's your favourite colour, Jenny?' he asked.

'Yellow,' I replied. 'It is such a bright, optimistic colour.'

'Yes, but a difficult one to blend, match and sell in the world of fashion,' he said.

I couldn't believe how the time flew by. We had talked non-stop for four hours and I felt as if I'd known him for ever, but there was still that tingle of excitement of a new relationship.

He drove me back to my hotel, this time in a green station wagon that belonged to the factory. Later, I would discover that he and his brother Roberto were on the Red Brigade's hit-list. They were prime targets for kidnapping and had been advised to use a different car each day and to vary their usual routes between home and the office or factory.

The chemistry was still there – with or without the Porsche. As he opened the car door and helped me out, I felt the frisson of anticipation again. He held my hand as we walked across the road – it sounds corny, but when we touched, it literally took my breath away. I had never felt like this before, it was as if I was being transported into another world. I knew instinctively that he was feeling it, too. He kissed me goodbye gently on both cheeks – his moustache felt softly tickly...not at all unpleasant.

'Are you all right for money?' Paolo asked gently as he said goodnight.

'Yes, of course,' I insisted.

Back in my shoe-box room, I lay awake wondering what would happen next, unaware that he had settled up my hotel bill and paid my next week's room rent as well.

4

Shopping, Skiing and Falling in Love

The next morning, I woke up to the sound of a knock at my door. The florist was there with an armful of yellow roses. There were 60 in all, beautifully presented in a fabulous pot. It was such a large arrangement they could hardly get it through the door of my tiny room.

I looked at the label – obviously, I knew who had sent them, but I was curious as to how he had put into words what was happening. There it was: 'I think these are your favourites – I hope you like them. Looking forward to seeing you later on. With much affection, Paolo. X'

Yes, they are…yes I do…and so am I!

All the staff at the Caravell Hotel in front of the station were alive with the gossip of it all. They'd never witnessed anything quite like this before.

'Signorina Jenny… Signore Gucci is on the phone again,' called Marco from the reception desk, just loud enough for everyone on the ground floor to hear and to react to the latest development in what had to be the most interesting relationship the hotel had ever seen.

On the phone, I thanked Paolo for the previous night and the flowers, so thoughtfully chosen in my favourite colour. He said that he had a dinner arrangement with some friends for the following evening and wanted me to join him.

The dinner party was held at the home of one of Paolo's friends and the other guests were a mixture of couples and single people. Some spoke English but, when the conversation drifted back into Italian, Paolo patiently translated for me so that I wouldn't feel uncomfortable or excluded.

I quickly realised some of the implications of dating one of the world's most powerful and wealthy men, apart from the fact that you can always get the best table in any restaurant, even if you haven't booked. Relations with his 'friends' were always cordial, but not close. He didn't let people get too close to him – he liked to keep his distance.

As we went out and about together, he would introduce me with pride in his voice. I was thrilled to hear him say to people, 'This is Jenny, my girlfriend.' In sophisticated Italian society, most of the men would be with their mistresses, so no one raised an eyebrow.

He was very well known in Florence and, wherever we went, people would react. Lawyers, accountants, professional people and staff

Paolo and I share a loving moment.

in restaurants – everyone would greet Paolo and they were respectful to me, too. They all knew that his marriage was terrible and they saw him looking so happy with me, so they had to agree that the relationship was a good thing. I think it was obvious that our affair was special and not just a fling. Perhaps, through the eyes of society, my being a student of opera was also something in my favour.

However, many of the Italian women I met were pretty frosty towards me. It became apparent that they didn't like foreigners – especially English or American women – coming over and, as they saw it, 'taking' their men. They tended to be polite and civil towards me when Paolo was around, but not warm. But I couldn't care less. I was so happy with Paolo that the outside world and what other people thought didn't worry me at all.

The first few weeks of our relationship fell into a pattern – we'd meet for dinner after his working day and chat together as if we had known each other all our lives. At the end of the evening, he would walk me back to the small hotel in front of the station and chastely kiss me goodnight.

We talked easily together and chatted about everything. He told me about his childhood and how he had started out (as was expected of a young Gucci) by running errands in the shop. In those early days, the family lived above the shop in Rome's Via Condotti. Paolo had been a reluctant errand boy and, even at a young age, he had felt resentful, believing he was worth more. He had also not taken well to the position of sales assistant, again finding that it went against the grain with him to be deferential to clients. Apparently, he had always been proud and haughty. It was taken for granted that he would follow in his father's footsteps, but Paolo had had one of his first rebellions at the age of 20 when he decided that the Gucci family business was not for him. Instead, he found a job advertised with the airline BOAC that was based in India. He told me that he had always dreamed of travelling and so he decided to apply. But it was not to be…apparently, he had been out late the night before and overslept on the morning of his interview, arriving at the BOAC offices too late – the position had already been filled. The House of Gucci was to be his destiny after all.

We also loved to talk about fashion. Up until a couple of years before we met, Gucci had traded only in leather goods. It was Paolo who instigated the ready-to-wear lines; without him, there would have been no *prêt à porter* range. Together, we would go through magazines like *Vogue* and *Harpers* and he would turn down the corners of pages with interesting designs and things he thought would suit me or for future ideas.

I confessed to adoring fur coats. I know I am hypocritical because I love animals, too, but it was at the time Italy was just beginning to style fur in a grand way and becoming a world leader in fur designs. Paolo and I would spend ages discussing the little details of various outfits such as putting a frill here or an extra button there.

Once, he dropped me back at the hotel with an envelope stuffed full of money. I didn't know what to say but he made it easy. 'Look, Jenny, you are a student and I want to help you. There is no obligation whatsoever. Please buy yourself some of the lovely clothes you were talking about.'

How could I refuse? Obviously, I didn't know at the time that this would be the first of many clothes that Paolo would buy me but I did know that I had to choose carefully. In the end, I selected one expensive item – a beautiful, navy-blue Yves St Lauren tailored cardigan with pockets – it was divine. I went for one really classy item – that was my style.

I am sure that the designer carrier bag didn't escape the eagle-eyed Marco guarding the hotel entrance. There was something of a knowing smirk in his voice when he called out that Signor Gucci was on the phone.

'What did you buy?' he asked immediately.

When I told him, he said that I should get a skirt as well. 'You can always go into the Gucci shop and choose anything you want.'

'I couldn't possibly,' I protested, 'I just wouldn't feel comfortable doing that.'

After a rather late dinner one evening, Paolo wanted to take me right up to my shoe-box room to say goodnight, but Marco, who was on duty, was having none of it. 'This is a respectable hotel, Signor Gucci…no men are allowed in the female guests' bedrooms.'

'Don't be ridiculous,' snapped Paolo. 'I just want to see her up to her room. Do you honestly think if I wanted to make love to her I would do it in this rotten flea pit?'

On and on they argued, Paolo pointing out that he resented the implications that were being made and that anyway, from what he'd heard, there wouldn't even be space in my room for two people. He was shouting and had really lost his temper by this time and they almost came to blows as my honour and Paolo's pride were defended. The other guests were not impressed by the disruption but were no doubt fascinated when they saw that it was one of the famous Guccis who was losing his cool.

No friendly wake-up call or cup of tea for me the next morning. Later, I apologised to the owners. The apology was not accepted. I was told in no uncertain terms that my companion's manners were disgusting.

Paolo wasn't bothered – in fact he had a plan. We had been dating for four weeks, and we still hadn't even kissed properly, when he said that he wanted me to move out of the hotel.

'Please come and stay in my house in the country. You won't be under any obligation to me and I know you'll love it there.'

It was pretty tempting – my shoebox was horribly cramped and, since the row, the staff had been rather unfriendly. Paolo put together a pretty powerful argument, also pointing out that he was not allowed to stay at the country house himself at the time due to the terms of his legal separation agreement before the divorce from Yvonne was finalised.

And so it was one cold, dreary day early in 1977 that a chauffeur from the Gucci empire helped me move my few possessions from the hotel to the next phase of my life. Leaving the city of Florence behind and driving through the Tuscan countryside, I knew instinctively that my new 'home' had also doubled as some sort of bachelor pad for Paolo. Although I strongly suspected that this was where he had taken his girlfriends in the past, it didn't really bother me. I was so excited at the prospect of being with him. I really wanted to make love with him – the sisterly kisses on the cheek were no longer enough.

The journey also provided time to reflect on the past few weeks and how fast everything was moving. I knew in my heart that I already loved this amazing, charismatic man. Maybe it was in his genes – his mother was British and his father Italian. Perhaps it was the slight English reserve alongside the passionate nature of the Italians that made him completely irresistible. Whatever it was made me feel quite hot and bothered, despite the chill of the weather.

Paolo's place in the country turned out to be magnificent. It was an apartment within a mansion that had once belonged to a count in the small village of Pozzolatico. The rooms were huge and cavernous with high ceilings and Florentine-style, red-polished tiles. The furniture was simple and rustic with soft chairs that just invited you to flop on to them. It was all typically Tuscan in style with a large eat-in kitchen, complete with a huge marble table. He hadn't added much in the way of personal touches but it was still charming. The bedroom was huge and dominated by an iron-posted bed made up with crisp, fresh linen.

After the chauffeur had left, my only company was Maria the maid who later would teach me not only how to make the best bolognese sauce in the world, but also Italian. I had to speak Italian to survive. Later, I would become friendly with a neighbour, a beautiful girl from San Francisco who was living with a Polish artist, and she also helped me with the language.

Paolo would phone up and pop over when he could but he was frantically busy at work and our relationship remained steadfastly platonic.

After about ten days in Pozzolatico, I was almost pulling my hair out with desire and, during one phone conversation, I told him that I was worried about our relationship – somehow things just didn't feel right. I felt uncomfortable and I wanted to know what was going on. He immediately took control of the situation.

'Don't worry, Chi-Chi [his nickname for me], I am coming right over,' he said.

It wasn't that I was unhappy – I'd managed to overcome the sensation of feeling stranded once I had discovered the country bus service. This twice-daily bus picked up farmers and peasants from throughout the Tuscan hills taking them and me through narrow, twisty roads into Florence. My Italian was also coming on in leaps and bounds and all the locals were really nice to me. I had other neighbours to talk to as well. Across the road from the house was a bakery that had been there since 1756 and the owners gave me the most delicious, freshly-baked bread each morning.

I was also keeping up with my singing. A few weeks before, Paolo had arranged for me to audition with a singing teacher in Florence, insisting that I must never go back to Rome. Gino Becci was *the* baritone just before Tito Gobi; he had sung alongside all the greats, including Maria Callas.

It hadn't been easy to get him to see me as he was then working with the Bilbao Orchestra and insisted categorically that he was no longer teaching. After some gentle persuasion, the great man agreed to hear me sing so that he could recommend someone else to coach me. I had gone up to this gorgeous house clutching two pieces of music – a Bellini piece and one from Puccini. We started with the Bellini, and the great maestro accompanied me on the piano.

I was just getting going rather nicely when he exploded, 'Stop, stop, stop.'

'Why?'

'Well, it's all wrong,' he sighed, 'why are you putting in all those extra notes?'

I explained that it was the way that I had been taught the piece.

'*Bella*,' he said, 'I'll teach you for six months and show you how it should be done. You are truly gifted. You look like an angel and you've got the voice of an angel.'

So that was how the great Gino Becci came out of retirement and taught me in between going to Bilbao. And I subsequently became a regular passenger among my Tuscan neighbours on the Pozzolatico-Florence bus.

After my outburst to Paolo on the phone, I hadn't planned what I would say to him when I saw him face to face. But the moment I looked at his concerned expression and heard his worried voice asking me what was wrong, it all poured out. 'I don't know what's happening, but I think I'm falling in love with you,' I heard myself say.

He put his head in his hands and the muffled words came out. 'I am so glad you said that first because I know that I am utterly in love with you.'

And then we kissed properly…and kissed…and kissed…and held each other. But we still didn't go to bed.

It was then that he invited me to his ski lodge and I knew that this was it. He explained that he owned a ski lodge near Florence in a resort called Abetone. I knew that not only would this be a make-or-break weekend for our relationship, but also that I had nothing suitable to wear. What London girl has a ski wardrobe? Not me.

So Paolo took me shopping. It was a bit like Julia Roberts in *Pretty Woman*. I was a trim size 8 and I needed everything – from top to toe – for a weekend in a ski resort. We chose navy-blue ski pants, a tight, zip-up ski jacket and sweater to go with it, beautiful gloves, everything you can imagine, including the most fabulous, great big Mongolian lamb boots. I was so shell-shocked I could hardly speak. He was so attentive and made such a fuss of me.

Paolo drove us up to the ski lodge on the Friday night – it was snowing as we climbed higher through the Tuscan mountains. There was a wonderful calmness between us, that familiar feeling that we had been together for decades rather than just a matter of weeks. We were in complete harmony, both aware, somehow, of the inevitability of it all.

It was a wonderful weekend and, of course, we slept together. It was the most natural thing in the world. We spent loads of time in bed talking, cuddling, drinking cups of tea and making love again and again. The sex was perfect – he knew exactly which buttons to press. We were both experienced and knew how to satisfy each other.

It was exciting because I was in love with him but not with that unbelievable urgency that sometimes happens at the start of an affair; it was calmer and more beautiful – not lustful and haphazard!

We always had great sex right up to the time when I left him – we never had any problems in the sex department – ever. We were totally compatible in every way. It was romantic and fun, we had a great physical relationship.

Fortunately, he wasn't into sexy underwear – it wasn't important to him – although I did have pretty undies. I found it cold at the ski lodge and wore woolly socks and took a hot-water bottle to bed, like an old, married woman, but he never gave it a thought. He'd just hunker down and kiss me and cuddle up to keep warm.

We didn't do any skiing – I had never learned and, although Paolo loved to ski, he didn't want to leave me. It was a weekend of lots of sex, and eating and drinking, and walking and talking and getting to know each other better.

We went shopping, too. He was the most wonderful shopper and loved shopping for everything – jewellery, clothes, socks, household items – in fact, anything except food and groceries. He loved *objets d'art* and was fascinated by merchandising. Ours was a match made in heaven.

I learned that although he loved opera, he didn't know too much about it. Later, he developed a good ear and, when he watched me perform, he could tell whether I was on form or not.

Monday morning came round horribly quickly and I realised that we would have to return to the real world. When he kissed me goodbye at the Pozzolatico apartment, I was distraught and tearful. I really didn't want him to leave.

'I insist that you go into the Gucci shop in Florence and choose whatever you want,' he said again. This time he sounded much more serious and maybe he was also trying to cheer me up, suggesting that we might meet up in the city for lunch.

I told him that although I appreciated his generosity and the new collection was gorgeous, it made me feel somewhat like a two-bit hooker. But he would not take no for an answer and gave me a card with the manager's name on it. He told me that the manager would be expecting me at a certain time.

Well, it was an offer I couldn't really refuse – what girl could?

I was terribly nervous – in fact, walking into that beautiful shop in Florence for the first time was more nerve-wracking than singing an aria on stage. But I needn't have worried. True to his word, the manager was waiting.

'Signora Garwood, how are you?' he said oozing Italian charm as he took my hand and kissed it. 'Mr Paolo says that you are to have anything you want.'

I had been thinking in terms of a pair of shoes. I couldn't believe the amazing selection of variations on the classic Gucci loafer. I had no idea they were made in such a range of colours and styles. Some had a small, stacked heel and were decorated with a narrow, gold chain while others had the traditional snaffle-bit design on the top. The assistant explained that they were also made in seven different leathers, including patent, lizard and ostrich. Unfortunately, they didn't come in my size or shape of foot. My feet were somewhat wider than the standard Italian's. I selected a different style to try on and – like Cinderella – they fitted perfectly.

'No, no, no, no, no…not just shoes,' insisted my new best friend, 'Mr Paolo would want you to have a bag as well.'

In the end, I chose an exquisite navy-blue, suede clutch bag and a pair of the cheapest shoes in the shop. They were navy-blue court shoes and were still horribly expensive but I thought they'd go really well with the Yves St Laurent cardigan/jacket. I was like the queen bee in the shop – all the assistants were buzzing around me offering advice and help. They wrapped my purchases beautifully. I had spent hundreds of pounds on two items that I loved, but the whole experience made me feel uncomfortable.

Paolo wasn't able to make it for lunch but he called me in the afternoon and asked how I'd got on. I told him about my selection, thanking him but making it clear that I felt really uncomfortable about spending his money. He just seemed surprised that I'd spent so little!

Those were heady days of falling in love and getting to know each other better. He would try and spend every spare moment with me. Often, he'd come racing back to our apartment at lunchtime – it would take about half an hour each way. We wouldn't always end up in bed – sometimes we'd just talk about what we had been doing and cuddle. During this period, he could never stay over a whole night. He wouldn't do anything to jeopardise his divorce, as he desperately wanted a legal separation from Yvonne. Although we would greedily grab at the short times we could spend together, there was never any talk of marriage. Instead, he would say things like, 'Be patient, I'll be with you one day soon, I promise.'

But I wasn't really bothered about getting married. I'd had one wedding and I was in no hurry to marry again. I thought my life was blissful as it was: I was in the midst of a fabulous love affair and I still had my music.

5

Meeting the Family

Florence in February is frightful. The cold and damp seems to seep into your bones.

It was on another chilly, wet afternoon in late February 1977 that Paolo dropped a bombshell. 'I want you to meet my father,' he said quite out of the blue.

I knew that it had been an especially busy time for Paolo at the factory, and I was learning what went on behind the scenes to put together and launch the twice-yearly collections. Paolo was responsible for the ready-to-wear clothes and there is no doubt in my mind that he was an extremely talented designer. He was always innovative and often would have to argue with the rest of the family about the introduction of his forward- thinking ideas. For instance, it had been his idea to incorporate fabric and leather together on items such as skirts, jackets, boots and bags, and it worked brilliantly, especially in that winter collection of 1977. Eventually, I had almost the entire collection, including these gorgeous, knee-high boots made of olive-green leather with a strip of tweed material insert which matched the suit or skirt.

Twice a year, all the items – all the shoes, bags, scarves, swimwear, absolutely everything – would be assembled for the buyers around the world. About 45 of the top store managers would descend on the Florence headquarters for 'The Meeting' and to make their selections to sell in all the Gucci shops and franchises around the world. It would be at a dinner during this period that I was to be introduced to Paolo's father, Aldo Gucci.

My reaction to the invitation was quite straightforward. 'Paolo, I can't possibly go – I am absolutely not ready for this.'

But he was having none of it. 'You'll have a wonderful time…they'll all make a fuss of you. I promise you it will be a lovely dinner and I want you to be there.'

It was as simple as that. Paolo also told me what to wear, selecting the new outfit from the collection he had picked out for me in Rome. I had another beautiful Gucci bag and my wardrobe was now dominated by this new kind of fabric which was cashmere and silk woven together –

Snapshot from the Gucci family album – from left:
Roberto, Olwen, Giorgio and Paolo in Rome in 1975.

I had twin sets, silk shirts, the softest cream-leather boots and a whole range of outfits in tones of wine and burgundy.

But for that first meeting with Aldo Gucci, I wore a beautiful tweed skirt with scarlet and dark-green tones. It was lined with the softest chocolate-coloured Napa leather that felt like butter. It wasn't reversible but a kilt style, so when I sat down and crossed my legs it fell open to reveal the gorgeous lining. It was made of a cashmere and wool mix. My shoes were classic Gucci stilettos in moss green and, on top, I was wearing a deep-tan sweater in vicuña wool. Vicuñas, I had learned from Paolo, live high in the Andes and are similar to llamas. I could now affirm from first-hand knowledge that, when their fur was knitted together, the result was fabulously soft and warm.

'Aa-aa-ah...' Signore Gucci Senior managed to put three intonations into his greeting. 'You must be the Eeenglish Jenny – how nice to meet you.'

Aldo's manners were as impeccable as his grooming and his charisma was enough to fill six rooms. His reputation with women was legendary and, at 72, he still had that magnetism.

As a youngster helping out in the first Gucci shop in Florence during the 1920s, it had become immediately apparent that the young Aldo could use his charm on all the female customers to great effect. He had been a very handsome young man with the type of chiselled features and blue eyes that made him attractive to women throughout his life. These attributes, together with a flirtatious nature and captivating manners, were a winning combination that undoubtedly reflected in the sales figures when Aldo was on duty. For this reason, his father, Guccio Gucci – the founder of the empire – turned a blind eye to the exploits of his third-born; that was until the shop received a royal visitor one day who was not happy.

This Princess Irene – who would later marry George II of Greece – had called in not to buy any Gucci luggage but to complain to Guccio Gucci about his son's affair with one of her servants. The princess insisted that she could not continue to take responsibility for the girl if the affair continued. Aldo must stop seeing her or the young Olwen Price would be sent home to her family in England.

Olwen, a trained dressmaker, was working as a ladies' maid in the princess's household in Florence when she met Aldo. The couple had probably got to know each other during her visits to the shop to pick up purchases for her mistress. The affair moved to the next level during several romps in the Tuscan countryside during their days off.

Aldo, realising that this was more than another passing affair and probably also suspecting that Olwen was already pregnant, did the decent thing and announced to his father and the irate Princess Irene that he intended to marry her.

The couple were married in England on 22 August 1927 at the Roman Catholic Church near Shrewsbury in Shropshire. Olwen had converted to her husband's faith. The groom was 22 and the bride 19.

When they returned to Florence, Olwen was forced to live with her in-laws and things must have been pretty strained in the cramped apartment, especially when baby Giorgio arrived early the following year. Later, two more boys were born – my Paolo in 1931 and Roberto a year later.

It was not a happy marriage, although, over the years, Olwen learned to play by the rules. She stayed at home looking after her boys and shying away from public functions. She also had to live with her husband's constant cheating and various mistresses. No one knew any longer whether it was a chicken or egg situation – did Aldo cheat because his wife refused to go to public functions with him? Or had she become something of a recluse and stay-at-home mother because of his humiliating behaviour? It was probably the latter. Aldo's women were usually picked from the various Gucci shops, including Bruna Palumbo, who was probably the love of his life and the mother of his daughter, also named Patrizia.

Throughout his life, Aldo had been the driving force behind the expansion of the Gucci empire. It had been Aldo who had, after massive arguments, managed to persuade his father to open the store in Rome way back in 1938. No expense was spared, much to the concern of the older Gucci, who watched the bills mount up with horror. But Aldo knew that he could turn the Rome shop round to make it a profitable jewel in the Gucci crown. He was proved right, as the world's jet-set, movie stars and royalty would make it a must-stop shopping destination. Through the decades, the rich and famous – such as Sophia Loren – would be spotted breezing through its double glass doors and emerge some time later clutching their exclusive purchases.

Early on in my relationship with Paolo, I, too, had touched the iconic door handles and breathed the smell of its luxurious interior. But that visit to Rome had not only been for shopping. It had been arranged that I would meet Paolo's mother. We hit it off and, straightaway, I knew that I really liked Olwen from the moment we met and I am pretty sure that the feelings were mutual. We got along well. Physically, she was a small, blonde woman, sweet, kind and softly spoken. Long ago, she had decided not to rock the boat and to accept her life and the sham that her marriage had become. Meeting her for the first time, it was apparent that she was not a happy woman, despite living in a magnificent home on the Via della Camilluccia – one of the most exclusive addresses in Rome – and being surrounded by all the trappings of wealth.

She lived in only a few rooms of the large family home on her own, apart from the servants, and she had made one room in the basement her special little sanctuary. It was here in this room, decorated in a typically English style, that she felt most comfortable and chose to serve me tea.

Paolo had told me that, during the war, his mother had been something of a heroine, working alongside a group of Irish priests in Rome helping Allied prisoners to escape. On several occasions, she had risked her life for the cause and narrowly escaped detection after hiding shot-down British servicemen in her house. Within the Gucci clan, it must also have been awkward for her fighting her own war on the side of the Allies from within an Italian family. When her father-in-law, Guccio, married Aida, he had taken on her son by a previous relationship. Ugo was always considered something of a thug in the family and had found his vocation wearing the uniform of the Italian fascist party. After Italy's capitulation, he, along with other fascists, was held in a prisoner-of-war camp run by the British. It was then that Olwen had also shown her loyalty to the Gucci family. Using her Allied contacts, she successfully appealed for the release of her brother-in-law.

Looking at this rather sad, gentle woman, I found it hard to imagine how brave and heroic she had been before being crushed by her overbearing husband, whom she still loved despite his rejection of her. She was, however, fiercely protective of her sons and made it clear that she approved of me as I had brought a smile back to her Paolo's face. 'I can't remember ever seeing him so happy,' she said in her soft voice. 'But, be careful,' she warned. 'Don't underestimate Yvonne.' She had recognised how unhappy he had been in his marriage and was genuinely pleased that we were together.

My meeting with Olwen had gone well…but what about Paolo's formidable father? Back at the dinner party, he had a suggestion: 'You know what…why don't you sit beside me?'

My heart sank. I really didn't want to be separated from Paolo and, in addition, I could see Aldo's current mistress, Chantal Skibinski, looking daggers in my direction. Chantal was originally Polish and, as well as her relationship with Aldo, was the director of European public relations and international fashion co-ordinator. She was a very attractive woman, in her mid-thirties, and was wearing so much jewellery that I wondered how her neck was strong enough to support it all. She was obviously rather put out but remained superficially charming towards me. She was obviously good at her job, too.

'Yes, I'd like you to sit here beside me so that I can get to know you better.' Aldo was not a man to be thwarted.

'Fine, yes of course, I'd be delighted,' I beamed.

The dinner was in a private dining room of the Hotel Villa Cora in Florence. There were about 20 of us around the table, including the American contingent. Once we were within chatting range, the formidable Aldo was clearly not someone who minced his words.

'Sooooo, you like-a Paolo…'

'Yes, I do.'

'Well, I like you.'

'Thank you very much.'

'I hear you sing.'

I nodded, fearing where this line of conversation might be leading.

'You wanna singa tonight?'

'No, I don't!'

'Aa-aa-ah…are you shy?'

'No, but I am full of vodka and wine and a heavy Italian meal and I wouldn't be able to breathe properly.'

Phew, but no sooner had I managed to steer him away from that thought, than he was on to the next.

'I want you – with Paolo – to be my guest at Regines in New York in a few weeks' time, then you'll come down to Palm Beach with me.' Gosh, he was a fast mover.

'I'll have to ask Paolo first.'

'No, you won't. You can come with me.'

'No, I can't – I don't think that would be a good idea.' Then, getting closer and whispering into his perfectly manicured ear, I breathed, 'Let me tell you a secret.'

'What, darling?'

'I love your son,' I whispered, 'so I couldn't possibly go away with you. And anyway, what about her?' glancing in Chantal's direction.

'Oo-oo-oh, don't worry about her. So-oo, you love-a my son – he's a good boy…a bit stupid, but a good boy.' This was his description of the 47-year-old man I loved.

Back in the mid-1970s, the relationship between Paolo and his father was not too bad. Obviously, there were the usual conflicts and arguments about how the business was run and often Paolo had to struggle to get his design ideas accepted, but back then there had been a fondness and warmth between both men. I suspected the dynamics of the relationship were not that different from what had gone on a generation before between Aldo and his own father, Guccio.

In the early days, it was acknowledged that Aldo was the business brains of his generation of Guccis. Constant conflicts with his father had followed, mostly about the costs involved in his grandiose expansion plans and dreams of opening Gucci stores throughout Europe and even in New York. Why not take the merchandise to the people instead of expecting the customers to travel to Italy to shop, he had argued.

At this stage, Aldo's siblings were also involved in the business. His sister Grimalda worked in the stores and his younger brother Vasco was in charge of the factory in Florence, where he was later to take under his wing the young Paolo, nurturing his artistic and creative talent.

It was Rodolfo, the youngest child of Guccio and Aida, who had shown no interest in the family business and would later become a thorn in Aldo's side when they became partners. Rodolfo was a remarkably handsome young man who had harboured a dream of a career in the movies but his father (Paolo's grandfather, Guccio) was having none of it and, in his typical bombastic style, dismissed the notion as absolutely out of the question. But destiny had other plans and, at the age of 17, as an errand boy for the family firm, Rodolfo found himself delivering a Gucci package to a film director in Rome's Hotel Plaza. The director saw his potential and invited him to make a screen test. It probably proved a far easier challenge than winning his father's approval of his new career. But he was determined and, over the next few years, under the screen name of Maurizio D'Ancora, carved out a fairly respectable career as a comic film actor.

In one of his films, *Together in the Dark*, he played opposite an actress called Sandra Ravel. In the script and in real life, the two fell in love and Sandra – whose real name was Alessandra Winkelhausen – became another Signora Gucci in 1944 in a romantic wedding in Venice. Four years later, when their son Maurizio was born, Alessandra persuaded her husband to return to the family business.

It would be 47 years later when Maurizio's bloody murder would be reported in headlines around the world. As the scandal unfolded, his ex-wife Patrizia Reggiani was found guilty of arranging her husband's killing. But all that was a long way off in the future and it was at this reunion in a private dining room of the Villa Cora Hotel where I first met Maurizio and Patrizia Gucci in far happier times. They were an attractive couple; Maurizio, having inherited his father's Hollywood looks, was tall and toned beside his petite, dark wife. Patrizia had regained her trim, pre-baby figure, despite having given birth to Allessandra a few months previously. It wasn't difficult to admire their baby daughter, who was very cute and well behaved. In those days, Maurizio was based in New York and they seemed like any other happy, close family enjoying a business break and being back in their home country of Italy.

Aldo's attention span was short and, after admiring his great-niece, he turned his attention back to me and I was reminded that this was the man who had dedicated his life to the creation of the Gucci brand concept we recognised today. It was Aldo Gucci who was credited with coining the famous phrase 'Quality is remembered long after price is forgotten'. He was a stubborn, single-minded man who was used to getting his own way. His father, although strong-willed in his own right, would have eventually been forced into giving way and, once again, heading to the bank to negotiate loans to fund his son's expansion plans. And here I was making the remarkable man burst into spontaneous laughter at some joke I'd just told – we both shared the same sense of humour. I could tell that Paolo was also pleased with the way everything was going.

The meeting had been a great success and, as well as winning over Aldo Gucci, Maurizio, Patrizia and their baby, I had managed to build up some friendships with the American buyers, many of whom were gay. I've always had a magnetic appeal to gay men – I adore them.

The atmosphere was upbeat and happy when Paolo and I said goodbye to his father.

'Paolo, you have to bring her to New York next month.'

It was more of a command than a request.

The travel arrangements were made and I packed two enormous Gucci suitcases. It was actually quite difficult to know what to take as, from New York, we would later go to the family home in Palm Beach and then on to Haiti, but Paolo assured me we could shop locally if I needed anything.

It was the first time I had travelled outside Europe; it was the first time I had flown anywhere first-class; it was also the first time I had ever been inside a VIP lounge and tasted the advantages of travelling with money. It would become very easy to get used to. Unfortunately, I couldn't experience all these firsts with my usual enthusiasm – in fact, I was feeling very sorry for myself as we left London. I had the first symptoms of 'flu which gradually got worse as I spent most of the Pan Am flight lying sprawled across Paolo's lap feeling very frail. The delights of first-class and its luxurious extravagance were quite lost on me.

We were whisked through Immigration and Customs and a limo took us to the St Regis Hotel on Fifth Avenue. Once in our suite, I collapsed on the bed in a sweaty, feverish heap. I couldn't believe it…for as long as I could remember – in fact, since the first episode of *Kojak* on Saturday night TV – I had wanted to visit New York, and here I was in the Big Apple and feeling dreadful.

Paolo was sweet. He arranged for medicines from the pharmacy and told me not to worry but just to rest. He wouldn't be free for sightseeing anyway as his diary was full of work appointments.

One afternoon a couple of days later, when I was beginning to feel a little better, I glanced in the mirror and realised how dreadful I looked. My hair was lank, my skin had an unattractive, post-'flu pallor, my nightdress was sticking to me and I really needed a bath and a visit to the hotel beauty parlour and hairdresser. As soon as I felt strong enough, I was dying to get outside and explore the city. So far, I had only been able to admire its familiar skyline from television shows. From my window, I could also watch the shoppers and commuters battling through the unseasonable city heat. Apparently, the outside temperature was over 80°F, and I thanked God for air-conditioning.

It was then that Paolo popped back to the hotel between meetings to see how I was feeling. 'Poor little Chi Chi,' he said, pushing the hair off my clammy forehead. 'Is there anything you want? Is there anything you fancy from room service?'

We sat on the bed and he held me in his arms. I felt tearful and frustrated at being cooped up in the hotel room when the whole of New York City beckoned.

'Don't worry, we've got another four days here and you'll feel better soon.' His hand patting and stroking my back and shoulder felt comforting. 'Then we've got a lovely holiday in Palm Beach and Haiti to look forward to.'

It felt good to relax against him, and to let him look after me.

'I want to ask you something.'

I must have been drifting off, as his voice seemed to be coming from a long way away.

'Will you marry me?'

What! I must still have been feverish or delusional or both. Nothing had prepared me for his proposal and I was also horribly conscious of looking far from my best. I really had no desire to get married again and everything felt so perfect as it was.

'Maybe we should just stay as we are…as lovers,' I suggested. 'Then I can continue with my singing and we can still be together.'

'No, I am not looking for a mistress. I want you to be my wife. I love you too much – I couldn't bear it if other men were looking at you and you were to go off with someone else.'

It all felt so right with that inevitability that I had sensed since I first met him.

'Yes, I will.'

He grabbed hold of me and hugged me.

'Don't kiss me,' I warned, 'or you'll catch the 'flu.'

'I don't care,' he said, 'I am so happy.'

So we kissed long and hard to mark our engagement…and he didn't catch the 'flu.

6

Sables, Pigeons and a Ring

Before fully accepting Paolo's proposal, there were one or two things I knew we needed to agree on. I was 29 years old and, although Paolo had two grown-up children – Elisabetta, who was just four years younger than me, and Patrizia, who was then 23 – I knew that I wanted to have a baby. I'd never been crazy about babies or children before and, as I have mentioned, I was notoriously unmaternal by nature. However, I could feel my body clock ticking away.

I was with the right man, the love of my life, and all those natural instincts were kicking in. I just hoped that he wouldn't think himself too old to be a father again. So I told him that one of the conditions of my acceptance was that we could have a child.

'Oh yes, of course, I want one, too,' he responded.

Next was a more unusual request. 'I will also want a full-time nanny.'

He looked a bit surprised and listened as I explained the logic. 'When we are married, I want to be with you as well as the baby. I want to be free to travel with you so that we can spend the little bits of free time you have, together.'

He readily agreed.

Little did we know that the journey to a pregnancy would be far from straightforward and that I would have to undergo many tests and an operation before my lovely Gemma was conceived five years later.

With everything settled, Paolo Gucci became my fiancé. The ring would come later when we returned to Italy, but first there was an engagement present to be bought and New York to be enjoyed.

The heat-wave continued but at least my temperature was now back to normal and I was feeling and looking much better after visiting the St Regis Hotel's beauty salon. My wardrobe wasn't exactly suitable for steamy New York. I had brought the wine/burgundy winter collection and selected a wine-coloured suit and black patent shoes for the visit to the furrier…phew, it was hot!

I was passionate about fur and Paolo wanted to buy me the coat of my dreams as an engagement present. He asked me what I would like and I chose a fox-fur coat. This fox-fur look was very fashionable at the time, but Paolo had other ideas.

'Everyone has fox,' he said. 'I want you to have something more special.'

I wasn't totally convinced…until I tried on the sable. It was gorgeous, soft and sumptuous and, as I caught my reflection in the mirror, I could see that it suited me to a T. The buyer was also gesticulating to me from behind Paolo's back, indicating that I would be crazy to have fox fur when sable – more than three times more expensive – was being offered. Even with a hefty Gucci discount, the coat was astronomically extravagant. I think it cost more than $4,000 and was by far the most expensive thing that Paolo had bought me.

Although I could parade around the air-conditioned hotel suite in my fabulous coat, it was hardly suitable for city sightseeing. There were no business meetings on the Sunday we spent in New York and so Aldo, Paolo and I had a normal touristy day – all three of us dressed in jeans and shirts. We explored Chinatown and ended up having a snack in Burger King in Times Square, just people-watching.

Palm Beach was fabulous – I just couldn't believe how gorgeous it all was and the Gucci waterfront mansion on North Ocean Boulevard was out of this world. It was a very different Palm Beach in those days – a place that attracted older people with mega-bucks, and I believe one of the owners of McDonald's was our next-door neighbour.

Apart from the staff, there were just the four of us – Paolo and me, and Aldo and Chantal, who was accompanying him on this trip. Without all the jewellery, Chantal looked more beautiful than ever. She had enviable Slavic bone structure.

A few months later – and many degrees colder – Chantal and I would have a funny, competitive confrontation over our furs. It happened at a special party for favoured clients at the London store in Old Bond Street. Aldo had apparently bought his mistress a long sable jacket. It was a cold night and I was wearing my fabulous engagement present over a cocktail dress when we literally bumped into each other. Chantal's fur jacket was draped over her shoulders. Her eyes glinted.

'Oh, Jenny, you've got a full-length sable,' she said, stating the obvious.

'Yes, and yours is gorgeous, too,' I commented without malice.

'Yes, it is, and I am sure it's much better quality than yours,' was her retort.

But, of course, I held the trump card. 'It's a shame you couldn't afford the full length.'

Later, I told Aldo about the conversation and he thought it was hilarious – he nearly wet himself. 'Jenny, you're dreadful. I love you but you are such a rebel,' he would say.

Back in Palm Beach and subsequently, it would be Aldo's favourite lover, Bruna Palumbo, who would take over the estate there and look after all his interests in the USA. Bruna, something of a Gina Lollobrigida lookalike, had been first spotted by Aldo, working behind the counter at the Via Condotti store in Rome. But I am pretty sure that it was Chantal who was using her charms and keeping Aldo happy on this, my first visit to Palm Beach.

Aldo always said that Palm Beach was the only place he could truly relax, but, in fact, I don't think he even knew the meaning of the word. These five days in Florida were meant to be a holiday but they were still full of meetings with the managers and accountants while visitors from other stores would also come over to discuss various issues. I particularly got on with Carlo from the Beverly Hills store.

Over a cup of tea one afternoon, Aldo explained to me that, ten years before, he had chosen a sleepy road called Rodeo Drive for the location of his sumptuous Californian store. It had been specially designed, he explained with pride, to attract the stars.

Aldo and I would often share a cup of tea in the afternoon. The others would take a siesta after lunch, but I was too young and energetic for that and, after a short nap or whatever with Chantal, Aldo would become restless and come downstairs and our English cup of tea ritual began.

He warned me about the dangers of sunbathing with my fair skin – a warning I should have heeded as the Florida sun was particularly vicious and I got horribly burned. The redness was not a good look that evening at a formal charity event we attended.

Throughout the stay in Palm Beach, my beautiful sable coat stayed in the wardrobe and, during the days, I lived in the prototype swimwear range. Aldo complimented me on the 'look' – I had two swimming costumes and two bikinis and two matching *pareus* (a sort of Tahitian sarong) in the very best Swiss cotton lawn, one designed with the trademark Gucci flower design. The white bikini had matching white thong sandals and the costumes featured specially-treated leather straps decorated with horse bits and adorned with the famous metal GG logo in a side panel.

Aldo took the credit for Gucci's latest design coup – he had a way of twisting the truth in an uncannily convincing manner. He was one of those people who could argue that black was white and was used to getting away with it. Paolo was absolutely furious that his father had once again 'embellished the truth' about what had actually happened.

He explained to me how every detail of the swimwear range had been his idea and that his father had been dead set against it. Aldo

74

had apparently raged, 'Gucci will NEVER sell swimwear,' his face getting redder with each word he shouted. 'Never, ever – it is completely the wrong direction for the Gucci name.' He was adamant.

'But, it's a progression for us…a way of moving forward,' Paolo had argued.

After four years of shouting and fist-banging, the prototypes (some of which I was wearing) had been produced. It was eventually agreed that a very limited collection – probably 100 or so pieces – would be put only in the Palm Beach and New York shops. They had all sold out within 24 hours and customers were clamouring for more. When I ventured out onto the beach, I would invariably be stopped and asked where my lovely swimwear had come from. And now, true to form, Aldo, who had been so dead set against the Gucci swimwear range, was claiming that it had all been his idea. This, I was to learn, was typical of him.

From Palm Beach, we parted company with Aldo, as Paolo and I headed to Haiti. A few weeks before, we had attended a function at the Haitian embassy in Rome and Paolo had confided in me his plan to change his nationality. He was feeling increasingly disenchanted with Italian politics, especially the powerful communist party, and had decided to renounce his Italian nationality and become Haitian. I think the last straw had been a proposal to ban the use of American Express cards in Italy – a 'crime' which could see you thrown in jail.

This was our first visit to the island and, when we arrived at the airport in Port au Prince, we both got a fit of the giggles. We had dressed in a hurry and I suddenly saw the funny side of Paolo's appearance – he was covered head to toe in GGs. He had 'Gucci' down the side of his shirt, a Gucci belt, Gucci canvas GG loafers, a Gucci bag, Gucci luggage, a Gucci watch… I'd never seen so many logos together on one person.

'Just look at you,' I giggled.

'Oh my God, I feel terrible. I hadn't realised,' he said.

Haiti under Baby Doc was poor and corrupt and we spent most of the visit waiting for an audience with the esteemed leader. Paolo dropped lots of $100 bills into the hands of various equerries, but the promised appointment never materialised.

The embassy people looked after us really well and proved gracious hosts, serving delicious meals and taking us on sightseeing tours of the island. At first, we were shielded from the poor areas and shanty towns but, later, I got my first bitter taste of deprivation and suffering.

This was to be the first of many visits to the island for Paolo and me and it was also the planting of a seed of an idea, which would improve the lot of hundreds of Haitians. Paolo reasoned that in such a corrupt country, to give money to the poor would serve no purpose, but if you could teach them a skill and provide them with work, that would be a different matter entirely.

His plan – which, in fact, took three years of the inevitable family obstructions to overcome and huge rows to endure – was to set up a small factory on the island where cosmetic bags and beauty and perfume bags and accessories could be made. Of course, the family, especially his uncle Rodolfo, went mad, arguing that the name of Gucci was synonymous with only Italian craftsmanship – nothing bearing the Gucci logo could ever be made outside of Italy.

Paolo pointed out that the production price would be considerably lower by basing it in Haiti and that the end products would not be destined for the flagship stores but would instead be sold alongside the new and growing perfume business.

Christmas at Palm Beach with Aldo.

With a bow round his neck, Paolo masquerading as a gift for his father.

Gucci Perfume International Limited had been set up in 1972. In this instance, it was Aldo who had had trouble convincing his brothers Vasco and Rodolfo to branch out into the fragrance market. On this occasion, Aldo had had the foresight to connect fragrances with the luxury goods market while his brothers, Vasco and Rodolfo, wanted to stick with what they knew – leather. Since then, the Gucci perfumes were sold in perfumeries, pharmacies and duty-free shops around the world. Paolo's Haitian cosmetic and beauty bags were to go alongside them.

Paolo had a conscience and wanted to give something back to Haiti so eventually, out of his own money, he arranged for a designer and expert pattern cutter and machinist from Milan and Florence to be flown on to the island to teach the locals. Of course, there would be other advantages to setting up a Gucci production line in Haiti. Inevitably, it would help with the process of him getting a Haitian passport which, in turn, would have attractive tax advantages. But he was convinced that the way forward was producing a cheaper second more accessible Gucci line. I know Paolo also looked into the possibilities of putting a factory in Yugoslavia, which would have been much more convenient for transport to and from Italy, but that idea was blocked by his uncle Rodolfo.

Paolo and I would make many visits to Haiti over the next four years – even my first driving licence was issued there until I passed my test some years later in New York. Each time I visited the island, I was struck by the warmth and friendliness of the people, as well as the brilliant colours of the bougainvillea that grew everywhere.

The next time I would land at Port au Prince Airport it would be for my wedding, but first it was back to Italy. The apartment at Pozzolatico felt cold and unlived-in when we returned late and tired after our travels. It had been a long journey by road from Rome Airport and it was going to take me a while to readjust to our pre-New York, Palm Beach and Haiti adventure.

Although we were engaged, Paolo's legal separation had still not come through and so, when we returned to Florence, things were pretty much as they had been before the trip. It felt rather unsatisfactory as Paolo kissed me goodbye and headed back to work, and he still had to sleep at his marital home. I was determined not to make problems and would, once again, throw myself into my music studies. But, as I stroked the soft sable of my beautiful coat, I was aware that there was still something missing...an engagement ring. I wasn't sure how to broach the subject.

'I think you've been very generous and I love my coat...but...' I hesitated.

'Do you want a ring?' He could read my mind.

'Well, yes, we are engaged and you've asked me to be your wife. I would like to wear your ring,' I said.

'I am so sorry,' he apologised. 'It never occurred to me. We'll go this Saturday.'

At this point, I think I should explain that Paolo had a rather unusual hobby – not your usual playboy stuff at all. He was, in fact, a pigeon fancier. He bred carrier pigeons and had an aviary for some 200 birds in Florence. Later, they would inspire him to incorporate dove and falcon motifs into his designs. Odd though it might sound, I would also come to be fascinated by these amazing creatures and join him on weekend evenings at gatherings in Modesa – between Florence and Milan – as he called his birds back after their long flights across the Adriatic Sea from Yugoslavia or wherever they'd been. I would sit there in the middle of a field, on a folding chair, with a flask of tea and slice of fruit cake reading a book and watching him call his pigeons home. Between landings, from time to time, he would come over and give me a kiss. But early on in our relationship, I resented the proportion of his scant free time that he spent as chairman of the Tuscan branch of the Italian federation of Pigeon Fanciers.

There was a meeting of pigeon fanciers the Saturday night we had set aside to shop, but at least we were able to spend the afternoon picking out my engagement ring. Of course, Paolo knew all the right people and we headed to Puccini's on the Ponte Vecchio. We spent about an hour making our selection and I was thrilled with my diamond-and-sapphire ring in an ultra-modern setting in yellow gold – it was a very chic design. Afterwards, he dropped me off at the apartment and headed off for his pigeon meeting.

It always felt strange to be on my own after spending time together and the big iron, four-poster bed seemed especially imposing as I climbed into my side. 'It won't be long before all the divorce paperwork is finalised and we can be together properly,' I daydreamed, flexing my fingers and admiring my fabulous engagement ring. My mind was miles away when my foot touched something inside the bed. I screamed and pulled back the covers, terrified at what it might be. And there it was – a small box, beautifully wrapped. It had a little note attached: 'To my darling – here's a little surprise for you.'

I snapped the box open to reveal a ring for my little finger that matched my engagement ring. It twinkled at me invitingly…it was gorgeous! I had the set and they looked wonderful together.

This was before the days of mobile phones and there was no way that I could reach Paolo to thank him, but I was absolutely thrilled. When he came round the next day, I leapt at him, squealing with delight, and thanked him over and over again.

The weather was getting warmer, talk of summer holidays was in the air and Paolo had discovered my guilty secret… I couldn't swim. I might have posed glamorously around the Palm Beach pool in the Gucci swimwear prototypes, but I didn't actually get very wet.

I think we had both realised early on that I would never make a skier – I didn't like schlepping around in the heavy boots and I hated wearing a woolly hat. Although I loved the snow, I was always very protective of my throat and chest and wore a mask to protect my delicate vocal chords from the freezing air – especially in Canada. But swimming was something else entirely. Paolo had told me that we would have lots of holidays in the Mediterranean and I would miss out on so much if I couldn't swim. So he arranged private lessons twice a week at a spa in Florence where, with the help of my fantastic teacher, I learned the necessary co-ordination and was quickly jumping up and down with as much joy as any child when I accomplished my first width and then a length of the Olympic-sized pool. It was much easier than ballet.

Yippee! I could swim and, thrillingly, Paolo had an amazing three weeks off work and had taken a house on the Costa Esmeralda at Porto

Cervo, in Sardinia. This exclusive resort had been developed by the Aga Khan and was where the seriously wealthy went to see and be seen. But, alone at last, Paolo and I were happy in each other's company. We would stroll out in the early evenings through the pale-pink designer boutiques, cafés and restaurants. Hand in hand, we'd watch the beautiful people and identify what they were wearing and guess at their jewellery designer.

It was also where we had our first row. I want to call it a 'row', but actually it was more one-sided than an argument. He lost his temper with me and I was dumbstruck by his over-reaction...and then I promptly burst into tears.

Like most Italians, Paolo was something of a gourmet who enjoyed good food and expected a high standard in his kitchen. On this particular evening, we both wanted to stay in and so had enjoyed browsing the local market for produce that morning and selecting a fish for dinner.

I have always prided myself on my culinary skills and was very happy to cook for my lover. However, being faced with this unfilleted fish rather threw me. I decided to – and here was my unforgivable error – remove its head and tail before cooking it. When Paolo saw his head-and-tail-less meal, he went ballistic. His rage was totally disproportionate to my mistake. I couldn't understand why he was so angry – I had never seen him like that before. I had never heard anyone in my family ever speak to each other like he screamed at me. Without warning, he totally lost his temper.

Although we made up later, I was left feeling rather confused and unhappy by his ugly outburst. Maybe Paolo was more similar to his father than I had realised.

7

Designer Wife and Diplomat

On our return to Florence, I was a woman on a mission – I was busy house-hunting; not just selecting bricks and mortar, but picking out what would be our first home together.

I had never been exactly thrilled with the Pozzolatico apartment, especially knowing its history as Paolo's knocking shop. One day, I was vividly reminded of his earlier exploits there when I discovered his secretary's slippers under the bed. Like everyone else in the Gucci family – and probably most of Florentine society – I was aware of Paolo's long-standing affair with his secretary.

Paolo, in common with all his Gucci relatives, had chosen a mistress from within the firm and his relationship with Giliola had been on and off for almost five years when he and I got together. It was, therefore, hardly surprising that Giliola, who spoke fluent English with everyone except me, was decidedly unfriendly and reluctant to put my calls through to Paolo in the early days. She had been a thorn in Yvonne's side and I was determined not to end up in the same position as Paolo's first wife.

Paolo makes a chain of the world famous Gucci scarves to form a cordon at the opening of Gucci, Atlantic City.

The slippers incident culminated in my throwing the fluffy mules at Paolo's head in disgust and him promising me that it was over with Giliola once and for all, and that he loved only me. Some weeks later, after a coffee and a long chat, Giliola and I actually realised that we liked and respected each other. She also stood firmly by my side during the awful 'fishbone incident' that uncannily tied in with one of the high points of my musical career – an invitation to sing at the Vatican in June 1978.

I was aware of having swallowed a fishbone during a dinner with clients but, after a brief choke, I didn't really think any more about it until the middle of the night when I started to feel very unwell and was finding it difficult to breathe. Paolo took me to the hospital first thing the following morning but was not able to stay with me as he had a long-standing, very important meeting with some buyers from Germany, so Giliola was dispatched to hold my hand and interpret. Both of us were open-mouthed in admiration at the six drop-dead gorgeous student doctors who were working on trying to retrieve the stuck bone from my throat. Actually, my mouth was being forced open as my tongue was pulled out with gauze until it started bleeding in futile attempts to get at the obstruction.

By this stage, my throat was visibly swollen, I had no voice from all the gagging and I was in agony and feeling pretty sorry for myself. Paolo called to find out how I was doing and when Giliola – my new best friend – told him, he sprang into action. A few well-connected phone calls later and I was placed in the very capable hands of a top ENT specialist, Dr Anselmo, who decided that I needed emergency surgery. Although I tend to be calm in health crises, I was very worried about any damage to my vocal chords.

The next thing I knew was waking up with the two-and-a-half-inch fishbone smirking at me in a specimen jar beside the bed. I was sent home with instructions to eat only soups and soft food and to rest for a few days. However, being young and foolhardy, I was determined that I would not miss the opportunity I had to sing at the Vatican the following day. I had been so excited when my friend, Rico Garzilli, an American Jesuit priest and a brilliant musician and composer had, through his role as dean of the Vatican College, arranged for me to perform 'Ave Maria' and some of the pieces he had written. Fishbone or no fishbone, I would not let my old friend down – and I didn't.

Singing in such an historic setting and in front of all the priests was an unforgettable experience although, with hindsight, it was a stupid thing to do. It could have permanently damaged my voice and, in fact, it did affect its tone and range for some months afterwards. But I was elated when I caught the train back to Florence. There was a smile on my face as I curled up in my first-class seat and fell into a deep, exhausted sleep.

House-hunting through the most select areas of Florence was a wonderful experience. Paolo was still unsure about Italy's political future and so had decided not to invest in property in his homeland. So it was from a shortlist of rental properties that we made our final selection.

There was no doubt that the address, an exclusive plaza just behind the Piazza Michelangelo, was one of the best in the city. It was a five-bedroom and five-bathroom traditional Florentine house with a huge kitchen and pantry. The lounge was decorated in a simple, tasteful style with antiques and linen chintz soft furnishings with Sardinian rugs on the tiled floors. I loved it from the moment I turned the key in its magnificent front door and immediately made arrangements to have my piano shipped over from London. But it was the bedroom that really decided the choice for us. A huge bed with a surprisingly comfortable horse-hair mattress dominated the room…and it had a view to die for. Double French windows opened out onto a small balcony where you could stand for ever drinking in the picturesque Tuscan countryside dotted with cypress trees and red-roofed villas. It was breathtakingly beautiful, even for a city girl like me.

Despite having a rural feel, Paolo still hankered for the countryside and so took over the project of converting an old farmhouse on a large plot of land near Galluzzo. It included fields of olive trees that produced the most delicious olive oil you have ever tasted. This was before the days when olive oil was fashionable, but I used it for everything and we also gave it away to friends and family. Just imagine if we had marketed it under the Paolo Gucci brand name as 'designer' olive oil – I am sure we would have made a fortune.

Once we had settled into our new home, my next project was winning over Paolo's two daughters. It was important to me that we should get along well together. From earlier meetings, I knew that Elisabetta, who was petite with a movie-star smile and a sunny disposition, would be a much easier proposition than her younger sister. Patrizia was a real beauty with satin skin that tanned easily and a curvaceous, perfectly proportioned figure…and a difficult character.

In a way, I could understand her attitude; she loved her father but he ignored her. She had witnessed her parents' unhappy marriage and then I had come into his life and it was as if he had pushed her further aside. In fact, I found Paolo's attitude to his daughters cold and distant – it was difficult to understand. Perhaps it was all because of his upbringing and the way that his own father had treated him.

Patrizia had a nasty habit of behaving badly to attract his attention. On one occasion, in a horrible mood, she came round to our house with her boyfriend on a scooter and started to hurl abuse at us – she had decided that she hated her father and me and wanted to tell us so at the top of her lungs. It was a five-minute walk up the driveway to the house and Paolo simply chased her away as if he wanted her out of his sight.

I would often intervene on the girls' behalf. Sometimes they wanted money to travel (both were students then) or for a car and Paolo would refuse to help them. He'd demand that they earn their own money – but who would give a Gucci girl a holiday job?

'Oh, come on, Paolo,' I'd plead, 'you can afford it and it would mean so much to them. Lisabetta has set her heart on going to Greece and Patrizia really does need a car to get about.' In the end, he would give way – but he wasn't generous or warm with them. Fortunately, things were patched up between the girls and me later and, despite a few hiccups over the years, I grew tremendously fond of them both.

Even at its worst, the relationship with my stepdaughters was considerably easier than the confrontations that Paolo was enduring with his family around the boardroom table and my experience in the role of mediator would prove helpful in the future.

The devoted housewife - cleaning Paolo's shoes in the kitchen in Florence.

It felt as if we were always travelling during this period of our lives when we were based in Florence – I don't think we were ever anywhere for more than three weeks at a time. I went everywhere with Paolo – Madrid, Paris, Barcelona and New York – for meetings or to visit suppliers. I remember especially being fascinated, getting to know the silk suppliers and learning about the design and printing process for the scarves. We were a good team and would delight in combing the fashion magazines together and discussing colour schemes and ideas.

It was part of family folklore that the iconic 'Flora' headscarf had been created by a happy accident. Apparently, Princess Grace of Monaco visited the Milan store and Paolo's uncle Rodolfo had rushed out of his office to welcome her. As she prepared to leave, he had offered her a souvenir gift from the collection and she had modestly suggested that she might like a scarf. At that stage, Gucci only produced a very limited and not very imaginative range, including one with the traditional saddle stirrups design, and Rodolfo found them completely unsuitable for the princess. Thinking on his feet, he asked what type of design might appeal and Princess Grace had apparently suggested that maybe something with flowers would be nice. According to Rodolfo – who had been known to exaggerate – he had a flash of inspiration and pretended to the princess that, by some amazing coincidence, Gucci designers had been thinking along the same lines and just such a scarf – full of magnificent flowers – was currently under production.

The story goes that Rodolfo explained to the designer that he wanted a complete *burst* of flowers – not just a design around the edge – and the colourful bouquet was to be printed on a large square of top-quality silk. This scarf would show flowers from every angle, however it was tied or worn.

The famous 'Flora' scarf had been born. Versions of the design with ladybirds and butterflies as well as the flowers – including the smaller sized 'Mini Flora' – would be sold in their thousands around the world. It also marked a new and important component of the Gucci business – silk. Prince Rainier had also given a Gucci scarf to each female guest at his wedding to Grace Kelly in 1956. Recently, I read that Gucci has now reissued their Flora collection, making the vintage items even more collectable. I wish I knew what had happened to mine!

One day at the end of November 1977, Paolo suggested that alongside a hot-weather wardrobe I should also pack all of my divorce and nationality paperwork, as we were off to Haiti for a business trip and to finalise his divorce from Yvonne...and to get married. His Haitian divorce followed on from the legal Italian separation and was later to prove very controversial – as was our subsequent marriage.

We were married in the Port au Prince Town Hall in front of their emblematic registrar – complete in his bowler hat and spats – on 2 December 1977. That morning, I had had my hair and nails done in the hotel beauty shop before dressing carefully in a short, blue-silk Gucci dress that had been designed by Paolo and picked out by him for the occasion. At midday, he slipped a wedding ring of baguette diamonds on to my finger and we agreed to whatever the registrar was saying (it was all in French) and signed various papers and I became Mrs Paolo Gucci. The Haitian ambassador's son was our witness and a couple of friends from New York were our only guests.

It was a lovely day, although I was sad that my family couldn't be there – it was too long a flight and my parents wouldn't have been able to stand the Haitian climate with its exhausting combination of heat and high humidity. As it was, my hair needed tons of lacquer to prevent it flopping in the sticky air. The wedding was followed by a lunch in the island's top restaurant and Paolo and I got very emotional – we both cried.

We stayed on in Haiti for a few days' honeymoon before returning to Florence for Christmas. I had planned a real family Christmas – my parents and Sue were joining us for the holiday and Paolo's girls had also agreed to come over.

Just as everyone was settling in, the shit hit the fan. Someone in Haiti tipped off the press in the USA and, from there, the story had leapt across the Atlantic – PAOLO GUCCI DIVORCES IN HAITI AND MARRIES JENNY GARWOOD – was on the front page of Italy's favourite *Corriere della Sera*.

Yvonne went berserk and was only slightly pacified by the thought that the marriage couldn't be legal. Various lawyers were called in to back up her claim but Paolo really wanted to make sure that his divorce and our marriage was, in fact, above board. He hired a specialist professor of law at Harvard to investigate. It took a year and we became the basis of a legal precedent. But there it was in black and white – our marriage was legal.

Paolo and me on our wedding day in Haiti.
I was so happy then and had no idea how things would turn out.

When it came to attempting to nullify it – when I wanted a divorce – it would also prove impossibly complicated. Years later, going through the papers I signed on my wedding day, I discovered with the help of a translator that one of them was a pre-nuptial agreement. I had had no idea that Paolo had included this document for signing alongside the other marriage certificates.

Still, to this day, I don't understand why he was so desperate to marry me. I wasn't that keen on the idea, having had one failed marriage already and, although I loved him, he could have had me as his mistress and settled for a quiet, trouble-free domestic arrangement. For some reason – he always said that he never wanted to lose me – he was adamant about getting married. Now, looking back, I, too, am very pleased that he got his way.

The first year of our marriage was a very happy time. For the most part, Paolo appeared able to cope with the family battles, although there would be the inevitable stress around the times that the collections were presented. When we were in Florence, he would always come home at lunchtime and sometimes I would meet him at the factory. It was set in beautiful grounds with carefully manicured gardens, where some of the staff would have picnic lunches in fine weather. At this time, Gucci goods were produced in a state-of-the-art factory on the outskirts of Florence at Scandicci, close to one of the main *autostradas* feeding the city. Although the original factory on the Via della Caldaie, where Paolo learned his craft beneath its high-frescoed ceilings, had been closed, its principles still held good.

After Vasco's death in 1974, Paolo was placed in charge of the modern Florence factory and its 600 staff of designers, cutters, pattern-makers, and leather and metal workers. Gucci had always been renowned for being a good employer and artisans working there in their brown or white coats considered that they had a job for life. These people were among the most skilled leather workers in the world. It was fascinating to watch them at their craft and see how the iconic Gucci bags were made. In one area, gas torches were used to heat lengths of bamboo so that they could be bent to make the famous handles.

Paolo's office was upstairs and had glass walls through which he could oversee the whole operation from the ordering of the raw materials – such as the gorgeous cashmeres and softest leather hides – through to their manufacture and, eventually, to where they were dispatched to Gucci outlets around the world.

There was a family story that had been prevalent since the days of Paolo's grandfather, Guccio Gucci. It was said that all newborn Gucci babies were given a piece of leather to smell in their cribs to engrain the family business into their blood. Maybe this did happen in the early part of the century, but certainly Paolo never mentioned it to me. I don't know whether he had a piece of leather in his pram or not, but I do know that the business was in his blood. He was known to be the most creative of all the Guccis and was always coming up with new ideas, most of which were shot down at the board meetings, which led to endless frustration and furious rows.

There were many myths about the early days of the Gucci brand and some – such as its saddle-making roots – were actively encouraged. Aldo himself would refer to the Gucci saddle-making past in interviews with journalists but, in fact, no Gucci ever made anything for horses. Many years later, Paolo's cruel treatment of horses would make headlines around the world and a horse statue was to feature prominently in the breakdown of our marriage, but at this time he was kind to animals – he had kept racing pigeons since the age of 11 and, as an adult, developed a passion for Arab horses. Aldo once famously referred to Paolo as his 'thoroughbred son…who unfortunately no one had ever learned to ride'.

Concerning animals, Paolo shared with me a terribly sad story of his childhood that seemed to sum up his father's ruthless streak. As a youngster, my husband had adopted a little mongrel dog. The boy and dog had been inseparable and, in a household where there had been no pets, Paolo adored his little companion and usually they went everywhere together. One day, he came home from school to find that his little dog had 'disappeared' – apparently, his father had simply got rid of it, for no apparent reason. Even all those years later, Paolo's eyes had filled with tears when he told me the dreadful story of his father's vicious cruelty and the scars that it left. He never forgave him for that.

It has been well chronicled that, back in the 1890s, Guccio Gucci's passion for high-quality luggage had, in fact, come from working at London's Savoy Hotel in his youth and seeing the trunks, suitcases and hatboxes used by its rich and famous guests. At the end of the 19th century, the young Guccio had been forced to travel overseas in search of work, as his parents' straw-hat making business in Florence was failing. So the luxurious Gucci empire grew from straw hats and a keen eye for quality luggage – not saddles.

The decision to incorporate the trademark canvas-and-leather combinations was born out of necessity. Paolo had told me that, during the war, it was impossible to get enough top-quality leather from overseas – I think much of it had come from Scotland. It was decided only to use the scarce tanned leather on the crucial bits of the bags and cases – like corners and straps. The brilliant craftsmen then skilfully incorporated the canvas and the rest was, as they say, history – a history which I loved to hear passionately imparted from the lips of my husband.

For Paolo and me, the hectic travel schedule continued during the early part of our married life. We were a partnership as well as a married couple. As we had agreed on our engagement, I was not going to be a stay-at-home wife. We enjoyed each other's company and were pretty reclusive, really. I still worked on my voice coaching when possible and even gave an occasional concert in Florence. However, apart from my family, Patrizia and Lisabetta and their boyfriends, and a good friend of mine from England, Vicki Mackenzie (who was a journalist with the *Daily Mail*), we rarely entertained at home. Like all couples who are in love, we were wrapped up in each other and completely happy in our own company. Of course, Paolo's work schedule was extremely demanding and, if I'm honest, I sometimes found it hard to keep up with him. He seemed to have boundless energy. On one occasion, his family doctor, who had known him all his life, took me to one side, pointing out that I looked particularly exhausted.

'Paolo is a phenomenon,' he said, 'you'll never be able to keep up with him, Jenny.'

But I was determined. 'I must. I want us to be together as much as possible and that means travelling with him.'

The doctor then advised a change of diet that would increase my stamina. I was to cut down on the pasta – my usual choice – and include more red meat. I followed his recommendations and was more or less able to stand the pace. Our 17-year age gap hardly seemed a problem!

Fashion was still a favourite topic of conversation and Paolo would always ask my opinion. Together, we'd look at the latest editions of *Vogue* and *Harper's* and he would pick out clothes he wanted me to buy.

We were great travelling companions. In our first-class seats, we would tweak designs and select buttons at 30,000ft and I was constantly amazed by his creativity – he was a brilliant designer. Usually we agreed, but not always. He could be very dictatorial and belts were a frequent bone of contention between us.

As a singer – even a slim singer, as I was then – I have always had an aversion to being restricted at the waist. I have never had an 'hourglass' figure and belts – especially wide, leather belts – have never suited me. Paolo was always trying to get me to change my mind about belts and once – to further his cause – he bought me a magnificent and very expensive leather coat. I hated it on sight and knew that it would look terrible. Indeed 'sack' and 'potatoes' were the words that sprang to mind when I put it on.

'It is supposed to be worn with a belt to nip in the waist,' Paolo helpfully pointed out.

Just to prove my point, I went along with the charade. The end result offended even my stylist husband's eye. The price of winning the argument paled in comparison.

'Well, it's staying in the collection,' he stormed. 'Other women have waists. Italian women have waists and it will look wonderful on them.'

He was always the boss during our fashion discussions, but he would at least listen to his un-curvy, English wife's opinions.

Paolo loved colour and, as with all his creations, he used it in a quirky and unusual way. He'd throw splashes of yellow into a navy-blue collection, for instance, and I believe that he was the first designer to put chocolate-brown and blue together. People were shocked at the time but, later, many other designers would copy his ideas.

He was also an instigator with his business proposals. Although the Gucci brand was world-famous and selling well in the 1970s, he could see the opportunities for starting a second somewhat cheaper line that would be more accessible. He wanted to call it 'Gucci Plus' and worked day and night on the business plan and designs. Time and again, he would present his ideas in the boardroom only to have them thrown out.

'Rodolfo is a talentless idiot,' he would storm. 'He might have been a good actor, but he's a lousy businessman! All he does is interfere, rub Aldo up the wrong way and suppress his poor son, Maurizio. He should just stay in the Milan store and not get involved in executive decisions.'

Originally, Guccio Gucci shares had been divided into thirds between Aldo and his brothers Vasco and Rodolfo. Vasco, a heavy smoker, died of lung cancer in 1974 and, having no children, left his shares to his widow. His father, Guccio, had always made it absolutely clear that no shares should ever be given to female members of the family, so Maria was bought out and the company then divided equally between Aldo and Rodolfo.

Later, Aldo gave away 10 per cent of his holding to be divided between his three sons – Giorgio, Paolo and Roberto. Although 3.3 per cent individually would not make much of a voice at board meetings, collectively it gave the three brothers the balance of power between their father and uncle.

Rodolfo did not follow his brother's example and ceded absolutely nothing to his only son Maurizio. This put Paolo's cousin in the unhappy position of not owning a single Gucci share during his father's lifetime. Of course, this would lead to endless personality problems and complexes in the young man who was already stifled by his overbearing father.

So Rodolfo, the former Hollywood actor, controlled half of the company – as he constantly liked to remind everyone. The people working in the shops would collectively sigh when he made his rounds. He had a habit of pointing up at the chandeliers, for instance, and saying to anyone who would listen, 'Half of that chandelier is mine, you know.

Half of everything is mine – I should be consulted on everything and my decisions must be accepted.'

Paolo's plan was to make the Gucci brand more attainable, especially to younger customers. His argument was sound: 'I know that the future lies in diversifying. By bringing in a second line, we don't have to sacrifice the Gucci quality. By using other factories outside of Florence, we can still achieve the same level of quality and save a fortune in the process.'

Gucci Plus was his dream…it would be his own label. It wasn't really that he wanted to break away from the family to get it. If his family had agreed, he would have been happy to work on the new line within the family business. But he was blocked at every turn. It was frustrating for him and actually made him very sad.

Later, of course, later his idea was proved right. Armani and Valentino both came out with successful second lines.

Without permission from the board, Paolo continued to work on Gucci Plus. He created the designs, approached suppliers and looked at manufacturing costs in other countries. Obviously, word got out and, for once, Rodolfo and Aldo were in agreement – Paolo would have to be stopped.

Imagine how hurt and angry Paolo must have felt when he arrived back at the Scandicci factory after lunch one day to find an embarrassed security guard blocking his way. His office was cordoned off and the locks had been changed. He had been fired – for what would be the first of several occasions.

8

Black Sheep – Rifts and Reconciliations

I couldn't bear to see Paolo so unhappy.

It was as if all the stuffing had been knocked out of him: he appeared completely beaten and dejected and it was all so unfair. He had always been an upright and athletic man, but suddenly his whole demeanour had changed. He was deeply hurt; it was almost as if he had been abused. He told me that he felt as if all the work he had done – his designs and the success of the Scandicci factory – had been for nothing. To add insult to injury, Roberto would be brought in to replace him and Paolo didn't rate his younger brother's abilities.

After some consideration, I decided to get involved and intervene on Paolo's behalf. I was not afraid of my father-in-law and I knew that although I might at times irritate him, he had always respected my feisty nature. We had already had a major confrontation at the Palm Beach house. On that occasion, somehow I had been left out of the loop on the fact that lunch was starting earlier than usual at 12.30 and I was upstairs doing something when everyone else had gone into the dining room.

By the time I arrived at the table, the dozen or so other guests – who were mostly Gucci managers and executives – were already seated round the table. Aldo was in a thunderous mood and, when he turned on me, I could see his face was red and a vein in his forehead protruded menacingly. Everyone went quiet: they knew the signs.

'Who do you think you are, coming late to the table?' he thundered. Before I had a chance to answer, he snarled, 'I'll tell you who you are…you are nothing. You are a nobody, a nothing!'

My hackles rose. 'I beg your pardon,' I said surprised, but not contrite. 'Please don't speak to me like that. I am late and I apologise.'

'You are nothing,' he said again. This must have been his favourite put down, but it wouldn't work with me. Out of the corner of my eye, I could see the other guests shifting uncomfortably in their seats. I was obviously expected to quietly back down, and go to my place. But that was not my nature.

'I am a nothing, am I? Well, if that's what you want to believe,' I said levelly. He was obviously used to bullying his family, but he wasn't going to bully me. 'Why don't you sit down and calm down? You are very badly behaved,' I said, as if to a naughty child.

Gucci men – Paolo is sitting with his Uncle Rodolfo and Rodolfo's son Maurizio, who was famously killed by his wife Patrizia.

The manager of the New York shop looked as if he was about to have a heart-attack. He was horrified that I had dared to talk back to Aldo Gucci. 'You can't speak to the chairman like that.'

'He might be your chairman, but he's my father-in-law and he's totally out of line. I am very angry with him.'

I took my seat with dignity and, eventually, the storm abated and normal conversation resumed. Later, I would learn that Paolo could behave like his father at his worst – completely irrationally. Often, as I've said before, he could be cold to his daughters but, because he was so sweet and loving to me, it would take a while for me to register this other side of the Gucci personality.

Having already been prepared to stand up to Aldo, and bear the brunt of his scornful anger, I was more than ready to discuss Paolo being locked out of his own office. I picked up the phone.

'Hello, Aldo...it's Jenny here.'

'Oh, hello, Jenny,' he said neutrally.

'Can I come and see you?' I would get a lift to Rome with Paolo's daughter Patrizia and her boyfriend, who were returning the following day.

'Of course you can come and see me...' This was the charming Aldo I remembered. 'When do you want to come?'

'I'm coming tomorrow.'

'Fine, see you then.'

Click...the line went dead. It was as easy as that.

Patrizia also wanted to speak to her grandfather about getting a job within the Gucci empire. She was desperate to work and no one would employ her, although with her volatile character she would have fitted in perfectly. I decided also to put in a word on her behalf and felt that she would have more success in getting what she wanted if I broached the subject with Aldo first.

Patrizia went first to her grandmother's home and I got a cab to the Via Condotti store. As I headed upstairs to Aldo Gucci's office, for once I barely noticed the iconic displays as I passed by. I hardly glanced at the browsing customers, although I am not sure whether I would have even noticed had there been anyone famous around the place. I was more concerned about what I would say and how my unpredictable father-in-law might react.

'What's all this about?' I asked, after receiving a warm hug. 'Why have you sacked him? Paolo's spirit is broken and he's very upset.' I was later to discover that it had actually been Rodolfo who was responsible for having Paolo's office locks changed and instructing the security guards not to allow their director into the factory. However, I doubted that Aldo had stood up for his son.

'No, he's not, he's fine,' argued Aldo.

I insisted that he was far from fine. Then he took the wind right out of my sails. 'OK,' he said, looking at his watch. 'Let's go for lunch.'

On the way out, through the store, Patrizia spotted us and went crazy. No doubt she threw that tantrum because I had her grandfather's attention. Little did she realise that I was also going to put her case to Aldo over lunch.

'She really needs a job,' I pointed out. Lisabetta was already carving out a name for herself as a popular and successful member of the ready-to-wear team at the Florence shop.

'OK, I'll see what I can do,' Aldo murmured; he seemed to be in a very amenable mood that day.

Roberto would much later, when we were out of the way, be persuaded to give his niece a menial position in the Florence factory. Paolo was then furious with his younger brother for what he considered to be yet another insult.

It was a known fact in the world of Gucci that women were second-class citizens and would never be included in its management. I remember Paolo explaining the situation of his poor Auntie Grimalda. Despite having dedicated her life to working in the first Gucci shop and supporting her husband, Giovanni Vitali, by bailing out the business during its early years, her father had disinherited his eldest child – just because she was a woman. Guccio Gucci died of a heart-attack at the age of 72 just days after Aldo opened the first New York store in 1953. Grimalda was 52 at the time, still married to Giovanni, but childless. She was shocked and disappointed not to have been left any part of the Gucci business. Although she loved her brothers, she wanted to have a say in the direction of the company and even went to court in an attempt to change her father's Will. Unfortunately, her case was lost and a family precedent was set.

Grimalda was a sweet and pretty lady and she never appeared to harbour any bitterness or resentment towards her family. I know that her brothers, and later her nephews, all looked after her financially. She always made an effort with her appearance and, when I first met her, I was struck by this smart lady who was immaculately groomed, with her hair carefully coloured and styled and she usually wore a lovely gold necklace. She remained interested in the business all her life and, during our visits, Paolo would bring her up to date on everything that was happening. Wisely, she tried not to get involved in the various rifts or take sides – especially between her brothers. She told me that her father was partly to blame for the family feuds. From an early age, he had always tried to pit Aldo against Rodolfo and vice versa, believing that sibling rivalry would

In our courtyard in Florence, wearing Paolo's collection – olive green suede and silk…gorgeous! © *Terry Fincher/Photographers International*

make both boys more competitive and work harder. I am sure that it was a good thing that Guccio didn't live to see how the jealousies and battles for power would spill over into the generations to come.

My meeting with Aldo was instrumental in his decision to suggest the New York move. He needed help with the business there and it would put a healthy distance between Paolo and his Uncle 'Foffo'. It seemed like a good solution all round. Having witnessed Patrizia's outburst in the shop, he also had a long talk with my step-daughters. He explained to them how unhappy their parents had been together, that life moves on and that they should stop being so difficult and resentful. He also mentioned that there were two sides to every story, pointing out that their mother had had an ongoing affair for the last 14 years. I am sure this did some good and we weren't regarded as the complete 'baddies' after that.

So our meeting had many benefits although, I am sure, it did nothing to change Aldo's attitude and behaviour towards Paolo. Actually, I don't think he was able to control his temper even if he had wanted to. It was the way that he reacted to anything that he didn't want to hear or if he was crossed in any way – he would just go mad. I am sure that he loved his sons in his own way, and that 'own way' was controlling and manipulative. There was something wild and confrontational that was ingrained in all the Gucci men – they could be charming one minute and behave like barbarians the next. Board meetings always brought out the worst in them all and it never failed to amaze me how they could all be screaming at each other and at each other's throats but then, moments later, they would all go out for lunch together as if nothing had happened.

It wasn't only Paolo who would be in the firing line. Rodolfo and Aldo would also have screaming matches with Paolo's older brother. Giorgio, who was three years older than Paolo, and had actually been the first son to rebel. At the age of 41 in 1969, along with his then girlfriend Maria Pia, he opened his own boutique in Rome.

I had always really liked Giorgio. He was somewhat quieter and shyer than the other members of the family, more like his gentle mother Olwen, whom he also resembled physically. True to family form, Giorgio had had an affair with Gucci sales assistant Maria Pia, who later became his second wife. Their parallel business was on Rome's Via Borgogna, a street that ran parallel to the Via Condotti where the iconic Gucci store was situated.

Giorgio, fed up with being bullied and having to go cap in hand to his controlling father for money, had decided to branch out. The Gucci Boutique he ran with Maria Pia catered for younger clients and he chose his stock from the Gucci collections of handbags and gift items wisely. He knew everything there was to know about handbags – he was a genius, a world expert on the subject – and his business thrived, much to the annoyance of his father.

Uncle Foffo – as they called him – was also unhappy at his nephew's success and demanded his share of the profits. He was absolutely relentless. This was Giorgio's baby and the fact that it was turning into a gold mine was a credit to his hard work and talent. Nonetheless, Rodolfo would be a frequent and unwanted customer at Giorgio's Gucci Boutique. He would storm into the shop, cast a scornful eye over its merchandise, terrorise Maria Pia and demand half the profits. Like his brother Aldo, and with his theatrical background, Rodolfo could throw a memorable temper tantrum when the mood took him.

'This is all mine,' he'd explode. 'It's not yours – you'll be hearing from my lawyers,' he'd threaten.

Not to be outdone, Aldo would also frequently hurl abuse at his oldest son in his shop in front of his customers and employees. They were both absolute bastards. In a press interview at the time, Aldo said that his son Giorgio was 'the black sheep of the family'. 'He has left the cruise liner for a rowing boat…but he will be back!'

His prediction proved right. Giorgio and Maria Pia gave up the fight in 1972 and their business was reabsorbed into Guccio Gucci. The couple continued to run it but with somewhat fewer unwanted visits and shop-floor outbursts from Rodolfo and Aldo.

Roberto was a year younger than Paolo and was something of a hybrid British-Italian mixture. Within Italy, there are also distinct regional characteristics and Tuscans are known by the rather dubious epithet 'the French of Italy'. Notoriously, they are credited with being haughty and arrogant alongside their love of culture and the arts and the Guccis could trace their Tuscan merchandising roots back to 1410. Certainly, Roberto and his wife Drusilla looked down their Tuscan noses at me. Although, to be strictly accurate, Drusilla had a Roman nose, coming as she had from a noble Roman family. However, whatever shapes their noses were, I was definitely an inferior being.

I was at the Palm Beach house when I first met Drusilla; the incident was short and not very sweet. 'You are with Paolo,' she said... I wasn't sure if the inflection in her voice meant that it was a question or a statement, but there was no time for me to say anything before she went on, 'I don't know what to say. You look ridiculously young. How old are you?' There was no pause for me to respond. 'What? Seventeen?' This was definitely not meant as a compliment.

'No, actually I am 29,' I replied, finally managing to find my voice.

'Well, you are far too young.' Apparently, we were not going to be friends. She turned on her immaculate Gucci court heel, walked away and managed to studiously ignore me for the rest of the week.

As a former sales employee, Maria Pia was also not good enough for Drusilla. The pecking order for Gucci women was difficult to understand and I had no idea where my position was. It was apparent whenever we met at family gatherings that Maria Pia, in turn, barely tolerated me. I remained neutral – their attitude really didn't bother me at all.

Drusilla and Roberto were definitely the most prolific and religious of the Guccis, producing four sons and two daughters between 1956 and 1967, and to their credit, they managed to avoid the family pitfall of naming any of them Patrizia. The three Patricias already in the family caused enough confusion as it was. There was Aldo's daughter by his mistress Bruna, Maurizio's wife and Paolo's daughter, all with the same name.

Roberto was also the most obedient and docile of the boys. He was usually quietly respectful of his father. Perversely, Aldo would give indications that, rather than admiring these qualities in his youngest son, they seemed to annoy and rather bore him.

It was Paolo's cousin, Maurizio, and his wife Patrizia, who were the friendliest towards me at first. I liked Maurizio, whom I always found to be kind and sweet, not at all judgemental. Perhaps his tolerance of me was due to the difficulties he had had to overcome in achieving the family's acceptance of his choice of wife. Rodolfo had gone absolutely mad with rage when, at the age of 22, Maurizio had come back to the Milan apartment to tell him that he had fallen in love.

Since the untimely death of his mother, Maurizio had been stifled by the overbearing Rodolfo. Alessandra Winkelhausen, the former Hollywood starlet, had been ill for a long time before succumbing to cancer at the age of 44; Maurizio was just 5 at the time of her death.

Paolo had told me how unhappy his cousin's young life had been. Although, without a doubt, he and his brothers had suffered growing up with an autocratic and moody father, at least they had been part of a family. Besides two family retainers, Maurizio had only had his father, who was determined his son would be raised in an unfashionably strict and regimented environment with a deep understanding of the value of money. There would be no fast cars or jet-set lifestyles for the young Maurizio. In their place were strict curfews, limited pocket money and regulated skiing holidays at the family home in St Moritz.

Rodolfo also instilled into his repressed son the responsibilities that went alongside being a Gucci. As the boy became a tall and lanky teenager with straggly, dark blond hair, Rodolfo explained that most women were gold-diggers who would do anything to get their claws into a Gucci. So while most of his peers would spend the long summer holidays partying in the jet-set capitals of the world, Maurizio was sent to New York to work for his Uncle Aldo.

For the most part, the shy and rather diffident Maurizio accepted his lot. That was until he succumbed to the charms of the beautiful, dark-haired girl with the violet eyes and an uncanny resemblance to a petite version of Elizabeth Taylor. Possibly no girl would ever have been good enough for Rodolfo's only son but, certainly, Patrizia Reggiani fell well short of the necessary criteria. Her father, Fernando, was a successful businessman, who owed a major Milan transport company. He was not – as Patrizia liked to joke – a truck driver.

Her mother, Silvana, came from a far humbler background. Her family had run a restaurant where, as an 18-year-old waitress, she had fallen in love with a 42-year-old customer. Fernando was married and considered something of a pillar of the community, but this didn't prevent him from acknowledging and looking after his 'other family' when Patrizia was born in 1948.

A few months after his wife died, Silvana and her 8-year-old daughter moved into the family's comfortable Milan home. Some years later, Silvana and Fernando were married and Fernando officially adopted the little girl he adored. As she grew up, he showered her with expensive gifts. She also had an impressive clothing allowance that she spent on quite provocative outfits for the party-girl image she was creating. Her father generously added the fur coats and jewellery. I suppose she could have been described as an 'It' girl today. Her father's money had been earned too recently to qualify for the 'society' bracket.

When Patrizia and Maurizio met they were both said to be the same age (22), although later it would come out that Patrizia was, in fact, somewhat older – certainly she was a great deal more experienced than her new boyfriend. It was well known in Milan social circles that Patrizia would marry money. However, only those who closely knew Rodolfo could have foreseen the lengths that he would go to in order to stop the match. When Maurizio failed to respond to his father's usual bullying tactics, he turned his attention to threatening Patrizia's family. When everything failed and Maurizio continued to see his girlfriend in secret, Rodolfo resorted to throwing his son out of his home, disinheriting him and cutting him off without a penny.

It was in this state – clasping his Gucci suitcase – and without any money in his pockets, that he arrived at the Reggianis' front door. Fernando offered a home and a job to Maurizio on a couple of conditions – that he should continue with his law studies, and that no hanky-panky under his roof would be tolerated. He would also take his daughter away on a long trip to see whether the relationship was really serious or not – would it be a case of absence making the heart grow fonder, or out of sight, out of mind? Time would tell.

When father and daughter returned from their trip around the world in September 1971 it was clear to see that the young couple were more in love than ever and determined to be together. When word reached Rodolfo that his son was going to marry the upstart girl – whose name he couldn't even bear to mention – he concocted a new plan. He had, in fact, done everything in his earthly power to keep Maurizio away from Patrizia and he was amazed that his son's rebellion had lasted as long as it had, and that he had not yet returned to the Gucci fold. There was only one further course of action he could take…he would go to God himself.

The way Rodolfo would make sure that his case would reach his Maker was through the cardinal of Milan, so an appointment was made. He tried every argument to get the wedding stopped, even begging that his Holiness the Pope himself be informed of how totally unsuitable a wife Patrizia would make. But there were no religious grounds whatsoever to cancel the nuptials and Maurizio and Patrizia were married in grand style on 28 October 1972. Not one of Maurizio's relatives attended what Paolo later said had been one of the society events of the year.

The married Maurizio was a much more confident young man than the one who had previously been squashed by his father's overbearing personality. In the time that he had lived in the Reggiani household, he had finished his studies, gained legal qualifications and enjoyed working in his father-in-law's transport business. Patrizia was convinced that, eventually, her husband would be reconciled with his father and be able to take his place again in the Gucci business.

In the meantime, from across the Atlantic, Aldo had been watching his nephew's life unfold and considered that Maurizio might be the right man to take over from him in New York. His three sons were already tied up with the Italian side of the business – Giorgio was looking after his shop in Rome, while Roberto was in Florence and Paolo was clearly creative and making his mark on the design side of the business, and learning more of the trade at the Florence factory as he prepared to take over from his Uncle Vasco.

Aldo played a part in persuading his brother to see sense, forgive Maurizio and accept his beautiful, young wife. He also spoke to his brother 'Foffino' about his plans for his nephew in New York. It was due to Aldo and some behind-the-scenes manipulation from Patrizia that Maurizio and his father were reunited after a separation that had lasted two years. In true Gucci tradition, they greeted each other warmly as if nothing had happened and plans were made for the young couple to move to New York.

Patrizia was thrilled and excited about living in the United States. She had always had a gift for speaking languages and her English was fluent. She was also socially ambitious and determined to be a success among the highly-competitive New York social sets. This was the Patrizia that I had met on my first visit to the city before Paolo and I were married. The new mother of gorgeous baby Alessandra was warm and welcoming to me. I didn't know then how diplomatic the baby's choice of name had been. Choosing to name her after her late and much-loved paternal grandmother had delighted Rodolfo and had undoubtedly helped cement the reconciliation. Later, I would realise that Patrizia was friendly towards me only because I was not perceived to be a threat. Things would change when we moved into what she considered to be her territory.

When that happened in 1979, Patrizia was well on her way to achieving the social status she craved. Certainly she had the 'right' address – a penthouse in the bronze-tinted, glass sky-scraper built by Aristotle Onassis and known as Olympic Tower. The story goes that she was so determined to live in the magnificent Manhattan apartment that she approached her father-in-law herself to ask him to buy it for them. Whether or not it was by way of an apology for his earlier mistreatment of his son and daughter-in-law, or whether he considered it a good investment is unclear; eventually, though, Rodolfo gave in and the apartment was duly purchased.

Paolo and I were often invited there for lunch when we were in the city and we were always impressed by the opulence of their home and lifestyle. Huge picture windows looked out onto Fifth Avenue, while the interior had a chic, modern, if somewhat flashy feel with leopard skins draped over the sofas and modern chrome-and-glass furniture. Incidentally, the arms dealer Adnan Kashoggi was their next-door neighbour.

While all might have become cosy between Maurizio and his father, back in Italy, Paolo was finding it increasingly difficult to work with his uncle Rodolfo. It was impossible to get a straight answer regarding the company's financial situation and Paolo would often come home and tell me that 'the bastards [Aldo and Rodolfo] have hidden all the money'. Despite being a company director (he'd been reinstated after the 'cordoning-off' incident) and shareholder, he was denied access to the company accounts. There were always undercurrents of discontent, games were being played, traps set and stunts pulled.

Paolo also felt smothered creatively and was especially furious when, after putting together nine successful and highly acclaimed collections, Rodolfo had sacked him and brought in another designer.

It was the last straw. In desperation, Paolo spoke to his father in New York.

'A change of scene will do you good,' said Aldo. 'Why don't you move over here and look after the shops? It will be a fresh start for both of you, and maybe it will even help Jenny's singing career.'

I was thrilled... I had always loved New York.

9

Dallas Days and New York Nights

It was New Year 1979 and Paolo and I were excited about starting a new life together in New York. I was always a city girl at heart, whereas he hankered after the countryside. Despite this difference of opinion – and the fact that Italy and especially Florence were in Paolo's blood – we were both happy to embark on this new adventure.

Paolo had been officially appointed vice-president of marketing and managing director of Gucci Shops Inc and Gucci Perfumes of America, with an executive salary to go with the titles. There was a bounce to his step and it was wonderful to see him once again bursting with ideas and enthusiasm.

At first, we moved into my father-in-law's second apartment on Fifty-Fourth and Fifth Avenue until Bruna – Aldo's mistress and now constant companion – complained that it was time we moved out and got a place of our own. It was convenient and an easy walk to Paolo's office in the Gucci Fifth Avenue store, so we chose a small one-bedroom apartment in the same building. Our exact address was 25 West Fifty-Fourth Street and we had our new home all done up in soft beige – it was chic and elegant and we were very contented there for a while.

However, Paolo's satisfaction was short-lived. The apartment was not considered grand enough for a man of his status and position. Once again, I was instructed to contact real-estate brokers and come up with a short-list of properties for his later consideration. I was happy to do this and selected one or two possibilities before falling in love with a terribly expensive triplex on Fifth Avenue. Not only did the apartment cost an arm and a leg, but even then – in 1980 – the maintenance fees were around $4,000 a month. Despite that, we both decided it was worth it. That was until one of the Gucci accountants dissuaded us. He pointed out that being on eighty-ninth Street was the 'wrong' end of Fifth Avenue. 'You should never,' he warned, 'go above eighty-sixth Street.' Anyone who knows New York will realise that time has proved how wrong he was.

On one of our evening strolls around the city – people-watching and checking out the competition by comparing window displays in the other designer stores – we spotted a fabulous town-house for sale. It was just off Fifth Avenue and belonged to a major Wall Street broker. Negotiations were soon underway and, eventually, Paolo bought it. We employed Noel Jefferies, a brilliant young architect and designer, to refurbish our new home. We'd seen and admired his work in exhibitions and he and his wife Lynne remain my close friends to this day.

With Noel and Paolo's combined creative talents, the house ended up looking incredibly beautiful but, unfortunately, we were destined never to live there. It was the time of the revolution in Iran and the deposed Shah's senior treasurer made Paolo an offer for the house that he simply could not refuse. A year after buying the town-house, it was sold at an enormous profit and, as usual, the money was paid offshore somewhere.

Despite being a successful business venture, Paolo was upset to see the house go. He had put so much of himself into the project and had really formed an attachment to the place. I was more pragmatic – we were still travelling a lot and I was sure we'd find somewhere else. Today, that town-house is worth around $10 million and its previous owners include Calvin Klein.

We were still travelling a lot of the time and every three months we popped over to Lugano in Switzerland to – as we jokingly put it – 'visit the money'. I really enjoyed these jaunts that began with a train journey to Milan and a night in the Principe di Savoia hotel where we would pick up a car and then drive over the border into Switzerland. I adored Lugano – it was picture-postcard perfect – and even suggested we buy a home there, until I realised that it would be a very boring place to stay for more than a couple of days. 'Visiting the money' was nothing like 'going to the bank'. It was more like a business meeting held in someone's expensively decorated lounge. Usually, two very discreet men in suits would politely welcome us and Mr Sganzini, Paolo's financial lawyer in Switzerland, would also be there. I only once visited the safety deposit boxes like you see in films; that was when Paolo wanted to deposit some property deeds. Afterwards, he would ask whether I wanted to go to a restaurant for lunch and my answer was always 'no'. We had a favourite ritual of sitting on a terrace (it was usually cold and I would be swathed in furs) to eat the most delicious bratwurst in crispy rolls. They tasted heavenly and Paolo adored hot dogs. It seemed like the height of happiness being wrapped in fur, eating a delicious sausage sandwich with the person you love in beautiful surroundings.

I remember on one occasion – we had probably been married for about five years – casually mentioning between mouthfuls that I had always wanted a Piaget watch. Paolo excused himself, disappeared for a short time and returned with the most magnificent one as a present.

On the return journey, we usually stopped over again in Milan for shopping and to meet up with Maurizio and Paolo's uncle Foffo (if they were speaking) before heading home.

When we weren't travelling, our New York days settled into a comfortable routine. I continued with my singing, I studied and also had evening classes – these helped enhance my theatrical experience. I also learned 'middle-of-the-road' music (which I actually loathed), but it did help to expand my repertoire. The theatrical classes gave me confidence to perform, which was just as well as, on a couple of occasions, I had to step in at short notice to present Gucci fashion shows when the PR person had become sick or when Aldo suddenly decided he didn't want to do it. Apparently, I had so impressed my father-in-law that he asked me to travel with him and become more involved in the PR side of the business. He said that I was better at it than the professional team who were paid upwards of $200,000 a year for their efforts. Paolo wasn't keen on the idea, making it clear that, as I was his wife, he wanted us to be together. I really enjoyed being involved with the Gucci public image and my theatrical training stood me in good stead for my times in the spotlight. Aldo also liked to call on me to help entertain overseas buyers, so I always had to look my best – perfectly groomed and, of course, immaculately dressed at all times…just in case.

Paolo actually had quite simple tastes – he loved to put his feet up and read his favourite Italian newspaper. I would always find a source for the *Corriere della Sera* wherever we were in the world and make sure he had his copy each day. He also enjoyed it when my musical friends popped round. These occasions would often evolve into spontaneous musical

With Paolo's father, Aldo, meeting American choreographer, Jerome Robbins, and philanthropist interior designer, Mica Ertegun, at the Metropolitan in New York.

soirées around the piano – there was always a piano in our home. They were contented and happy times for us both.

My father-in-law had realised his dream of taking Gucci to America in 1960 when he opened a boutique in the St Regis Hotel where, 17 years later, Paolo proposed to me on my first visit to New York. In 1961, Gucci stores appeared in Old Bond Street, London, Palm Beach and, in 1963, the first Paris shop opened. Soon, they would be in the best addresses all over the world.

When Paolo and I moved to New York, the final touches were being added to the new store on Fifth Avenue. Aldo had taken me around the building which was clearly 'his baby'. It had been an enormous undertaking – with the first four floors completely gutted before being totally reconstructed. Glass-walled elevators – very much ahead of their time – took customers and visitors up to the different floors. Aldo's office was on the top floor – the 16th.

Much to the annoyance of New York shoppers and the incredulity of the fashion media and New York business world, true to their Italian heritage, Gucci shops in the United States closed for lunch. Aldo always insisted it was a better policy for all his staff to take lunch at the same time – in the case of New York, it was 12.30–1.30pm – rather than risk poor service due to sales assistants taking staggered lunch breaks.

In fact, the service in the New York store was notoriously lax and even, on occasions, rude. Most of those who worked there were young members of Italian aristocratic families, wannabe actors or pretty actresses and models. They were working at Gucci as some sort of rite of passage or on a kind of temporary 'work experience' – they certainly didn't consider it as a long-term career choice and most felt infinitely superior to the customers.

These 'assistants' became notorious for the snide remarks they passed in Italian behind customers' backs. Although they believed that the put-downs would not be understood, sometimes they were and some customers would take a kind of perverse pleasure in repeating them at parties. They became a sort of status symbol and people would almost compete with each other for who had had the worst Gucci experience.

It was quite bizarre and I remember a few years earlier the *New York* magazine ran an article about Gucci entitled THE RUDEST STORE IN NEW YORK. Amazingly, despite the inconvenient lunchtime opening hours and rude staff, there was never any shortage of customers – an estimated 9,000 a day shopped at Gucci stores in America.

The PR team were anxious about their chairman's reaction. However, Aldo, being Aldo, found the article immensely amusing and sent its writer a huge bouquet of flowers thanking her for the 'good publicity' – all the more surprising as my father-in-law always prided himself on his charm and good-manners.

Paolo liked to come home for lunch and, afterwards, we would relax in front of the television. Our favourite daytime soap opera was *All My Children* with its improbable storylines of unrequited love and failed romance. He would arrange for it to be recorded for us when we were travelling. We also enjoyed watching *Dynasty*, and would compare the similarities of the Ewings and South Fork to the Guccis in the other popular series of its day, *Dallas*. We definitely had a lot in common with those characters – Paolo would cast his uncle Rodolfo in the role of the scheming JR – although he really wasn't clever enough – and Aldo would make a more manipulative and short-tempered version of Jock Ewing, the family patriarch. I supposed that if Patrizia was the bitchy Sue Ellen, it would make me into a blonde version of Pam; while Paolo would then become a balding Bobby. There was no doubt that Paolo's younger daughter could behave like Lucy who was known as the 'Poison Dwarf'. I wondered if any of my Gucci relatives sat on their sofas with their feet curled up beneath them, cuddling their respective partners and playing the same television soap mock casting game and, if they did, would each identify themselves as a more flattering character. The true soap opera of the Gucci Family, would, in fact, end up starring Patrizia Regianni and Maurizio with the final episode closing on the cliff-hanger of the gunning down of Maurizio in the red-carpeted foyer of his office in Milan. Forget the fictional riddle of 'Who shot JR?' this storyline was true despite being so far fetched that you absolutely couldn't make it up.

Although we enjoyed the simple pleasures of exploring New York and cosy evenings at home in front of the television or popping out to the movies, there were also plenty of smart occasions involving evening dress and I had a fabulous collection of gowns in my wardrobe to choose from. My jewellery collection was also growing, and among the latest additions was a magnificent emerald and 3-carat diamond ring Paolo had had specially made for me to mark our second wedding anniversary.

For members of New York society the invitations arrive thick and fast. It is possible to have your social diary fully booked – or even, for some occasions, double booked, for months in advance. It is hardly surprising that there is a condition aptly named 'New York Burn-Out'. I remember Paolo saying on several occasions that he was exhausted and couldn't take any more events We even declined an invitation to one of Adnan Kashoggi's famous parties – he was known as the Great Gatsby of the Middle East – but we were tired out and simply couldn't face it.

We did, however, support the family when required. Aldo put his name to several charities, especially the Boys' Clubs of America. He

Always a huge opera fan, I didn't miss the chance to ask Placido Domingo to sign my shirt.

was also a personal friend of the late Luciano Pavarotti and he would host various gala benefits with the famous tenor and opening nights at the Metropolitan Opera and the ballet where we would sit in the royal box. I have many wonderful memories of this time listening to my hero Pavarotti's magnificent voice and meeting and talking to him after the performance.

I am also a huge fan of Placido Domingo and I was thrilled to meet him on another occasion. I especially remember Pavarotti's opening night in *Don Pasquale* with the late Beverly Sills, who sadly also died in 2007. Afterwards, the family hosted a fabulous reception in the exclusive Gucci Galleria. This was a special area on the fourth floor of the store used for entertaining important customers.

With New York society watching, it was very important to look good for such occasions and I made a careful choice for the Metropolitan Museum Costume Ball that year. I had found a beautiful and unusual dress by a young Florentine designer. It was quite exquisite, tiered with a large frill underneath covered with a layer of real silk paper taffeta on top. It was so elaborate that it's hard to describe, but I remember that it had a gently flared shape with some pleats and an area of embroidery down the front. Its colour graduated from a dark, chocolate-brown at the top to a pale, pinky-beige at the bottom. I had chocolate-brown shoes and evening bag.

It was a terribly individual dress, completely unique and a real head-turner. I was tall enough to carry it off and Paolo smiled his approval when he saw me in it. The arrangement was that Paolo and I would share a limousine with Maurizio and Patrizia, and we would arrive at the ball together.

We met up first at their apartment in the Olympic Tower. Patrizia greeted us looking very elegant in a pale-pink shift dress covered in shimmering opaque sequins; it suited her petite frame perfectly and she looked lovely.

She took one look at me and almost burst out laughing.

'Jenny, you look quite charming,' she sniggered insincerely. 'What an unusual dress...' in a tone of voice Sue Ellen would have been proud of. Fortunately, I had enough confidence in my choice of outfit not to be bothered by the snide remark and smiled happily at the photographers as we stepped on to the red carpet. Flash bulbs popped throughout the evening and the press was very much in evidence to capture the cream of New York society in action.

I woke up the next morning to a furious phone call from Patrizia. 'How dare you!' she shouted.

I had no idea what she was going on about.

'I am Mrs Gucci in New York – not you!'

I was none the wiser.

'Go to the newsagent's, then you'll see.'

So I did – and there, on the front page of *Women's Wear Daily*, was my picture and I had to admit the Florentine dress did look magnificent. The inside story hailed the stylish new arrival on the New York social scene – Jenny Gucci, wife of Paolo. It was hardly my fault that poor Patrizia didn't get a mention.

But she was not giving up that easily. Patrizia was irrationally terrified of losing her social position, which was absurd. Paolo and I were never attracted to that way of life and were happy to live our private lives quietly, preferring to spend the little free time we had together relaxing with our feet up or eating informal suppers around the kitchen table with friends and my family.

Patrizia was determined that there would only be one 'Lady Gucci' in New York. She decided to take her issues to Aldo demanding that I wouldn't have a high profile role. She didn't want anyone surpassing her. The fact that Patrizia was used to behaving like a *diva* (although she couldn't sing) and that I had the ability to impress with my voice was a huge feather in my cap and the source of massive envy on her part. Status meant everything to Patrizia Reggiani and years later, when I would think back on all our meetings and conversations, that fact – that status meant *everything* – kept returning. Could her motive to do the unthinkable have been not just money and straightforward jealousy of a younger woman, but a fear of losing her prestigious position as the wife of Maurizio Gucci? At the time I would publicly announce, 'never in a million years', but looking back on our time together in New York, perhaps the signs were there – even though, she and Maurizio appeared like a normal – albeit high powered and attractive – couple who were comfortable and casual with each other and who had two gorgeous daughters.

Aldo told me later some details of the confrontation about me. Patrizia had stormed into his office: 'You cannot have two Gucci women starring in New York…and it has to be me', she had shouted. Apparently he had told her not to be so stupid. 'Jenny is my daughter-in-law and she is great company and also very talented – you are just going to have to get used to it.'

To outside appearances she accepted the situation and was always cool and charming to my face; but, behind my back, she didn't use my name instead referring to me as 'that stupid English girl'.

I remained friendly with Maurizio, while his wife and I were coolly courteous to each other in public but, clearly, we would never be close. I wasn't bothered at all by the occasional contretemps. Like Aldo, I also had other things on my mind…babies.

Now that we were settled in New York, Paolo and I decided that we would try for a baby but nothing happened immediately so I had started taking a fertility drug. Neither of us was happy about the drug and Paolo was especially concerned about its possible side-effects, so we made an appointment with a highly recommended doctor. It was not the first time that Paolo had held my hand while I suffered the indignity of having my insides poked about.

In the early days of our relationship, I had had an IUD coil that had apparently become dangerously infected. I dramatically collapsed outside the British consulate in Florence, haemorrhaging and with a temperature of 104°F. I was rushed into the emergency room of the nearest hospital, which was run by nuns. There, I was strapped down and bravely, or perhaps foolishly, rejected the offer of an anaesthetic. Paolo was called and came rushing to my bedside. I squeezed his hand so tightly that he winced. The doctor counted one, two, three…and twisted and pulled. The pain was excruciating but the relief was amazing. It was like having an infected tooth removed.

Although the doctor had been accomplished, there was no doubt that the IUD had left me with some sort of long-term damage. The New York gynaecologist wanted to investigate further. This time, there would be an anaesthetic for the planned laparoscopy and, depending on what it revealed, further surgery would be needed.

Two-and-a-half hours later, I was groggily coming round from the operation to discover that the IUD had, as I feared, left massive internal scarring that had affected one ovary and that one of my Fallopian tubes had somehow got entangled in my bowel. All had been corrected and, apparently, the other ovary looked fine.

Five days later, I left the hospital with the advice not to do anything special on the conception front, to forget temperature-taking and all the other checks and measures, and simply to relax and let nature take its course and leave my one functioning ovary to do its stuff.

Happily – however fraught his professional life – Paolo and I had always enjoyed an active sex life, so no problems there.

After an initial honeymoon period, working with his father again was causing Paolo more headaches. He'd come home and tell me that his father was behaving like a domineering autocrat. Even with small things, he was being impossible – Aldo always insisted that the handbags were stuffed with white tissue paper. Paolo had decided – for no real reason – to change this trend and began introducing coloured tissue paper. Aldo had gone mad, opening all the bags and discarding the paper on the floor. 'Don't you know?' he screamed, oblivious of the customers' raised eyebrows and uncomfortable sideways glances from the staff. 'Coloured tissue paper fades – that's F-A-D-E-S…' He spelled it out as if Paolo was stupid.

Creatively, my husband was also feeling stifled and he craved the freedom that would allow him to start his own Paolo Gucci line of products. He still dreamed of opening a chain of shops under his own name in all the cities where Gucci already existed. These would not be in competition but, like Giorgio's Rome store, would target a completely different market – younger, with less money to spend. However hard he argued that there would be no conflict with Guccio Gucci, his father would have none of it.

For his part, Aldo was realising that the 3.3 per cent shares he had given to each of his sons had left him in a vulnerable position in the boardroom. Rodolfo's various complexes further muddied the waters. Despite his Hollywood credentials, he had always been jealous of his elder brother's success and charisma. He was also concerned about Maurizio's future as a major player in the next generation, convinced – perhaps correctly – that Aldo's sons, especially Paolo, had more power and influence. He was also aware that Aldo was surreptitiously moving the mainstream Gucci business over to the subsidiary company of Gucci Perfumes in which Rodolfo had only a 20 per cent share. Therefore, he decided to flex his muscles and began putting the pressure on his brother for a larger chunk of the Gucci Perfume business. Aldo said, 'No way!'

Sometimes, it was as if they all hated each other, as if there was a genuine dislike and a constant simmering of deep-seated anger. It was as if everything that each one did was motivated by revenge as part of some weird payback system. They had all suffered abuse from their fathers and all of them were continuing the cycle. Aldo and Rodolfo had both been bullied by their father, Guccio Gucci, and his shadow hung over them throughout their lives. Now they were using exactly the same tactics with the next generation. In turn, I had already noticed the warning signs from Paolo in how cruelly he could behave with his own daughters.

From my position on the sidelines and from all that Paolo told me, I was aware that another major confrontation was brewing…and then my husband received a summons from his father to meet him at the Palm Beach office. Even with my premonition and limited experience of how family meetings could escalate out of control, I could feel my mouth hanging open in disbelief as Paolo told me what had happened and how he had been lucky to escape this particular meeting with his life.

It took place around the conference table in Aldo's office in the Palm Beach store. Aldo asked Paolo for his allegiance at the forthcoming board meeting where he intended to block Rodolfo's advance. He could be pretty sure that Giorgio and Roberto would tow the line, but he was concerned about his middle son – Paolo was the stubborn, awkward one who wasn't afraid of his father and would be quite prepared to stand up to him. Aldo needed Paolo's 3.3 per cent vote…and Paolo felt this was the moment he could negotiate for his own Paolo Gucci business.

'How can you expect me to support you in your fight with Rodolfo when you won't even listen to my ideas?' he told his father.

This was not the way Aldo had expected the conversation to go and he could feel the familiar sensation of uncontrollable anger welling up inside him. He pushed his chair back, stood up quickly and began to pace the room in a futile attempt to keep his growing rage under control.

Paolo was also angry and filled with righteous indignation. He, too, stood up. 'Remember, you fired me – I didn't ask to be fired!' he reminded his father as he had recently been sacked again. It seemed as if this was quite a normal situation and Paolo appeared pretty unconcerned when he told me that he was officially 'unemployed' once more. 'If you won't let me work within the company, then you must give me my freedom to work on my own,' he continued.

Aldo's pacing became faster, as did his heart rate, the vein on his forehead standing out menacingly. He must have thought, how dare Paolo try and manipulate me like this? To Aldo, it was bribery, pure and simple. If I give him the freedom to break away to do something totally alien to the whole Gucci brand, then he will give me his vote. If not, he won't. It was preposterous!

The rage erupted. It was beyond the point of no return. Aldo Gucci was totally out of control. His hand reached down to the table and found the heavy glass ashtray, a Paolo Gucci design – how appropriate! 'You son of a bitch! Why won't you do what I tell you?' he screamed, and, with all his force, he flung the table centrepiece in Paolo's direction. If his aim had been true and it had hit his son's head, Paolo would have been killed. As it was, it missed by a couple of inches, hit the wall behind and smashed into a million pieces.

Paolo knew then that his hopes of winning over his father were as shattered as the crystal glass shards around him.

10

Easter Eggs and an Olive Branch

The Gucci window displays were famous in the flagship New York store. No one – not even the most jaded, bored or pampered shopaholic – could walk past without looking covetously at the latest fabulous outfits, and admire their faultless cut and luxurious fabrics so cleverly and temptingly teamed with the absolutely 'must-have' accessories. Paolo took particular pride in these displays, believing them to be not just creatively satisfying, but also an important showcase of Gucci merchandise.

Among the many topics of disagreement between father and son was the advertising budget and the money that should be spent on promotional catalogues. Aldo firmly believed in the old-school method that publicity should be by word of mouth, while Paolo constantly appealed for a more sophisticated publicity strategy.

It was strange because, when dealing with the press and media, they saw things from the reverse perspective. Paolo couldn't care less what was written about the family, while Aldo (probably more sensibly) did try to filter the stories that came out, especially when they were about the notorious family board meetings. I was still learning that although the Gucci men could be perfect gentlemen, they also behaved like animals when they got together. For this reason, there was a skilled PR team kept at full stretch. Aldo, who adored being the centre of attention, really enjoyed being interviewed. He was skilled at turning on his charm to good effect. Invariably, the interviewer – especially if it was a woman – would leave completely won over by the guru of Gucci.

Aldo was also more impressed by celebrities than either Paolo or I, although I am in awe of people who have a huge talent…particularly if that talent involves music and singing, but other types of fame leave me pretty cold. My father-in-law, on the other hand, had a tendency to fawn over all those people who are just famous for being famous. Of course, money also talked for Aldo and, from his executive suite on the top floor of the Fifth Avenue store, he was always informed when a big sale had gone down – some wealthy customers would spend up to a quarter-of-a-million dollars at a time!

The Fifth Avenue premises had been tastefully designed to appeal especially to the super-wealthy. Handbags and accessories were on the first floor, men's fashions on the second, and ladies' on the third. Aldo also instigated an exclusive 'golden key' system allowing access to the Gucci Galleria. I loved the super-rarified atmosphere of this fourth-floor haven where the likes of Jackie O were regulars.

There was an impressive art collection there, including an original Van Gogh and a Gaugin, too. Aldo proudly confided to me that this collection was worth an estimated $6 million. This was a haven for the very VIP'est of

Performing in New York in 1980.
I am wearing designer couture made
for me by Paolo.

Gucci's élite customers. They were invited to sit down and sip the best champagne amid the limited-edition Gucci jewellery. And, if a 'normal' Gucci bag wasn't enough, this was where you could try out a bag with solid gold trimmings. Items like these carried price tags of $10,000 or even more.

Aldo only ever gave out a thousand of these 'golden keys' – no more were made – so you can imagine how sought-after they became in certain New York society circles. I was lucky because I didn't need a key to allow me access to the fourth floor – as a Gucci, I could pop in whenever I wanted.

One spring Sunday afternoon, Paolo and I were discussing his work and, once again, he was sharing with me how much he missed being involved in the creative side of the business. I complimented him on the new window display. Paolo told me that a Nicolo Minnelli, the fashion co-ordinator at the Beverly Hills shop, had designed it. We both agreed that this man, Nicolo, who turned out to be a good friend of Bruna's, was some sort of genius. It had been arranged that he would look after the window displays in both stores.

Paolo and I had arranged that afternoon to have a stroll through the city together with my father-in-law, just the three of us. When we met up with him, Aldo suggested, 'Let's go to Chinatown. You wouldn't believe the amount of tat and cheap rubbish there!' It seemed like a good idea. It would certainly be a different area of the city to explore.

It was interesting to absorb the sights and smells of this huge immigrant area of New York. We walked along quietly together, occasionally pointing out unusual things and I felt that I was witnessing a rare moment of Gucci harmony. Unfortunately, it was short-lived. Aldo had an idea – and the next thing we knew were being bustled into a tiny cramped Chinese shop.

'Don't you think they'll be perfect?' he asked, holding up a cheap, garishly hand-painted egg. In his hand was something the size of a hen's egg, sporting a $3 price tag.

'Perfect for *what*?' asked Paolo. The tone of his voice was bordering on confrontational and distinctly apprehensive but also curious as to what his father could possibly have in mind.

'It's Easter coming up. We can buy loads of them and use them to decorate the shop window.'

Paolo was incredulous. 'You can't possibly put those in the Fifth Avenue shop!'

'Yes, I can. As usual, Paolo, you don't know what you're talking about...' Aldo was becoming prickly at the possibility of being thwarted.

But the window display was Paolo's responsibility – Aldo might be in charge of the Palm Beach store, but New York was Paolo's.

'Dad, it's simply not going to work,' Paolo said, reasonably. 'They look cheap and tacky – everyone's going to know where they came from.'

'It *is* going to work – they'll look wonderful,' he replied, and on that note he bought the entire stock from the Chinese owner who had somehow managed to maintain an enigmatic expression throughout.

We walked home in silence, with both father and son presumably thinking about how they could stop each other from carrying out their plans. Paolo was absolutely determined that no Chinese egg would ever find its way into his shop window; Aldo was equally resolute that it would.

First thing Monday morning, and the race was on. Paolo got to Nicolo first. The fashion co-ordinator was also horrified at the thought that his chic and stylish display could be ruined by such tasteless decorations... over his dead body, he said dramatically.

Paolo tried to reason with his father. 'Look, Dad, Nicolo says the eggs are terrible – you cannot put them in the window.'

But Aldo was not giving up that easily. He called Nicolo in to see him and threatened to fire him unless the eggs were put in the window. With the job he loved on the line, Nicolo's artistic integrity went out of the window – literally. He simply had no choice.

When Paolo returned to work after his lunch break, he had a fit. There, at 6in intervals around the base of the window, were the Chinese eggs. He contacted Nicolo to find out why he had had a change of heart and, on discovering the reason, he demanded the window key from the shop manager. Paolo collected all the eggs and stormed upstairs to the executive suites. In his father's office, he threw the Chinese eggs across the desk.

Paolo was livid, 'Don't ever, *ever*, do that again – the windows are mine!'

Father and son screamed and swore at each other for several minutes. The eggs were never seen again; it was not a happy Easter.

Fortunately, at home life was more harmonious – which was more than could be said for our latest colour scheme. We were on the move again and, this time, it was as if we had come full circle – back to the original 'family' block just off Fifth Avenue and a super-convenient, five-minute walk to the shop. Paolo had converted our first one-bedroom apartment into an office and we had bought a larger, two-bedroom home on the twelfth floor.

Together, we chose a soft grey and aquamarine colour scheme throughout. The kitchen was redone with pale grey units and tiles and it looked great. Paolo had decided to order the light-grey fabric that would be used to cover the walls of the rest of the apartment from a favourite supplier in Florence. It also made sense for us to be out of the apartment while it was being done up, so we moved back to Florence for a few weeks.

The opening of the Chicago Gucci store.

I was preparing lunch for my husband and his assistant and good friend, Joseph Olivieri, at our Florence home when the two men volunteered to pop out to pick up a loaf of bread for the meal. Imagine my shock when they returned an hour later having made a detour from the bakery to the design shop, and once there had totally changed the decoration colour scheme of our New York home. Apparently, the supplier couldn't provide the pale-grey, velvet-like fabric or the aquamarine alternative we had selected, so Paolo had gone for something completely different – a deep maroon/rust, suede-like fabric for the walls and, to go with it, emerald-green lacquered furniture! Thinking about it now, I suppose it wasn't too dissimilar from the typical Gucci red and green that had evolved from horses' girth straps back in the days of Paolo's grandfather.

For my home, it was not a look that I could imagine and the reality – when it was completed – was as gloomy and dark as I had feared. I was very cross not to have been consulted, but although our home looked quite shocking, it was – to say the least – unusual and, in a way, very chic.

Whenever I visited friends' apartments, I was always immediately struck by how light, cheerful and spacious they all seemed in comparison to ours. It was like living in some dark, velvet womb, made even more claustrophobic when the ceilings had to be lowered to put in all the necessary additional lighting. Then there was the emerald green lacquered furniture and woodwork. Even my piano was stripped and re-covered in green lacquer!

I screamed, 'Noooo, not the piano, too!' but my complaints fell on deaf ears. I lived with that colour scheme for so many years that I looked ginger when I came out!

Although I didn't like the colour scheme and it certainly would not have been my choice, I was not at all unhappy. On the contrary, I was in love and living just off Fifth Avenue in New York – my favourite city in the world. I could not have been more content. Life was one wonderful adventure after another and I loved every minute of it. I never knew what to expect next, so when Paolo came home one hot summer's day in August 1981 and announced that we would be going together on a business trip to Japan, I was especially thrilled as this would be my first visit to the Far East.

Even with the comfort of first class, the flight from Rome seemed interminable and we were pretty exhausted when we arrived at Tokyo airport and then faced a four-hour limo ride through gridlocked traffic to our hotel. We decided on a small snack before going to bed, little knowing that every dish included raw fish. Together with the jet-lag, this turned out to be a lethal combination. I was horribly ill all night and felt very queasy the following day when we took the bullet train to Osaka to visit a pen factory.

Paolo and I were treated like royalty during the visit. Pale-faced, doll-like women presented us with trays of small delicacies before bowing and backing respectfully out of the room. It all felt very strange and a bit scary. I couldn't get over the hundreds and hundreds of factory employees, all wearing the same clothes and working side by side, creating these beautiful enamel pens, their bicycles parked outside ready to take them to their strange homes and fishy food. My stomach lurched again.

'Is Mrs Gucci happy?' I heard my name mentioned and snapped out of the reverie that had led me sickeningly into a Japanese kitchen with the all-pervading smell of raw fish.

'Yes, I am fine,' I smiled weakly. Actually, I felt hungry and disorientated but I didn't want to complain.

'Can we get you anything?' asked the kindly factory manager.

'I am feeling desperate for something sweet,' I admitted. 'My dream would be for a piece of cake – ideally chocolate flavoured – and a cup of tea.' I knew it was an impossible request and that cake of any type didn't appear to exist in Japan in those days.

'Riptons tea?' his secretary piped up.

'Oh yes, Lipton's tea would be wonderful!' Paolo gave me a look as if to say 'You'll be lucky,' as he struggled on manfully swallowing his green tea.

A few minutes later, this dream food arrived. The 'Riptons' tea was only very slightly fishy and tasted like nectar, and wherever the individual chocolate cake had been sourced, I didn't care – it hardly touched the sides on the way down – it was delicious. Paolo, with his passion for cake, looked on enviously until a similar trayful was found for him.

It was true that we, Mr and Mrs Gucci, were treated at the very least like royalty but Paolo, on his own, was given almost God-like status in this country that was just waking up to the designer goods revolution. There were two Gucci shops in Tokyo and, once identified as a genuine 'Gucci', Paolo would be prodded and touched by adoring fans. Crowds gathered outside the store windows as people pointed him out and waited for a glimpse of their hero. Paolo hated all the attention and I teased him that he would make a hopeless pop star.

One evening, we were invited to a famous geisha house in Kyoto as the guests of the chairman of the board of the chain of Takashimaya department stores. As was the custom, our Western clothes were removed and we were given kimonos to wear for the evening. However, it would take more than a kimono to make me feel anything but conspicuous in this alien environment. I felt completely out of place – large, blonde and clumsy beside the petite elegance of these geisha girls with their white-powdered faces, painted lips, wigs and tiny feet. Their little white hands were all over Paolo, who I could tell was feeling horribly uncomfortable and getting rather grouchy. It wasn't helped by the unaccustomed sitting position. We were cross-legged on cushions on the floor and, as time dragged on, our knees, hips and backs were beginning to complain.

I managed to eat a little plain boiled rice and some tempura, but it was the delicious plum wine that was slipping down the best. As Paolo was the centre of attention, I was pretty much ignored, but, after several glasses of this wonderful concoction, I was feeling warm and friendly

An interview with me which appeared in Today newspaper in 1986. The green piano was still attracting attention!

towards everybody, even the most acquisitive of our Japanese female companions. She had scornfully pointed out in perfect English that she liked to shop in Harrods and that she had a larger diamond ring than mine at home.

'Oh, your wife is a singer?' Suddenly everyone turned and looked at me with new respect.

Two Japanese accordion players were summoned. Translators informed me that although they had an extensive Japanese classical repertoire, the only Western music they knew was from *My Fair Lady*.

And so it was that I found myself standing barefoot on top of a table in a Kyoto geisha house singing 'I Could Have Danced All Night' and ending on a perfect top C.

Everyone went wild. Rapturous applause followed and demands to sing it again and again and again. I lost count of the number of times I sang this same song, but it was either seven or nine. Paolo thought it was hysterically funny...he couldn't stop laughing. We both laughed and giggled at the memory all the way back to the hotel where we happily collapsed into the softness of our Western mattress.

The Japanese visit was a success on many levels. It was interesting to talk to the buyers and establish what would sell well there compared with other countries. Apparently, men in Tokyo in the early 1980s were only interested in buying plain grey suits; if we introduced another colour, it would be refused.

We stopped over in Hong Kong on the way back and visited some garment factories there. Paolo was in charge of all the fashion lines then and, although everything was made in Italy, he was looking for suppliers for his dream of starting a Gucci second line.

Things were also looking up in the Gucci camp at home. Paolo was to be made a peace offering from his father. His work and family situation had been impossible since the 'ashtray-throwing' incident and, I think that for once even Aldo knew that he had gone too far and wanted to make amends. With his media ear finely tuned, he was also aware that the incident had attracted a lot of negative publicity. It was one thing to be seen by the public and customers as quirkily Latin and fiery in temperament, but it was quite another to be viewed as a homicidal maniac.

Aldo decided to make the peace. It was December 1981 when he called to invite us to spend Christmas with him and Bruna in Palm Beach, it was as if nothing had happened.

'Aldo, we'd love to,' I said diplomatically, 'but we've already arranged for my parents and sister to come to stay with us in Florence.'

'Then come and share some Florida sunshine after Christmas, around New Year.'

It felt like the right time to make a new start so Paolo and I agreed to the plan.

The Florida sunshine was as welcoming as our greeting. It never failed to amaze me how the troubled Gucci men could embrace warmly as if nothing had happened after the most terrible fights.

As with everything in the Gucci family, it was a complex olive branch that Paolo was offered by his father. It involved a huge re-structuring of the entire company, bringing all the smaller subsidiaries, including Gucci Perfumes and the parent company under one umbrella to be known as Guccio Gucci SpA. The new conglomerate would be quoted on the Milan stock exchange. Aldo would remain as chairman with 17% and Paolo would be his vice-chairman.

This was all well and good, but what about the original issue that had caused the rift in the first place – Paolo's desire to have his own brand? Aldo had also come up with a solution for that. A new division of the company would be formed, with Paolo as its director, and it would be called Gucci Plus.

It seemed like a dream come true. This would mean that Paolo could design and market the second Gucci brand that he had always dreamed of. In exchange, both father and son agreed to drop all the existing lawsuits against each other – and there were many – and Paolo would have to give up the right to design goods under his own name.

When Paolo explained all the conditions to me, I was thrilled for him. A big salary came with the new job – $180,000 a year – and it also included a generous severance pay for his old one. I couldn't understand why he remained sceptical.

'I just don't trust them,' he told me.

As it turned out, he was right to be suspicious. Further questions revealed that all his design proposals for the new line would have to be passed by the board. Surely, this would prove exceptionally tedious and, with his old nemesis Uncle Rodolfo at the helm, he'd probably never get anything approved. Nevertheless, in the new family spirit of optimism and convinced that right was on his side, some weeks later Paolo finally accepted his new position and signed on the dotted line. He was then summoned to present his ideas to the board.

The meeting was in March 1982. Paolo had worked for weeks on selecting his product lines and presenting his marketing strategy to the board. As always, I thought his designs were terrific – he had not lost his touch. But the board didn't see it that way. I couldn't believe it as he told me that, one by one, the board had rejected every one of his proposals, sometimes even before he had finished presenting it. He was not so much dejected as furious. 'I've been so stupid and gullible,' he said angrily. 'I've been tricked.'

'Why? How? I don't understand,' I stuttered lamely.

'They never meant to launch a second line. It was all a ploy to get me to agree not to break away on my own. I knew I was wrong ever to trust Rodolfo,' he said bitterly. Apparently, the board's official reason for not backing Paolo's ideas was that a cheaper line of products would go against the interests of the company.

Soon after the meeting, the board stitched Paolo up even further by taking away his right to sign for the new company. All his father's and uncle's promises and assurances were worthless.

Paolo would not take it lying down, though. For a long time, he had been questioning the Gucci finances and had, on many occasions, asked to see the books. Now he was demanding access to the accounts.

'Jen, I know they're hiding it somewhere. I just don't know where the money is, but I intend to find out. They're not going to get away with it!'

The next board meeting was scheduled for 16 July 1982 in Florence. This time, Paolo would be prepared. He had begun investigating the company and was discovering some discrepancies, including a notional subsidiary in Hong Kong. Not only this but he also felt that the way he had been banned from setting up the second Gucci line was highly suspect. He had put together a list of questions in Italian with an English translation on another sheet. Just to make sure everything was watertight, he had gone so far as to have the translation validated by the American consul in Florence. He also had a tape recorder in his briefcase and intended to record the meeting for later evidence.

It was a hot summer's day and family tensions were running especially high. I waited at home with my friend Vicki Mackenzie, who was a regular houseguest. As a *Daily Mail* journalist, she was especially intrigued by the way my new family operated. She'd often raise an eyebrow at some of the stories I'd tell her about the Gucci boardroom scuffles, like how Paolo had once thrown the handbag collection out of the window because they had been designed by his uncle and not passed by him for approval. Finding the bags strewn across the lawn the following morning, the security guards thought there had been a burglary.

Vicki had also witnessed the Guccis at work first hand. During her visits, we'd go to the Florence shop and have fun trying on clothes – even outfits we knew would look ridiculous, just for a laugh. We'd giggle like a couple of kids and then hush each other. It wasn't difficult to overhear the shouting and banging going on in the boardroom. It would sound as if a huge fight was taking place, yet, a few minutes later, the family would emerge smiling with their arms around each other's shoulders.

'They're a crazy family, Jenny,' she'd say. 'You're getting used to it, but I really think that at the least they're all completely unbalanced. Are you sure you know what you've got yourself into?' she asked, suddenly serious.

So that summer day, Vicki and I together and, with a fair degree of trepidation, waved goodbye to Paolo and wished him good luck...not knowing that he would need more than luck to get him through what lay ahead.

II

Thicker Than Water?

Everyone had his or her own version of what happened in the House of Gucci in Florence's Via Tornabuoini that fateful July afternoon in 1982, from those inside the boardroom to the shop clerks and startled customers whom Paolo rushed past as he made his bloody escape. Within hours, the whole city was buzzing with the scandal and, by the next morning, it had been featured on television, radio and in the newspapers around the world.

It was late evening by the time Paolo came home and told Vicki and me what had happened in the overheated boardroom above the shop. 'As usual, we all greeted each other formally before taking our seats at the long boardroom table. My brothers had come from Rome and Maurizio from Milan to be there,' he said.

As was his custom, Aldo sat at the head of the table, flanked by his brother Rodolfo on one side and his eldest son, Roberto, on the other. Paolo sat at the other end of the table between his cousin Maurizio and brother Giorgio. In between were an array of lawyers and various Gucci executives. It took only a few minutes for the thin veneer of civility to vanish.

All dressed up with somewhere to go: the opening of the Gucci store in New Bond Street, London.

The meeting was officially declared open and a secretary read the minutes from the previous meeting. After these had been approved, Paolo stood up and asked if he could make a statement. There were angry mutterings around the table and glances were passed, which clearly indicated that everyone knew that Paolo planned to cause trouble and should – at all costs – be prevented from doing so.

'I knew then that they were all against me and that I would not be allowed to have my say. I could feel their hostility,' he told us. 'I was especially disappointed that I didn't even have the support from my brothers. I couldn't believe that they didn't want answers as well. I had suspected that there might be trouble, but I had hoped that it would break down into a generation split – us versus my father and uncle. But it was not to be.

'I felt that I was well within my rights as a member of the Gucci family, as a company executive and a shareholder, to ask questions and to get answers. The fact that no one would talk to me made me more concerned than ever that they all had something to hide.

'My father asked me why I wanted to make a statement and the angry grumbles round the table got louder.'

Paolo then started to read from his papers. 'I want to say that, as a director of this company, I have been denied access to any of the company's books or documents. I want my position clarified before we go any further at all...'

People were now shouting him down and Paolo was convinced there had been some previous agreement between them to fire him from this new company as well. This could be his last chance and it was therefore more important than ever that he should have some record, some ammunition and some evidence.

Finally, he made himself heard: 'Who are the mysterious share-holders in Hong Kong and why are they being paid so much money?' He shouted the question across the room.

In the pandemonium that followed, Paolo could hear the voice of his father saying that it was none of his business, and lawyers calling for caution. He also noticed that the secretary, with her shorthand pad on her knee, was examining her nails and not taking any notes. She had obviously received an instruction not to minute anything Paolo said. This was very serious; he had to have some record and he was pleased to have come prepared.

That was the moment when he reached down for his Gucci briefcase and pulled out the tape recorder. 'I put it on the table to show how serious I was and the lengths I was prepared to go to get answers. I held the sheets of questions in one hand and with the other switched it on and began to speak. 'Are you refusing to answer my questions?'

One of the directors was on his feet. 'These are not questions which concern this meeting,' he said.

At that, Paolo threw his lists of questions down on the table. 'If you won't answer my questions and refuse even to minute them, then I will record my questions and your lack of responses.'

According to Paolo, that was the moment when it all degenerated into a brawl. At the time he found it difficult to know who it was who had injured him. He felt an arm around his neck as someone, he later surmised that it was his cousin Maurizio, attempted to hold him from behind. His brother Giorgio had sprung up from the opposite side of the table and tried to grab the tape recorder. In the scuffle, Giorgio's signet ring cut Paolo's face and blood started to trickle down from the wound on to his impeccable Gucci shirt, tie and suit. Stunned, Maurizio and Giorgio let him go.

Paolo pulled out a handkerchief and held it against the wound. At the sight of the blood, the room fell silent.

'Call the police, call the police!' Paolo shouted.

He grabbed a phone and called not the police but his doctor and his lawyer before running out through the main store leaving a trail of shocked customers and staff in his wake.

His doctor in Florence was Dr Nepi and Paolo's first stop was his clinic. After the consultation, Dr Nepi made a detailed report about his injuries. Paolo had told the doctor that as well as the lacerations, he had sight problems and an acute headache from the injuries and that he was in a state of shock.

When he came home, although pale, he actually seemed quite pleased that things had come to a head. As our houseguest, Vicki, of course, got the story for the *Daily Mail* straight from Paolo himself. After he told us what had happened, I gave him a Valium to help him relax and he quickly fell fast asleep. Vicki and I looked at each other in amazement. She was sweet and supportive, but I could tell that she was concerned for me.

At the time of the boardroom scandal, Paolo was 51 years old, Giorgio was 53, Maurizio was 34, Aldo 77 and Rodolfo was 70. They were all old enough to know better. Unlike its gleaming buckles and bits, the Gucci reputation was definitely tarnished.

The press, of course, loved the story, and readers lapped it up. Among those who read about the boardroom brawl at their breakfast tables the next morning was Jackie Onassis in New York. Apparently, she sent a cable to Aldo immediately. It consisted of only one word: 'Why?'

American *People* magazine spotted the similarities with the TV series. Under the headline MOVE OVER DALLAS, the story spoke of a family feud that was rocking the House of Gucci.

A less formal affair... Paolo and me at the Beverly Hills polo tournament
sponsored by – you guessed it – Gucci!

Prince Rainier of Monaco, together with his wife Princess Grace, both loyal Gucci fans, had phoned Aldo to express his condolences and to offer his support.

Journalists did not have to dig very deep to realise that this was not a one-off, spur-of-the-moment loss of temper, but something that had been brewing for a long time. Those with a good nose for a story also knew that this one would run and run.

Gucci lawyers were, of course, rubbing their hands in glee. Paolo used his New York lawyer, Stuart Speiser, to act for him. He filed several lawsuits against Gucci, and, this time, the charges included assault and breach of contract. As he explained to me, the latter was because, as a company director, he had been denied the right to investigate company finances. The details of his claims were all over the papers, both in Europe and the US. I remember that all of the claims added up to around $15 million and, as well as compensation for his injuries, they included the fact that he had been tricked by his father's so-called 'peace offering' into giving up the right to start his own Paolo Gucci line.

Apparently, Aldo had gone ballistic when he heard what Paolo was doing and, in typically litigious manner, filed a counter-lawsuit against his son. Ultimately, neither of them won and, as usual, it was only the lawyers who profited. The case was thrown out of the New York court because, according to the judge, it had all happened outside his jurisdiction, in another country – Italy.

Sometimes during our marriage it seemed as if Paolo was always consulting lawyers. There were so many cases and counter-suits being issued that it felt as if he saw more of his legal advisers than he saw of me. It is strange perhaps that, of all the lawsuits that Paolo issued against the Gucci family, only one ever came to trial. It concerned whether or not, after a decade of arguing with his relatives and a million dollars in lawyers' fees, Paolo could use his name to launch his own fashion line.

In 1988, a judge prohibited him from using the name 'Paolo Gucci' as a trademark because, he argued, it could be confusing to Gucci customers. However, it freed Paolo to use his name as an independent designer for other labels. In fact, the same ruling applies to me to this day.

138

I can use the tag: 'Designed by Jenny Gucci for…'

Paolo was moderately pleased with the ruling, now having some basic guidelines that would allow him to create his own designs.

With Gucci family relations at an all-time low, it seemed like a good time to get away for a while and England beckoned. Paolo had always liked England and had happy childhood memories of holidays with his mother and her relatives in Shropshire. There were also British ties from his father's side. Aldo was an Anglophile, aware that the titled members of the British aristocracy visiting Italy and shopping at Gucci had undoubtedly added to the Gucci reputation for elegance and class. Paolo's grandfather, Guccio, had also spoken fondly of his days at the London Savoy Hotel, so England's green and pleasant land was clearly in his blood.

Since the Fifth Avenue town-house redesign that had been sold before we even moved in, and wanting to move on to something completely different from our maroon-and-emerald-green lacquer New York home, Paolo was hankering for another creative project to sink his teeth into. As a man who preferred the rural life to the city, he craved a home in the English countryside and quite fancied himself as an English squire. I would have preferred somewhere in central London but Paolo was adamant. He bought two beautiful houses in Knightsbridge as an investment and I pleaded that one of them could be a UK base for us.

'If you live in London, you'll leave me,' he said.

He really was a bit paranoid about letting me out of his sight in those days. It was completely illogical and I told him so. I loved him, he was my husband, and I was happy and had no intention of leaving him. But he would not be convinced.

'You'll take other men there and have affairs,' he said.

'Don't be ridiculous! I just want to be near my friends and family in London,' I reasoned. But he would not budge and, of course, he got his way.

In the small village of Rusper, in the heart of the Sussex Downs, we found a manor house called 'Normans' that ticked all Paolo's boxes – it had originally belonged to Henry VIII's favourite cook, apparently gifted to him by the grateful monarch. This enormous, half-timbered manor house had been rebuilt in 1710 and had later undergone a drastic modernisation in 1930. Paolo was determined to restore this historical property back to its former glory. It was a huge and exciting project as layers of plasterboard were carefully removed to reveal original chimneys and authentic oak-panelled walls.

The restoration of Normans was an enormous project that would take three years to complete. With our hectic travel schedule it was impossible to keep on top of the builders, so it was agreed that my parents should move in to one of the wings so that my father could oversee things while we were away. Paolo loved my parents and was really good to them. This was a terrific arrangement as it also gave my father a sense of purpose. He was happy to be needed and enjoyed the challenge of the conversion that seemed never-ending.

The main house, together with several outhouses, was set in 75 acres of gardens and pasture. It had nine bedrooms, two living rooms, a study and dining room. Each layer of ugly wallpaper that was stripped and every section of plasterboard pulled away revealed more wonderful treasures below.

Later, my sister Sue would also move to the Normans estate. There was a two-bedroom cottage on the land and we thought it would be an ideal home for Sue and her daughter Lucy, a place where they could make a new start. Sue's husband had died when Lucy was just six months old. Paolo was always very kind and generous to my family.

Despite all the property Paolo owned, I think he loved Normans best because he thought of it as his home. It was somewhere later that Lisabetta and Patrizia would come with their boyfriends for holidays. It was also a huge outlet for his artistic energy as he always felt stifled creatively in New York. He was also aware that it was a good time to invest in property; it was going up in price all the time. So, alongside the main estate he also bought a nearby farm and three cottages in the village for staff housing.

Shrewd investments and the state of the property market – past, present or future – were the last thing on my mind one glorious late summer afternoon in 1982…it was sex that I wanted.

This outfit was chocolate brown – and Gucci – from top to toe.
© *Terry Fincher/Photographers International*

Paolo and I were in the main house at Rusper for an appointment with the architect who had phoned to say he was running a bit late. We looked at each other and instantly felt the spark of desire, realising we were both thinking the same thing. The workmen were busy away from the main house and we quickly found a bedroom that wasn't too devastated, cleared away the debris, tore off each other's clothes, fell on the bed and had wild, satisfying and fabulous sex.

The occasion was truly memorable, not because it was especially great sex – which it was – or because we were caught *in flagrante* by an embarrassed architect – which we weren't. It was unforgettable for a marvellous and miraculous reason…it was the moment Gemma was conceived.

I felt strange almost immediately. From Rusper, we travelled to Sardinia for a short break and I could barely stay awake. It was just a week after the Rusper afternoon sex and I told Paolo that I felt very odd. I was so terribly sleepy all the time. 'Could I have been bitten by some strange insect?' I wondered. Normally, I had loads of energy and loved to swim when we were on holiday. This trip, I couldn't be bothered to even put on a swimsuit and go to the pool.

Back in our rust-coloured New York home and I noticed my period was two days late. It seemed far too early, but – just for the hell of it – I went out and bought a pregnancy test. Paolo waited with me as we watched the strip change colour. It was unbelievable! Paolo literally jumped up and down with delight and we were both over the moon.

I felt lousy for the first three months but then things developed into a normal pregnancy. I was enormous but still managed to keep up with Paolo's pace and travelled with him right up to the end.

Paolo would be in the somewhat unusual position of having a baby younger than his own grandchild. His own daughters were not thrilled at the prospect of having a little half-brother or sister. Lisabetta already had a baby daughter – little Olympia – with her boyfriend and Patrizia was clearly unhappy at the idea.

Paolo had taken to being a grandfather in his stride. He wasn't exactly ecstatic and never played the role of 'doting grandad'. In this respect, again, he was similar to his father and grandfather. He told me that, as a small child, he had often felt uncomfortable with his grandfather. 'I always felt as if I had done something wrong,' he said. Grandfather Guccio was notoriously tight and hated wasting anything, a trait that he had clearly passed on to his children. There was a story of Aldo's petty meanness that went round the family – I don't know if it was true, but I suspect that it was. Apparently, he had been known to top up the bottles of mineral water with tap water!

So, in the Gucci family, the grandchildren were not spoilt or bought lovely presents from their adoring grandparents. The Guccis were far from the typical image of a loving, big-hearted and generous Italian family.

Paolo never really appeared particularly interested in his grandchildren (Lisabetta's son Cosimo came along five years later) and, I am sure that if asked, Aldo would have found it impossible even to name all his grandchildren. I never heard him ask after any of them or comment on their various development landmarks. He was, however, politely solicitous of my wellbeing and appeared genuinely pleased for us that we were having a baby.

Paolo continued to be caring and loving throughout the pregnancy. I am sure that if he'd still been involved in the design side of the business, he would have made me some maternity clothes. As it was, Gucci didn't make any, so as my tummy expanded, I was forced to shop elsewhere.

12

A Birth, a Death and a Prison Sentence

As my pregnancy progressed, I became enormous. It wasn't just that I felt large, I was *huge*. Sadly, I wasn't going to be one of those women with a neat little bump at the front – I expanded in every direction. However, my bulk didn't stop me travelling and I continued to accompany Paolo on his worldwide business trips right up to the end.

Throughout it all, Paolo was wonderful. He told me that I looked beautiful and showed his love in lots of little caring ways. We spoke about names for the baby and agreed that, whatever the sex, the first name would begin with a 'G' following in the footsteps of Guccio Gucci; we wanted another 'GG'– Giles we decided for a boy and Gemma for a girl.

Our baby was born at the Park Avenue Hospital in New York and Paolo had expressed the wish to be present throughout. However, after 22 hours of rubbing my back, he was sent home for a rest. Complications developed and I had to have a Caesarean at the last minute, but Paolo wasn't allowed into the operating theatre. Gemma came into the world on 3 June 1983 weighing in at a healthy 8lb 1oz. I had secretly wished for a daughter but I suspected that Paolo was a little disappointed not to have had a son.

He was quite rude about Gemma in the first hours of her life; he said that she looked Vietnamese and half-jokingly accused me of having slept with an Asian. Lying there, exhausted and in pain with post-partum anaemia and tubes connected to one arm and the other arm in a splint, I found his comments far from amusing.

To me, Gemma was (and, of course, still is) gorgeous, if a little demanding. In hospital, she cried loudest and always had to be fed before the other babies in the nursery. I couldn't feed her myself. One of my arms was stiffly bandaged as a vein had somehow been split at some point during my labour, so I could hardly even hold her myself for quite a while.

'At least you haven't had the baby in the normal way,' said Paolo, during one visit.

'What do you mean?' I asked, suspecting I knew, but hoping I wasn't right.

'At least there won't be a problem *there*,' pointing vaguely to the top of my legs.

'There wouldn't be a problem anyway, would there?' I was disturbed by what he was suggesting.

'Well, there would be if they'd massacred you,' said Paolo, before changing the subject.

From day one, although he loved the baby, he seemed to take pleasure from saying unkind things. There was an unaccustomed edginess to him that was worrying. It was as if he would see how far he could go with his barbed comments and then he'd apologise by bringing in a special gift and flowers by way of a peace offering on his next visit.

His behaviour after Gemma was born was strange and disconcerting. I suppose, in my heart, I knew that he still loved me but he was such a complicated person, it was hard to tell what was going on. With hindsight, I think he was finding it hard to adjust to putting me into this new role of 'mother of his child'. No longer was I his blonde girlfriend and mistress – I wasn't his toy any more. For the first time, I could sense him beginning to withdraw from me. Part of me panicked, but the other part knew that I was strong enough to cope with whatever happened.

I had never liked the way that Paolo behaved with his two older daughters – the lack of emotion and warmth that he showed always upset me. It was such a different relationship from the one Sue and I had enjoyed with our parents. My friend Vicki would often whisper in my ear, 'He's weird, Jen…' and she was right.

I suppose it was because – up until Gemma's birth – he had always been so wonderful to me that I had been able to dismiss these warning signs. His nasty, cruel and vicious streak, I would put to the back of my mind. I would make excuses for his behaviour – it's just because the girls remind him of his ex-wife, I'd think. After Gemma's birth, even his body language changed. Of course, I should have confronted him, but he became increasingly unapproachable.

Despite being hurtful, Paolo continued to be very generous. He bought me lots of presents, including a fabulous new fur coat – it was a full-length, golden sable with a hood. He just arrived home with it one day saying that it was gorgeous and he couldn't resist it. He was a mass of contradictions – generous but mean-spirited at the same time.

One day, when Gemma was a few months old, I was wearing the coat, together with some burgundy, suede trousers and matching accessories to do some shopping. Although I was slim, my shape had changed since the baby. I still had a Caesarean tummy and Paolo was not going to let me forget it. When he came home for lunch that day, he didn't mince his words.

'Some people in the shop today said that they'd seen you in town. They asked me whether you were pregnant again.'

'Why?' I asked innocently.

'They thought you looked pregnant with your stomach sticking out like that,' he said cruelly.

'Well, honestly, there's not much I can do about it. It's the Caesarean – I am eating very little and my weight is the same as before the baby,' I pointed out.

'Well, you should be careful…you must look after yourself, Jenny.

There are a lot of women out there…' He left the sentence hanging in mid-air.

After a few mouthfuls of pasta, he then brought up the subject of one of his staff. She was plain but super-efficient; she also had a massive crush on my husband.

'I'm having trouble with her,' Paolo confessed. 'All she does is stare at me all day.'

I really wasn't worried.

'She wants me to go out with her one night.'

I burst out laughing, which was not the reaction Paolo had wanted. 'Are you serious, or joking?' I asked with a smile.

'It's not funny, Jenny. I think she really likes me.'

'Well, good for you.'

If Paolo expected me to fly into a jealous rage and go storming over to his office and create a scene, he was sadly mistaken. I still felt secure in my marriage and – after hours of gazing longingly into Paolo's royal-blue eyes and offering to have his babies – she soon packed her bags and returned to Italy.

I don't think Paolo had an affair at this stage of our marriage – I really don't think he had the opportunity, even if he had wanted to. We were together most of the time and slept together every night. There were no business trips without me and we had a wonderful after-work routine. Most weekday evenings, we would meet up at 5.30pm or 6.00pm and go shopping together. I would take a pencil and notebook on these expeditions because they were really research trips around the leading Italian stores in New York.

First stop would be Ferragamo, followed by Fendi and then Sachs Fifth Avenue. The notebook would come out as Paolo sketched new ideas. His eye for detail was amazing, as drawings of buttons and unusual handbag clasps would appear on the pages. If there was time, we would also go to Bloomingdale's where Paolo could happily spend two hours checking out the menswear department. He truly loved every aspect of merchandising. Sometimes, we would stop off for a cocktail before going home to play with Gemma and give her the night-time bottle before bed.

Going shopping with Paolo was every woman's dream. He would pick up, for instance, a gorgeous suit, then say, 'Go and try this on, Jenny – I know it will look perfect with this blouse.' And when it did, he would immediately buy it and maybe even suggest another one in a different colour as well.

He would then pick out some shoes for me, knowing that Gucci footwear was too narrow for me but that Charles Jourdan fitted perfectly. Although most Gucci shoes weren't for me, of course, I had a pair of the iconic loafers. The loafers remained a part of fashion history, even being seen on the feet of movie stars, presidents and royalty on their days off. Paolo also had several pairs in suede that he especially liked to wear when we were on holiday, but mostly he was more a traditional, lace-up kind of guy.

My husband had trained me well and I was now a very good shopper, knowing what suited me and especially what Paolo would like. I looked particularly good in trouser suits and would sometimes have them specially made for me by Paolo's tailor. I would also buy suits by other designers such as Valentino or Yves St Laurent. Paolo was a very generous man to those he cared for – my parents, my sister, the nanny, friends and, of course, me.

If my friends couldn't afford a Gucci skirt or a bag that they had admired, Paolo would suggest that I pick it up for them. We had an open account at all Gucci stores and sometimes Paolo would pay it off and sometimes he wouldn't, depending on his relationship with his father at the time. I know that at one stage the bill at the Fifth Avenue store was well over $50,000 – and that was at wholesale prices!

Paolo and I had a joint credit card and, in addition, he gave me cash each month. All our household bills would be paid through his office. Money was never an issue and I don't remember ever being denied anything.

The Gucci company finances were unbelievably complicated – on paper, it appeared as if there was much more than there actually was. That's why Paolo was constantly trying to find out where the money had gone.

Both Aldo and Rodolfo used their positions to exert control over the next generation. 'You'll get money when I say you'll get money and not before,' was the usual phrase. Even as adults, Paolo and his brothers would have to go cap in hand for money handouts – a quarter-of-a-million here, fifty thousand there.

Rodolfo had always been unbelievably controlling over Maurizio and Patrizia's lives. After the endless attempts to stop his son from marrying Patrizia Reggiani, it was as if he could not now deny his daughter-in-law anything she asked for. Patrizia spoke openly about not wanting jewellery but, instead, had an acquisitive eye for properties. She had absolutely *had* to have a home in the Olympic Tower building and, later, she couldn't live without the luxury duplex in Milan, arguing that property was always a good investment. She might have had the keys to their doors but, as she would discover later, it was her father-in-law's name that was on the ownership deeds for all 'Patrizia's' properties.

It is strange how the very wealthy always have some little eccentric economies that they like to make. With Paolo's grandfather, Guccio Gucci, it was cutting the ham so thinly that it was almost transparent. Aldo's was paying for bottled water; and in Paolo's case, it was taxis. Even in New York, where they were dirt cheap, he would always push for me to take a bus instead – even when I was pregnant. I would tease him about this and we always ended up having a good laugh about it; I was still able to make him enjoy a sense of humour. I take the credit for having taught him to laugh at himself as well as other things.

One thing that remained appealing about the Gucci men was that, although they could be incredibly sophisticated in their tastes, they also enjoyed down-to-earth, simple pleasures. Both my father-in-law and Paolo were pasta freaks and could demolish a huge bowl of the stuff in record time; they also loved my home cooking. A particular favourite was roast chicken with a creamy mashed potato.

Paolo and I had several favourite places to eat out in New York and were great fans of a scruffy Thai restaurant on Eighth Avenue – this was before the days of Thai food being fashionable. A corned beef sandwich from the Carnegie deli would last us about three days. If we were entertaining, the Four Seasons was our favourite venue.

At home in our maroon-and-green Fifth Avenue apartment, I usually did the cooking and Paolo had taught me to make his favourite Italian dishes. I wasn't bothered with other domestic chores as we had a cleaning lady and someone else did the laundry. And, as we had agreed back when we got engaged, we also had a string of wonderful nannies for Gemma. The first one began immediately. She was a specialist in newborns and was brilliant with Gemma, establishing a very strict routine. I was happy to hand over responsibility as it took me a long time to recover from her birth. As soon as I felt better, life again fell into a pattern.

Paolo and me with our beautiful Gemma when she was a toddler.

Our sex life resumed and was as satisfying as ever and we began travelling again. Now Paolo and I would take one transatlantic flight and Gemma and her nanny would follow on a connecting flight the next day.

We spent a lot of time at Rusper where the £2.5 million restoration work was continuing. The pink nursery and adjoining nanny's room was one of the first parts of the house to be completed.

Paolo's position within the House of Gucci was complicated. Technically, he had been out of a job and was not receiving a salary since the boardroom scuffle, and yet at this stage he was still in charge of all the US shops – Beverly Hills, Chicago and the latest franchise was Minneapolis, Saint Paul, where we had four days of parties to celebrate the opening. Of course, Palm Beach remained Aldo's baby.

Aldo was a very fit 78-year-old, showing little sign of slowing down or, heaven forbid, retiring. However, his time at the top was running out as changes in the company were taking place in Italy. His brother Rodolfo was terminally ill and his nephew, Maurizio, was warming up in the wings.

Even the fashion hot spots were changing and, although Florence would always be Gucci's capital and birthplace, and Rome the city where the first collections were seen, it was Milan's star that was rising. Milan was also now the home base of Maurizio and Patrizia who, in 1983, together oversaw the opening of a new Gucci store also in the Via Monte Napoleone opposite the existing shop where luggage and accessories continued to be sold.

It was common knowledge in the family, but not outside it, that Rodolfo had been suffering from prostate cancer for some time. He managed to work and hold on firmly to his share of the company's reins almost up to the end of his life. Meanwhile, his only son Maurizio, who was the only Gucci of his generation not to own any company shares, prepared himself for his inheritance which would amount to half the company.

I had always got on well with Maurizio – we were almost the same age; I felt sorry for the way that he had been smothered by his over-powering father and could imagine how excited he would be about at last being in a position to make decisions and to leave his mark on the House of Gucci.

Early in 1982, Maurizio – together with his wife Patrizia and daughters (Alessandra was then 5 and baby Allegra) moved out of their fabulous Olympic Tower penthouse in New York and returned to Milan. As in New York, Patrizia quickly set about establishing herself as the queen of the social scene and carefully orchestrated her husband's promotion.

A few months before Gemma's birth, Rodolfo died. Paolo told me the news the same day – 14 May 1983. By that stage, their dislike for each other had gone way beyond deathbed reconciliations, although Aldo had been with his brother at the end.

Paolo was completely unemotional when he brought me the news. 'Uncle Foffo died today,' he said. 'I wonder what will happen now.'

Later, we found out that Rodolfo had actually signed over his 50 per cent share of the company to his son before his death to avoid inheritance taxes. The authenticity of the documents would later be questioned in yet another Gucci court case where it was claimed that his signature had been forged.

Stateside, the net was closing on Aldo as the IRS and the US Attorney's office began an investigation into his personal and professional Gucci tax liabilities. For many years, Paolo had been doing his own investigations – not planning to use his findings against his father, but hoping that they might persuade Aldo finally to give way and allow Paolo his dream of starting his own fashion line.

Here I have to set the record straight. Newspaper articles at the time said that Paolo Gucci put his father in jail – that was simply untrue. I would often hear Paolo's side of his frequent phone conversations with his father. They were always the same – he would plead to be allowed to branch out on his own and constantly warned his father about the risks he was running with the tax authorities.

'Don't you understand, Dad? I *have* to make more money. You're not giving me *any*! I have two families to support, alimony payments to make, children to pay for…I want to go out on my own. You're up against this tax thing and you're going to end up in prison…'

It was never said in a threatening way, more as a matter of fact and another reason to allow Paolo to break away. Unfortunately, his appeals still fell on deaf ears.

'Sod off! I don't care what you do,' would be a typical response from Aldo. Paolo was under a lot of pressure from the IRS who were pushing him into making a deal. He shared this information with his father, warning him that if he were to be called to take the stand, he would be forced to tell the truth…which is ultimately what happened. The matter was handed over to the grand jury.

Alongside Paolo's role in all of this was the fact that during his long and argumentative career, Aldo Gucci had made many enemies – among them was a senior company accountant who had been with the firm for 15 years and was due for retirement.

Paolo told me that this elderly man had taken Aldo aside and warned him to be careful as his tax situation was, to say the least, 'vulnerable'. True to his nature of shooting the messenger, Aldo lost his temper with the employee: 'You're a stupid old man who doesn't know what he's talking about – get out of my sight!'

A letter of dismissal was then fired off to the accountant, who never forgave his former boss. So when the IRS came knocking, he co-operated with them. You really couldn't blame the man. He had been treated dreadfully after years of loyal service. I am sure that if the situation had been handled differently – even if it had only been in the form of an apology – things might have worked out differently.

After a long investigation, in January 1986, 81-year-old Aldo Gucci eventually pleaded guilty to evading $7 million in income taxes over an 11-year period from 1972. He faced up to 15 years in prison.

The actual sentence, when it came, was more lenient, as he had paid off his tax debt by then. But still, when I switched on the television on 11 September 1986 and heard that my father-in-law was going to go to prison for a year and a day, I felt physically sick. It was all so unnecessary – the rivalries and rifts within the family should never have gone so far.

After sentencing, in a choked voice, Aldo told the court that he forgave those who had betrayed him. On hearing that, I looked across at Paolo. His face – though white as a sheet – registered no emotion.

13

Sleepless in West Sussex

After an appeal was rejected, Aldo served his sentence – which worked out to be just under a year – at the Eglin Air Force base in Florida. During that time, we had no contact whatsoever with him. No phone calls, no birthday cards, no messages and no visits. I have since found out that he was in frequent contact with other relatives, friends and business associates both by phone and letter, but we didn't exchange a single word with him. It might seem odd to other people, but the relationships within the Gucci family were very strange. I knew that if I had said to Paolo, 'Why don't we phone your father and see how he is getting on?' he would have gone nuts.

Although Paolo was extremely upset by his father's prison sentence, he refused to talk about his feelings. He didn't cry, but he was very down for several days after we heard the news that Aldo would indeed serve time in jail. I don't think he felt guilty about his role in what happened. He had warned his father scores of times and Aldo just wouldn't listen. Paolo also probably reasoned that, by steadfastly refusing to budge an inch on his second line project, his father had somehow got his just desserts.

The Eglin jail was known to be a relatively easy option for 'white-collar' criminals and, during my father-in-law's stay there, another fashion designer was also serving time for tax evasion.

So with this deafening, year-long silence between father and son, I was anxious as to how they would face each other when Aldo was released. But I needn't have worried. In fact, Aldo and Paolo bumped into each other in the lift in our apartment block. Paolo was amazed to see his father looking so well.

'Dad, you look fantastic!' as they warmly embraced and kissed each other.

And Aldo's reaction was just as gushing: 'I'm telling you, son, it was the best rest I've had in 30 years! I slept like a baby every night and, during the day, I did the prison laundry. In the afternoon, I got to sit in a deckchair and read a book – it was fantastic!'

So, no hard feelings then. Thank God for that!

Paolo and I continued to travel extensively when Gemma was a baby. The pattern was – as before – usually to spend three weeks at a time in England, New York and Florence. Paolo might have cut contact with most of the family by then, but when in Italy, we still saw his daughters and also his mother.

Although brave and courageous, Olwen had never been the same after a gang of thieves broke into her Rome home. She still lived in the imposing villa off the fashionable Via della Camilluccia and had been in the bath at the time of the attack. We were in Florence when it happened and Paolo's brother Giorgio phoned with the news. We set off immediately to see how she was. Although clearly very shaken by the experience, we learned that she had also been tied up, along with her staff, and forced to tell the robbers where her valuables were. Undoubtedly, she was a very determined and strong lady and maybe her wartime undercover work had stood her in good stead. She even coped admirably with all the media attention that followed.

When we arrived, press and TV camera crews, police and even private bodyguards surrounded the house, the latter organised by the ever-solicitous Aldo for additional protection. It was a while later that the full impact of what happened seemed to hit Olwen and, sadly, she suffered a stroke, which left her quite incapacitated. Despite her physical frailties, she was still able to stand up to her husband and deny him the divorce he requested in 1984. There are some reports that, eventually, Aldo got his way and married his long-term mistress, Bruna, in secret, but I never heard anything about it at the time.

One thing I always found amusing was the way Aldo would breeze in and out of his wife's home as if they were still together, despite the fact that they had not lived as a couple for years. What was even more surprising was that, when he and his mistress were in Rome, he would always have his chauffeur drive through the imposing electric security gates of Olwen's villa and drop off their dirty laundry – both Aldo and Bruna's! Aldo would reason that he paid for his wife's household staff, so there was nothing wrong in using them.

At that stage, Paolo and I could still laugh together about the eccentricities of the Guccis. In fact, during the most stressful times, we worked especially well together as a close partnership.

Another, and perhaps stranger, partnership was also forming between Paolo and his cousin, Maurizio, who had by now inherited 50 per cent of the company from his father and acted as if he was somewhat overwhelmed by the new authority it afforded.

After Rodolfo's death, there had been a criminal investigation against Maurizio for forging his father's signature on the paperwork transferring the shares prior to death as a way of avoiding inheritance taxes. Maurizio had literally run away to Switzerland and into hiding during the investigation, but returned to Italy when the court case came up. After he was eventually found 'not guilty', he then turned his energies into his new role as major Gucci shareholder.

During this five-year period in the early 1980s, a staggering 15 lawsuits were filed in the United States by Gucci family members – all involved relatives and I am pretty sure that all of them included my husband in some way or other. Although I was still very much in love with Paolo and supported him in every way that I could, I was aware of how confrontational he could be. Often, I would beg him to let go and make his peace with his family. I knew that they were all pretty crazy, but all these arguments and allegations didn't do anybody any good. So when Paolo and Maurizio began talking, I was pleased and encouraged his contact with his cousin.

After a lifetime of being suppressed by his father, Maurizio was very keen to make his mark and create a new Gucci. To realise this long-held dream, he would need to take control. Maurizio understood that Aldo would undoubtedly be as stubborn with his nephew as he had been with his sons. In Paolo, he found an ally. Together – over dozens of meetings and phone calls throughout the spring of 1984 – they hatched a plan. They agreed that at the next board meeting (which would be held in New York in September), Paolo would put his 3.3 per cent shares with his cousin's 50 per cent and together they would vote Aldo out of the position of chairman, allowing Maurizio to take charge. In exchange, they would set up a new company with Maurizio controlling 51 per cent and Paolo – with the title of 'president' – 49 per cent. Maurizio also agreed to pay his cousin $20 million for his shares.

I thought it sounded like a good idea, especially as it would allow Paolo to get on with designing and creating new lines, which was what he had always wanted. Aldo was then 79 years old and, with the tax investigation hotting up, it really seemed like a good time for him to consider retiring. Admittedly, the method of his going was somewhat underhand, but I was also thinking about the number of times he had fired and hurt Paolo.

It was hardly surprising that Paolo was beginning to feel the pressure. He was also examining the possibility of selling his shares to outside investors. This would, for the first time in the history of Gucci, give someone who was not a relative a voice in the family company.

There was a famous quote from one of the company lawyers at the time: 'I know every piece in the Gucci line, and I know that two-thirds of the price of every wallet goes to lawyers.' Certainly, Paolo's lawyers' fees must have been huge, but despite that – and the fact that he hadn't had a salary from Gucci for a long time – I was never aware of having to make any economies or cut back on our very comfortable lifestyle. We still kept all our homes and our staff and neither Paolo, little Gemma nor I ever wanted for anything.

Once I read an article in *Vanity Fair* about the family and it claimed that 'Paolo Gucci was constantly suing his father; and the father was paying for his son's lawyers to sue him. Every time Paolo would run out of money to pay his lawyer, Aldo would pay.'

I never heard anything about that, and I find it very hard to believe. I am not saying that Aldo didn't give Paolo money; I think from time to time he probably did. I was only aware of some vague investments and money from Switzerland being our source of income.

My husband, who had always been able to sleep through anything, was tossing and turning all night and then getting out of bed and pacing up and down, up and down – for hours on end. Frequently, I would wake in the early hours, stick out an arm and find his side of the bed empty. It didn't make any difference where we were – at our home in New York, Florence or in our restored Tudor bedroom at Normans in West Sussex – life with Paolo was like clinging on to a roller-coaster. One minute he'd be ecstatic, as some meeting with Maurizio or the investors wanting to buy his shares had gone well; and the next he would be depressed. He was full of questions – was this the right time to sell? Should he hold on longer? Should he go back to working at Gucci? Would it be a mistake to settle for only 49 per cent of Maurizio's new company? Would working for his cousin turn out to be as bad as working for his father? The man was in turmoil.

I would get up and put the kettle on. Paolo always found a cup of tea soothing. After pacing

Travelling in style -
Paolo and Gemma in Palm Beach.

158

a bit together, I would eventually coax him into a chair and listen to his concerns as the sun came up.

We had the same conversations over and over again. I would tell him not to worry, that everything happens for a reason (a philosophy I still hold true) and that I still believed in him and his terrific talent as a designer. Maybe breaking away from the family would turn out to be the best thing that had ever happened to him. Then he would start to tell me everything we would do 'when the money came in'. He spoke about the possibility of receiving as much as $40 million for his shares, but it seemed impossible to imagine such a sum of money.

'You've been such a wonderful wife and so supportive and I love you so much, Jenny,' he often told me in these dawn conversations. 'I don't know how I would have got through all of this without you,' he would say while gently stroking my hand. 'When the money comes in, I am going to give you some for your devotion,' he promised. 'If it's $9 million, I am going to hand over $2 million of it to you so you'll always have security,' he promised.

'That will be wonderful, darling, thank you, but let's see how much you get first. Whatever it is, we'll be fine,' I would reassure him.

I would also try and take his mind off his problems while he was at home. I knew that he was able to relax playing with little Gemma. In New York, we continued our evening outings to the beautiful designer shops, followed by a glass of wine for him and a cocktail for me, then feet up in front of a mindless television series. It was all good anti-stress therapy. Although Paolo enjoyed political debates and loved reading his *Corriere della Sera*, there was nothing like an episode of *Hill Street Blues* and the *Dallas/Dynasty* soap operas to take his mind off everything. I would make a point of cooking his favourite meals and even cleaning his shoes; in fact, I would do anything he wanted to make this difficult time easier for him.

There is no doubt in my mind that there was a cost to living under all this terrible stress for so long. For a period, I was persuaded by my doctor to take beta-blockers as a way of protecting my long-term health. I didn't need anti-depressants – I was never depressed in any way, more scared and frightened. I can only imagine the possible consequences that it all had on Paolo's condition.

Although, ever since I had met him and, I'm sure, for a long time beforehand, Paolo had boundless and enviable energy, he also had a problem with his liver. I will never forget the first time I saw him doubled up in agony, the pain so bad that, on occasions, he would literally pass out. These attacks would come unannounced about every eight months or so, and end after a few minutes just as suddenly as they had begun. Regarding his health, Paolo was not a typical male. He was not the sort of man to bury his head in the sand and ignore symptoms. Early on, he had visited a doctor and then a specialist in liver conditions. It was confirmed that, although very rare, Paolo was unlucky and a bout of Hepatitis A – caused by eating an infected chicken during a holiday in Saudi Arabia in 1974 – had left him with a damaged liver. He had been very ill after becoming infected, but during the early stages of cirrhosis, and when you are young, the liver can repair itself. Sadly, as Paolo got older, the extent of the damage became more noticeable. He was very careful with his lifestyle choices and only occasionally had a glass of wine, but still unbeknown to us, his physical health was failing. Unfortunately, it would also become increasingly apparent that his mental health was also deteriorating.

However, he still found the restoration of Normans at Rusper very therapeutic. The house was coming on slowly, and working on its design and planning helped distract him from his other problems. He shared with me his dream of breeding purebred Arab horses on the 75-acre estate and a stud farm was included in the plans. There would also be two swimming pools, a gym and a tennis court – Paolo really fancied himself as Lord of the Manor and he was never happier than when he was designing or creating something, whether it was a house or a handbag.

As with our maroon-and-green New York apartment, Paolo and I would discuss and choose colour schemes that bore little resemblance to what Paolo finally selected. He would listen to my opinions and then, if he didn't agree, ignore them.

One day, after spotting a Volkswagen Beetle in the exact pale, almost-metallic lilac shade he wanted for the upstairs walls, he was a man on a single-minded vision. He would not rest until he had located the exact same shade. His English secretary, Deirdre, was also set the task of locating the precise colour. When she failed to do so, Paolo instructed her to approach Volkswagen directly and buy it from them. So it was decided to use car paint on the upstairs walls. The smell was so strong that we – family and staff – all had to be evacuated for three days for fear of being poisoned by it.

The house was huge with eight or nine bedrooms, several bathrooms and various reception rooms. I had asked Paolo if I could have my own room – not for sleeping but just a private space where I could sing or do my own thing. We agreed where it would be and, before leaving to buy some groceries, I made a request to keep the original Tudor oak door. By the time I returned, the door had gone and so too had the room. For some reason, he just didn't want to let me have it. Although I was cross, I had learned by this stage to pick my battles and, to be honest, I never really felt that Normans was mine. It was always Paolo's house – his dream and his restoration project. He even thought it worthwhile to have another futile battle with his family for the right to use the Gucci logo on the front gate.

Although my family were there in the English countryside, in my heart I remained a city girl and continued to prefer our life in New York. However, it was not by accident that we were out of the States for that September board meeting. Maurizio would also be absent and had sent a proxy to the boardroom on the thirteenth floor of the Fifth Avenue store. I think he was probably off sailing on his yacht at Porto Cervo at the time. Believing it to be just a routine meeting where the first six-monthly figures would be agreed, Aldo had also not bothered to attend in person. So it was left in the hands of the three lawyers, two of them knowing what would happen and the third, like his employer, Aldo, was caught completely unawares. The motion to dissolve the board was passed with 53.3 per cent support – Maurizio and Paolo had won and Aldo's reign was over. But, for Paolo, it would prove a hollow victory and the pact with his cousin would be short-lived.

In the meantime, Aldo had arranged to hand over his shares – they amounted to 40 per cent of Guccio Gucci – to his other two sons, Roberto and Giorgio, equally. Paolo had been left out of the legacy as a punishment for his treachery. Aldo meant the gift to be a secret and both brothers had agreed not to vote with their new shares at meetings. Despite this, Paolo somehow still got to hear about how his father had cut him off. I was surprised at how levelly he took the news.

'Maybe he was right – perhaps I do deserve it. He never really forgave me for giving evidence at his tax trial,' he reasoned with a shrug of his shoulders. I believe that father and son were far more similar than they ever realised.

Things also ended up badly between Paolo and his cousin. After months of soul-searching, Paolo came to the conclusion that Maurizio hadn't stood by his side of the agreement regarding the new company that they had planned to form together. Afterwards, he told me about how it had all gone right up to the wire. The lawyers from both sides came up with proposals and counter-proposals late into the night. In the end, Paolo had torn up the draft contract and walked away from the agreement that would have given Maurizio 53.3 per cent control of the company.

I hadn't really understood Paolo's motives. He was a complex person and maybe the enormity of cutting himself off completely from his family business just proved too much. Maurizio was more than disappointed – he was angry, and it wouldn't take long before he would discover a way of making Paolo pay for his disloyalty.

Despite all these wrangles, Paolo was working again. I was happy to see that he had rekindled his plans to create his own line and was full of fresh and exciting ideas.

'Sniff this, Jenny…just touch it, do you think it's soft enough? What do you think of the colour?' as I was handed a leather sample for consideration. His sketchpad was filling up with pencil drawings and ideas for a new collection of belts, bags and accessories. Buckles, handles and other details were delivered daily for approval.

The 'PG' range was building up nicely – the leather goods were gorgeous and I knew that the bags, belts, shoes and scarves would be snapped up, but the ready-to-wear dresses were a disaster. I think he must have been desperate because he bought in these awful dresses. We had terrible rows about them, especially a range of satin, gypsy-style evening dresses. They weren't his design and I thought they were ghastly – they weren't even well-made and looked cheap and tacky – certainly not worthy of a 'Paolo Gucci' label. I kept telling him that they were completely unacceptable and I would take them down and hide them away. Then he found them and kept putting them back.

I didn't really mind about the arguments over the dresses, as it was great to see my husband so enthusiastic again – he was more like the old Paolo I had first met, before all the family battles and conflicts had taken their toll. I happily agreed to get involved in the launch of the new PG accessories line and, together with his secretary, we planned a big party in Rome to mark the occasion. Invitations were issued, caterers booked and the scene was set.

It was March 1986 and the party was in full swing. As the models wandered among the guests, I could see the fashion journalists chatting together as they examined the new collection. No doubt they were also gossiping about the Gucci family and speculating about the impact Paolo's breakaway would have. Although the items would retail at a much cheaper price than the traditional Gucci lines, they still looked classy (with the possible exception of the dresses, which I continued to hide up until the last minute). Clearly, Paolo had not lost his touch, and I was looking forward to reading favourable reviews in the next editions of the fashion press.

We exchanged a conspiratorial smile across the room. He looked more relaxed and happy than I had seen him for a long time. We had also agreed to take on board any constructive negative comments about the designs; these were prototypes and details could still be tweaked or changed.

Suddenly, the whole atmosphere changed – the gentle party chatter gave way to raised voices and I could see Paolo struggling by the door with some men. At first, I thought they must be gate-crashers, and then – to my horror – I realised they were plain-clothes policemen. What was going on?

The policemen were grabbing the whole collection – stunned models were handing over the bags, belts…everything. All Paolo's beautiful PG collection was being sequestered because, apparently, he had no legal permission to use his name on the designs.

He knew instantly who had been behind the plot – Maurizio. Paolo was furious and let everyone know it as embarrassed guests hurriedly finished their champagne and grabbed their coats. The fashion journalists among them had a hard news story this time. The Gucci family rarely disappointed and, once again, there would be plenty of column inches about them in tomorrow's press. Sadly, Paolo's designs would only get a passing mention – not for their style, but for their legal implications.

14

Bye, Bye, Birdies

Aldo was standing between us with a protective arm around our shoulders. Paolo was smiling broadly and, in that instant, I could just imagine how he must have looked as a little boy. His father is gazing proudly at his son and the returning expression on Paolo's face shows love and affection. Aldo has just given Paolo a present to congratulate him on the success of his third Gucci ready-to-wear collection. This isn't just *any* present – the gift inside this box is truly expensive – not just in hard currency but in the effort and thought that it had taken to track down.

There was a gasp of surprise from the relatives still seated at the table as Paolo lifted the lid. To us, it looked like any ordinary pigeon – to Paolo, it was the North American champion he had coveted for months. And his father had bought it for him.

'You, my son, you're always trouble – you always were and you always will be…but you *are* talented. The collection is wonderful – a true champion of a collection – like this bird!'

For once, Paolo was at a loss for words. The frustration and bitterness of family arguments is forgotten as he simply thanks his father for the best present ever with a kiss and a warm embrace.

Then I woke up, still in that warm, fuzzy, dreamy place and with a short-lived smile playing on my lips. Although it had been a dream, I could hardly believe that these events had actually happened just a few short years before – at the start of our marriage. I found it shocking how quickly things had degenerated to such a state. Since that family party and Aldo's wonderful present of the world champion racing pigeon, my father-in-law had served time in prison (a punishment everyone falsely blamed on Paolo) and my husband – after the most terrible of family arguments – had been virtually ostracised by the family, left a boardroom meeting bloodied but not broken; and spent hours in discussions with lawyers seeking retribution and the right to use his name as an independent designer.

Meanwhile, in a parallel life, Paolo still had his racing pigeons – a hobby he had loved since the age of 11. We had many fond shared memories of pigeons. At first, I had never been able to see the attraction of his hobby, but after a while I, too, had become quite fascinated by these beautiful birds. It was no coincidence that pigeons had featured in my dream the previous night, as they were very much on my mind after the conversation we had had that afternoon with the doctor.

This time, our doctor had been absolutely adamant that Paolo would have to give up his lifelong passion for racing pigeons. Although he had birds in New York and in Italy, it was only in Rusper that he spent real, what he called 'quality time', in the pigeon coop. But it was a practice that was sadly making him desperately ill. If he continued spending time with his beloved pets, it would ultimately kill him.

At first, we had thought that it was a coincidence that Paolo always became ill after visiting the pigeon coop. His eyes and face would swell up several hours later and then his temperature would soar to a terrifying 102 degrees Fahrenheit. Alongside the chills, fever and shortness of breath, my poor husband also had to put up with diarrhoea and vomiting during these attacks.

Paolo couldn't bear to think that he was suffering from a deadly allergic reaction to his prized birds and so we spent ages trying to find another explanation – anything at all to blame. My cooking was a favourite culprit!

But the doctor was certain in his diagnosis – Paolo had 'Pigeon-Breeder's Disease'. There was no cure and the only treatment was to stay away from birds. Knowing the pleasure this hobby had given him over the years, I understood that he was devastated at the prospect of giving it all up. His largest collection was in England, but he also kept some birds in Florence, where they were cared for by his chauffeur, Dino, who was also a pigeon fancier.

In the early morning light, I smiled as I remembered the adventure we had had years before in New York when Paolo wanted to get a pigeon loft as a home for his small US collection that now – after Aldo's gift – included a world champion. It had been a bitterly cold New York afternoon and Paolo was wrapped up in a full-length, black mink coat and I had on my sable to keep me warm. We were walking through Little Italy holding hands when Paolo gestured for me to look up at the grey sky. It was an amazing sight set against a *West Side Story* sort of skyline. Hundreds of racing pigeons were circling downwards as they reached their home.

Pointing to the top of an old brownstone building – with the fire escapes on the outside – Paolo said, 'There must be a loft up there.'

Nearby was a bar/restaurant. We went in and, in Italian, Paolo asked to see the manager. Just like in a movie, the whole place fell silent. Eventually, a real Mafioso-type came out. He did not look friendly.

'What do you want?'

Paolo explained that we had seen the pigeons circling and wanted to know who owned their loft.

Looking a bit serious in our Gucci suits!
© *Terry O'Neil*

167

'I don't know anything about any pigeons,' he said, 'now, go away!'

'I only want to ask about the pigeons,' said Paolo, who was determined to find a home for his champion.

'For the last time, I don't know anything about any pigeons.' This time it was said in a distinctly menacing tone.

So we left – in a hurry – convinced that we were going to be shot at any moment. We ran to the corner of the road where we collapsed into hysterical giggles.

Some weeks later, Paolo found an old shoemaker, Fabio Ritzo, also in Little Italy, who knew about pigeons and looked after Paolo's very well. When Paolo went to see his birds, they'd have coffee together and often race them on Sundays when Paolo was in town. At Christmas, Paolo would always make sure that there was a Gucci handbag for Signora Ritzo who, understandably, thought that he was wonderful. We never again ventured inside that menacing bar.

Now all this would have to come to an end. First, Paolo had lost his family and his work within the firm, and now his beloved pigeons. I was terribly sad for him.

My dream remained fresh in my mind and I remembered the glimpse of the little boy that had now become my 56-year-old crazy husband. During the early days of our relationship, that appealing 'inner child' had popped up quite often – in spontaneous laughter and warm, open smiles. Recently, those happy times we shared had become fewer and further between. Sometimes, it even felt as if I was a stranger at Rusper, that somehow I was intruding on Paolo's other life – his English life – while I was there.

No, that couldn't be. We were, and always would be a partnership…I dismissed the thought as an over-active imagination. He had just been going through an especially stressful period and, as soon as the buyout was agreed, things would be better.

It was true that over the last couple of years we had been apart much more than before. The running of all the properties had become my responsibility and, nowadays, often before his trips, I would find myself saying, 'Oh, you go on your own this time, I'll stay in New York with

Gemma.' There was always lots of administration work to catch up with. And had I imagined that he almost sounded relieved as he quickly grabbed his bag and gave me a cursory kiss goodbye on the cheek? 'OK, you know I'll only be gone for ten days or so,' not even trying to persuade me to join him, before rushing out the door.

As I wallowed in those half-dream-like, yet keenly perceptive moments that October morning in 1987, I resolved to make even more of an effort to bring back the fun and laughter into our relationship. The bedroom curtain was partly ajar and I could see that a wet English day was waiting. Gemma and I would put on our boots later and kick a few leaves around and maybe collect some conkers. Perhaps, if it cleared up later, she could go out for a riding lesson on her pony. Even at the tender age of 5, Paolo was insisting that she would make a fine horsewoman.

I felt warmth and a huge sympathy for my husband who I knew would already be grieving for his pigeons. I could hear him moving around in the bathroom after another disturbed night. Other sounds from further away indicated that this magnificent 17th-century house was gently coming awake. Always the optimist, I decided that it wouldn't take much to enjoy my time in the English countryside. I was incredibly lucky, I had a wonderful life and I still had my music – despite everything, I managed to fit in voice coaching and singing at various recitals.

With renewed determination, I would give my husband a surprise. A warm and loving, good-morning hug and a cup of tea would start his day right, too.

And what a day it would turn out to be.

Before sharing the climax of that autumn day – one that would change our lives and the shape of Gucci for ever – I need to go back several months to tell you what had been happening in the Gucci business world since Maurizio attempted to take control of the company and the breakdown of Paolo's pact with his cousin.

Although, technically, Maurizio had inherited 50 per cent of the shares, he was finding that he was restricted at every turn by Paolo and his brothers who had little respect for his business acumen. In fact, since the meeting where Paolo and he had joined forces and got rid of Aldo as president, things had not gone well for our cousin.

Paolo and I were aware that, after the death of his father, Maurizio was getting increasingly fed up with married life. He made no secret of the fact that he found what he considered to be his wife's interfering ways as restrictive as his father's. He had told Paolo that he had never felt free in his entire life. As a child and young man, he had been suppressed by his domineering father, and now, when at last he had his inheritance, he felt it was Patrizia who was cramping his style.

He had been unable to cut his ties to Rodolfo, but he could always leave his wife…and that's what he did. He said that he craved his freedom – he was just desperate to get away. There was no other woman involved at that stage.

So in May 1985, Maurizio packed a small case in the Milan penthouse he shared with his family – his daughters Alessandra and Allegra were then aged nine and four respectively – telling them that he was going to Florence for a few days.

Maurizio had never been good at facing unpleasant scenes, so it was the family doctor who was called in the next day to break the news to Patrizia that her husband was not coming home. To say that it did not go down well would be something of an understatement – Patrizia went mad and then, when she finally calmed down, she set about a concerted campaign to get her husband back. In this quest, she was supported by her mother, Silvana, and her best friend, Pina Auriemma, who had a strong influence over her.

At first, although living apart, the couple would still sometimes attend functions together and I believe there were a few attempts at reconciliation, but I always thought that this was just because Maurizio missed his beloved daughters. Although he still craved freedom, he wanted the family to be together for the first Christmas of their separation and so they arranged to spend the December 1985 holidays at the family home in Saint Moritz.

Well advised by her mother and best friend Pina, Patrizia had made extensive plans to woo her husband back. She had decorated the house beautifully, arranged the carefully selected gifts under the Christmas tree and picked out an irresistible selection of clothes to wear at their various engagements over the holidays.

I don't think Maurizio had any intention of ever returning to his wife. I believe this was one of those occasions when he just wanted to be with his girls for Christmas. Whatever his plans had been, the whole thing went horribly wrong from the start when he refused to join his wife at midnight mass on Christmas Eve, something they had traditionally done together throughout their marriage. But, perhaps the present opening between the couple was the final catalyst that sparked the dreadful fight that really marked the absolute end of their marriage.

Patrizia had taken ages over selecting some very expensive cufflinks – with diamonds and sapphires – for her husband, but was terribly disappointed when she opened the small parcels from him. Inside one was a key chain from his yacht and the other contained an antique watch. Patrizia felt both were a snub. He knew her taste was far from classic and that she hated antique watches, preferring something modern. She was not appeased when he told her that the watch was a family heirloom having belonged to his mother. A huge fight ensued and Maurizio left the following morning telling his wife that he wanted a divorce. Patrizia swore that she would never grant him a divorce and that he would never be allowed to see his children.

Later, Maurizio would use his properties as a way of getting back at her, denying her access to either their home in Saint Moritz or his yacht. However, despite all the bitterness, he did make sure that, each month, $35,000 was deposited in her bank account.

It is strange to remember the breakdown of Maurizio and Patrizia's marriage because there were certain similarities to what happened with Paolo and me. Although I was very different from Patrizia in so many ways, the final straw in my relationship with Paolo was also over a present – something that was meant to bring joy and happiness – and he, too, would change the locks on our homes so denying me access. But there the similarities ended – I never found a penny from Paolo in my bank account...ever!

I do sometimes wonder if Maurizio's decision to cut his domestic ties had somehow had an influence on Paolo and his increasingly bizarre behaviour. That, and the sudden realisation that he was wealthy beyond belief – money *can* buy you most things and maybe, like Maurizio, it was freedom that Paolo thought he wanted at this stage of his life.

The negotiations for the buyout of Paolo's Gucci shares had been going on for ages. It was Maurizio who first introduced Investcorp to the world of Gucci. In the mid-1980s, this was a little-known investment bank that had made a fortune for its oil-rich Middle Eastern clients by turning round the jewellery company Tiffany and Co in 1984. Following the Tiffany coup, and its share launch on the New York stock exchange, the bank was looking for another luxury brand that was in trouble...and Gucci fitted the bill.

Since the family had got rid of Aldo, Gucci's management under Maurizio was shambolic and appeared to be haemorrhaging money. Paolo would go mad as he discovered the costs involved in Maurizio's 'restructuring'. Keen to make his mark, Maurizio claimed to have cut out all the old dead wood; in its place, he claimed to have brought in what he called a highly-skilled team of middle and top management head-hunted from major international European companies.

I remember when, after combing through masses of company paperwork, Paolo discovered there was a company plane that he knew nothing about. 'Whatever do we need with a private jet?' he asked. 'It's absurd! Maurizio only travels between Milan and Florence – he never even goes to Paris – and everyone knows it's much easier to go by road. For heaven's sake, they are 160 miles apart – even the train only takes two hours! It's madness!'

There was no doubt that Gucci was in trouble and Paolo and his family – I had come to call them 'The Real Guccis' – were, for once, united in their condemnation of Maurizio's leadership. Behind the scenes, Paolo continued to make plans to set up his own business. These plans now included opening his own shop in New York.

Meanwhile, Maurizio's personal assets had been sequestered by the courts investigating the alleged forgery of his father's shares and, to add to the company's problems, Paolo instigated more legal proceedings. This time, they were against his brothers for tax evasion. What's more, while their cousin was on his self-imposed exile in Switzerland, Giorgio and Roberto had attempted to take over the company. It was all a horrible mess.

Maurizio was looking for a source of money that would allow him to buy out his cousins' shares while remaining president of the company. When he was introduced to Investcorp by a third party, it seemed like a perfect match; he especially liked the Tiffany affiliation, feeling that it would be a good tie-in for Gucci.

All the key players in the negotiations knew that Paolo should be approached first. Although Paolo owned fewer shares than his brothers, he was seen to be the one most likely to sell and, if his sale went ahead, Maurizio and his backers would have the overall control they craved. Then, finding themselves as only minor shareholders, it would only be a matter of time before his brothers would follow suit...which was, of course, what happened.

In true Gucci style, it didn't go smoothly. That much was obvious once Paolo went for a meeting with his lawyer, Carlo Sganzini in Lugano, expecting to finalise the deal. I was at home with fingers crossed waiting to hear that everything had gone through. My heart sank when I picked up the phone to a furious Paolo.

'You won't believe what those bastards have done,' he was shouting, 'they have put in a clause forbidding me to do any business in competition to Gucci...' Before I could comment, he went on, 'That means I would never be able to open a shop or use my name as a designer! They honestly thought I'd sign *that*! They're mad! They think I'm stupid? You know what I did, Jenny? I took the bundle of papers – there were hundreds of them – and threw them up in the air. I had walked out the door before they hit the floor – I'll be home tomorrow morning.'

So there had been a lot of lost tempers and anxious waiting before the deal was finally agreed. Which brings me back to Rusper and October 1987.

It was 4.15 in the afternoon when the phone rang with the news. I picked it up as Paolo was outside in the rain talking to the estate workers.

'It's Carlo Sganzini here. I'm phoning from Lugano. Is Mr Paolo there?' he sounded happy and relieved.

'I'll get him for you.'

I shouted to Paolo, who ran across the lawn and grabbed the phone.

Dripping in the hall, I watched Paolo's face light up and heard Italian words of 'Congratulations…excellent…very good!'

He hung up and hugged me.

'At last, Jen, it's done. The money is in a bank account in the Bahamas – all $40 million of it!'

We were almost dancing round in excitement. I went to put the kettle on, but Paolo had other ideas. 'Let's open some champagne! Go and get your parents – this calls for a real celebration!' It was ages since I'd seen him so happy.

My parents were also thrilled for him. They had been incredibly supportive throughout all the ups and downs. 'It's wonderful,' they said, 'now you'll be able to live the life you want, Paolo.'

'At last you'll be able to relax,' added my father. Both my parents loved him very much.

Everyone, including Judy the nanny and Paolo's secretary Deirdre, joined in the champagne toast to the future. But the great party atmosphere was about to be shattered.

The implications of having unlimited money were beginning to sink in and I suddenly thought of something I really wanted. I took Paolo to one side. 'You know what I'd really like? Mummy and Daddy are getting old and I'd love to take them on a cruise. It would be a trip of a lifetime and it would mean so much to them.'

He'd always loved my parents and had been very generous to them, so I was completely unprepared for his reply. His face suddenly turned cold, almost unrecognisable. 'No, it's *my* money,' he said in a chilling tone.

15

Temper-tantrums and Testosterone

The completion of Paolo's sell-out to Investcorp didn't just mark the beginning of the end of our marriage, it also marked the end of the century-old Gucci family business.

Although he didn't say anything to me, I am sure that Paolo's conscience troubled him – at least a little bit. He knew that he had not only sold his family heritage but also that his move would lead to the downfall of those 'Real Guccis', as I called them, like Aldo, who had built the company up to the global phenomenon that it had become. Despite having been involved in a tangle of lawsuits against his relatives for as long as I could remember, I don't think he had ever wanted to bring down the whole Gucci family firm.

A few months later, as predicted, Giorgio and Roberto followed suit and were each paid $70 million for their shares. But it took almost two more years before Aldo also finally caved in and sold his remaining shares in Gucci America to Investcorp. It happened in an emotional meeting in Geneva when my 84-year-old father-in-law, in person, dramatically handed over the documents. This all marked a significant landmark in the company's history, it was the first time since Guccio Gucci borrowed capital to set up his small business that an outsider had owned such a significant part of the company – 50 per cent to be precise. The rest was left in the hands of its appointed president, Paolo's cousin, Maurizio.

Paolo changed with the money. Always moody and quick-tempered, he became far more difficult to live with. Around me, he appeared agitated, angry and unable to relax. It should have been a really happy time for us, a time of planning for the future and collaborating together on the project for the new shop in New York, but it wasn't working out like that.

He had always been so generous and, suddenly, he wasn't any more. It was as if he didn't want me to have anything. I now know that actually he didn't want to be with me at this period. Later, I would find out that his thoughts were totally dominated by another woman and how he was going to get her into bed.

After his cold dismissal of my suggestion of a family cruise, I never again asked him for anything. Most of the time, I felt as if I was walking on eggshells. He would turn on a penny, like his father had before him.

Our beautiful home, Normans, in West Sussex.

I wasn't particularly concerned by his behaviour. I felt that it was all to do with the mixed emotions he was experiencing after the sell-out and receiving so much money. I thought that it was just a phase that would pass. I also devised a way of diffusing his temper tantrums – if he behaved like a naughty child, I would make a point of treating him like one. Or, another strategy I employed was simply to walk away. When we were in England, Normans was such a huge house that it took at least half an hour to find anybody; by that time, his anger had usually dissipated.

One afternoon at Rusper, Gemma, her nanny Judy, his secretary Deirdre, my sister Sue and my journalist friend Vicki all witnessed one of his irrational explosions. Paolo always had a sweet tooth and, when asked, would confess to enjoying a slice of cake more than a glass of wine. Our cook had happily obliged and, when we walked in that afternoon, there was a wonderful smell of home baking wafting from the kitchen. Still warm from the oven, a banana cake was temptingly waiting on a cooling tray.

I can't remember the reason why Paolo lost his temper, but I will never forget the picture of him grabbing a kitchen knife and stabbing at the cake until it lay in crumbled pieces all over the table and the floor.

Everybody discreetly left the room and I was left with him. 'Now that really was very silly,' I heard my motherly voice coming out. 'Your behaviour is appalling, especially in front of other people! Are you going to stay and explain to cook what you've done?'

Paolo was still babbling incoherently with rage.

'I think you should clear up all the mess you've made.'

'No, you clear it up,' he said sulkily.

'No, I'm not going to – you made the mess and so you must clear it up,' I responded.

And, oddly enough, after a bit of complaining, he did.

I took the same tack when he threw the cutlery all over the floor because he didn't like the way the teaspoons had been arranged in the drawer. It might have been acceptable behaviour to shout and throw things among the Gucci family and in their workplace, but I wasn't having it in my home.

Unlike years before in Florence, I no longer needed Vicki to point out to me how strange my husband's behaviour was. And even with his erratic track record, there was one event so completely out of character that I will never forget it. It also took place around the kitchen table at Rusper.

Paolo and I were having a light lunch with Deirdre, Gemma and Judy, and everything was comparatively normal until Paolo selected an apple from the fruit bowl. I had noticed him glance across at Deirdre and caught something – I couldn't quite put my finger on it, but there was definitely something in the look that passed between them.

Paolo then picked up a small paring knife and proceeded to carefully peel the apple.

'Why are you peeling it?' I asked. In all the years I'd known him, I had never before seen him peel an apple. For a second, he looked slightly wrong-footed before he regained his composure. When he placed the perfectly peeled fruit in front of his secretary, I noticed that there was definitely something going on.

After they both left, Judy turned to me. 'That was very odd,' she said.

I agreed that I found it most peculiar, too.

Deirdre seemed such an unlikely object for Paolo's fantasies. She was a few years younger than me and just didn't seem to be his type. I don't mean to be unkind, but she was a very ordinary, village woman – petite with dark, straight hair and always appeared to be lacking in style or personality. She lived on a housing estate in the village with her husband and two young children. It just didn't make sense…and yet…

I decided to confront him. 'What's going on? Are you having an affair with Deirdre?'

'Don't be ridiculous – I only peeled her apple!'

'How did you know she liked her apple peeled?' I realised that I sounded petty and suspicious.

'Because she told me.'

'She blushed when you gave it to her.'

'She blushes easily.'

Deirdre, solid dependable Deirdre, who had also become my friend over the years, whose children came over to play with Gemma and her cousin Lucy – it couldn't be true. Anyway, the conversation was over – at least for the moment.

Maybe I was suffering from an over-active imagination? Nothing really felt 'right' at that time. Even sweet Judy, the nanny, was behaving oddly. At first, I reasoned that she was having an off day, but, after a while, I felt I must talk to her. Surely it wasn't my imagination – she really *was* being rude and disrespectful to Paolo.

I had always been friendly to family employees like Deirdre and Judy, insisting they call me Jenny (not Mrs Gucci) and that they join us for family meals, outings and so on – they really were part of the family. I had always been especially fond of Judy: she was young and funny and fitted right in with the family. She also had a reputation for eating men alive. Perhaps it was these qualities that eventually led Judy in 2002 to a new employer – Catherine Zeta Jones – for a staggering salary, where her Welsh roots were employed to good effect with the film star's children, whose upbringing included them being able to understand and speak the Welsh language.

But back in 1988, I wanted to know what was going on and, reluctantly at first, but then with more fluency, Judy began to spill the beans. No doubt she was relieved to get it off her chest.

A few weeks before, she had, apparently, had an unwanted, late-night visitor. She had answered the knock at her bedroom door and found Paolo there in his dressing gown.

'Did you know that Jenny's away?' he asked.

'Yes, of course.'

Then, straight to the point, he had asked her to sleep with him. 'I'll buy you a car,' he offered by way of incentive.

'What sort of car?'

'I thought a Ford, maybe…'

'I'd want a f*****g Ferrari to sleep with you!' she replied angrily, slamming the door.

Judy found the whole encounter deeply disturbing and she had gone to the next-door house in tears, not sure what to do. She looked at me for a reaction. Somehow, it all seemed so ridiculous, and I loved her response…I couldn't help but smile. Soon, she also saw the funny side of it and we had a good laugh together.

But what was going on? This had to be more than some delayed mid-life crisis – my husband was in his late fifties and he had started to grow a ponytail, not a good look at the best of times, but truly ridiculous when, like Paolo, you are completely bald on top! He couldn't even cope with it himself. He'd come to me in the morning and ask me to tie it for him. Again, I'd find myself in this strange 'motherly' situation. After I'd done his hair, I'd pat him on the bottom and tell him that he could go out and play with his friends…many a true word is spoken in jest.

Could it be that he wanted to follow in Maurizio's footsteps? That he, too, craved his 'freedom'?

He had also bought himself (not Judy!) a fabulous silver Ferrari but he hardly used it. In fact, I think he felt uncomfortable about the attention it provoked. He never liked appearing flashy. Occasionally, we'd use it to go antique shopping – we'd roar through the English countryside and people would stare. Although he'd always loved cars, the Ferrari didn't give him as much pleasure as he had expected. Once we drove to Wales in it – it only took about an hour and a half – and when he got out the other end he said, 'You know what, Jen, I'm too old for this – it's a young man's car. I think I'll get rid of it.'

I thought it was rather sweet of him to admit it. So, like everything else in his life, Paolo's mid-life crisis (or whatever it was) was not what you might call 'straightforward'. He remained a mass of contradictions. Sometimes he was kind and considerate to everyone – my family and friends, as well as the children – and sometimes he was awful, angry and impossible.

But there was another aspect that was distinctly worrying…his health. Apart from the acute liver pains, I was increasingly concerned about his restlessness, and Paolo promised to see a specialist once we got to Florence.

I went with him to visit the doctor – not his usual Dr Nepi, but someone else in another practice – and I was very pleasantly surprised by Paolo's instant improvement. Having gone in for the appointment looking pretty dreadful and clutching his stomach, moaning about the state of his liver, a few minutes later he emerged a different man – he almost skipped out of the office he had so much energy.

'Whatever did they give you?' I asked. 'It seems to have had an almost instant success.'

'Oh, it was just an injection,' said Paolo evasively.

'What sort of injection?' Don't forget that I had been a medical secretary in another life.

'Just vitamins – I think B12 – because my liver doesn't function properly, I need regular vitamin shots,' he explained.

At the time, I never really queried it. Certainly, whatever the injections were, they made Paolo feel so much better – he was almost back to his old self. So much so that we planned a holiday in Gozo, an island off the coast of Malta.

'When we travel, I'll need you to inject me,' he said.

'Where?' I asked.

'In my bum.'

'No problem,' I joked. 'If you're a good boy, I won't hurt you at all… but if you're naughty…' I smiled suggestively, patting his bottom. He liked the innuendo and grinned back, grabbing me round the waist and pulling me into him.

Whatever problems we might have had with Paolo's extreme mood swings, they never spilled over into the bedroom. Our sex life together was always great.

Well, almost always. On that holiday in Gozo, Paolo was especially anxious and fidgety. Sometimes, he'd want us to sleep together and other times he would suggest that we took separate beds – I just put it down to the heat and him being over-tired and over-wrought.

Paolo always enjoyed female company and was happy to take 'his favourite girls' – his daughter and her nanny, my sister Sue, my niece Lucy and me – on holiday with us. He never minded being the only male – in fact, on one memorable occasion, he decided to join in to the extent that he surprised us all by dressing up in women's clothing so that he could be 'one of the girls'! Of course, we all thought it was hysterical. It was a joy to find out that, when he relaxed, I could still recognise the man I had married.

We all made a great fuss of him, and were really great company... when we were together. But on this holiday, Paolo also seemed to crave privacy and was constantly sending us all off to the pool or shopping with a 'I'll be down in a bit'. When he'd packed us off together, he would be constantly on the phone to England sorting out estate details (or so I thought at the time) with his secretary Deirdre. Every time we would say goodbye to him to go to the beach, pool or shopping, he had this old-fashioned phone receiver stuck to his ear. He seemed desperate all the time to be in touch with his secretary in England.

'What's so important that it can't wait a few days?' I would ask. 'Surely, Deirdre can manage without you 'til we get back.'

But Paolo was preoccupied, maintaining that there was a pile of accountancy and financing problems related to paying contractors in England.

The work at Rusper was continuing apace with the modernisation of the stable block and, indeed, it had been further complicated since my father and mother had moved away. My father had helped Paolo since the beginning of the project but, like the rest of us, was finding his behaviour just too difficult to cope with. Paolo would never pay the exact amount on a bill, my father had explained to me. Whatever the amount, even small bills for, say, £35, he would always knock something off and refuse to pay the total amount. English builders or contractors didn't know how to react – sometimes they'd reissue bills for the outstanding amounts and the procedure would go on and on. I don't remember any taking him to court for small outstanding bills, but this attitude also meant that, in a small community like West Sussex, fewer and fewer people would work for Paolo Gucci. He had acquired a bad reputation and made a very unfortunate name for himself in the village and surroundings. My father was especially concerned when he took the same attitude with the staff salaries. The estate payroll was growing each month and, again, Paolo was refusing to pay his staff all of their agreed wages. They'd come to my father begging for their money. It put him in an impossible situation.

Even with all these problems, my parents were still fond of Paolo and were grateful to him, but I think the real reason they left the estate was because they sensed that my marriage was in difficulties and they were of an age when they really didn't want to get caught up in something which could turn ugly.

My sister Sue and her daughter were still living in their cottage. Lucy adored her uncle Paolo, who was something of a surrogate father to her. Together on the sofa in their blue-and-white bobble hats and scarves, they'd watch football matches, like England playing Italy, after Sue had prepared him a lovely, home-cooked meal. After supper, Paolo would also give Sue some money to help with the housekeeping and for all her work behind the scenes with caretaking the estate when he was away.

Sue and I were close and would often discuss my crazy husband, so she wasn't too surprised one day when he asked her if she would inject him with his vitamins. Sue's a bit squeamish about needles and apologised, but she just couldn't do it.

I needed some answers that would at least partly explain Paolo's increasingly irrational behaviour. I was sure that there were many explanations, not least his Gucci upbringing, and an eminent psychiatrist would later back this up. But I did discover another contributing factor from an unlikely source – a blood sample.

Paolo had become quite secretive about his 'vitamin shots'. By this stage, he had learned to inject himself in his thigh and seemed to be doing so with increasing regularity. On our next visit to London, I persuaded him to see a specialist in Harley Street. I still had contacts there from my time as a medical secretary and spoke to a friend who happened to be an endocrinologist. I told her that Paolo wasn't at all well and that I was worried about him; she promised to phone me after the results were in for his blood test.

A few days later, I got the call from my friend. She couldn't keep the surprise out of her voice. 'In all my years in practice, I have never seen anything like it, Jenny! It really is most unusual.'

'*What* is?' I asked impatiently.

'Well, let's put it this way – your husband has the sperm count of a 17-and-a-half-year-old boy!'

'*What*? Well, he *is* a Gucci and they are a bit special,' I joked.

'No, seriously, Jenny, this is not normal at all. I am surprised that you aren't permanently pregnant. Unless you want another baby – be careful,' she warned.

Of course, these were the days before Viagra and what I had thought were innocent vitamin B12 shots were, in fact, pure testosterone – the male hormone. Maybe it was these injections that were making him so much more aggressive and short-tempered, or perhaps it was his conscience that was troubling him.

Paolo never did things by half measures, and he needed a replacement hobby for his beloved pigeons and he found it in Arabian horses. One morning at breakfast, he said to me, right out of the blue, 'You know I love horses? I think I might buy a few champions.'

Actually, I didn't know he loved horses. To my knowledge, apart from encouraging Gemma's riding lessons and occasionally stroking her pony's nose, he'd never expressed an interest in the creatures before. I looked at him quizzically.

No, from whichever angle, I found it difficult to equate Paolo with horses. Unfortunately, later, my misgivings would prove eerily correct. But, for the moment, it was as if almost overnight he had become obsessed with Arabian horses. He didn't go to horse races or anything like that; it was visits to horse shows, breeders and stud farms that became his passion.

In 1989, he was spending money like water and he also bought his own breeding farm in upstate New York. We chose Millfield Stables in Yorktown Heights together. It was a magnificent estate set in 32 acres of rolling lawns, had a state-of-the-art stables and riding school, a guest cottage and swimming pool alongside the main house with its four bedrooms (all with en-suite bathrooms), an enormous 40ft living room, library and range-style kitchen. Gemma and I spent most weekends and school holidays there and we both made friends in the area. Gemma's pony Beatrice was one of the first inhabitants of the stable block.

Meanwhile, an ocean away, similar scenes were being played out in West Sussex, where beautiful Arab horses began to arrive at the newly converted stables at Rusper. An army of grooms and stable hands were hired on both sides of the Atlantic to look after Paolo's new 'pets'.

At Rusper, the run-down barns and pig-sties of the adjoining farm had been bought, knocked down and, in their place, was a stable yard with freshly-painted white horse boxes and tack rooms with window boxes bursting with flowers. There was also a sand school and outdoor lunging ring. Horse boxes were driven nearly every day into the stable yard to unload their precious cargoes. Anglo breeds, large and graceful Shire horses and their foals, together with the most adorable miniature ponies, all kept the Arab brood mares and stallions company in the paddocks. The horse population changed regularly as newcomers arrived and other horses were sold on. At one time, there were a dozen miniature ponies that became household pets. These gentle creatures were delightful, and the children loved them. They were quite domesticated and were sometimes allowed inside the house and even, on occasions, as unusual passengers in the car.

Although Paolo Gucci never learned to ride – in fact, I think that only once was he ever spotted perched rather precariously on a horse – with his stables and paddocks full of magnificent horses, his country estate and his subscription to *Country Life* magazine, my Italian husband slipped perfectly into his new role of English country squire.

16

The Last Straw

'Designs by Paolo Gucci' – it had a certain ring to it. The ruling by the New York District Court in 1988 meant that, at last, Paolo could start his own fashion business under his own name. At first, he didn't seem to recognise the implications of the ruling and wanted to continue fighting; but I pointed out that it would give him amazing opportunities. He would be able to work on his own at last. Once he saw the potential, he wanted to shout the news from the rooftops but, instead, he decided on the next best thing – a page advertisement in *Women's Wear Daily*. There, Paolo also showed his creativity with words, composing a poem for the occasion and dedicating it to 'the retail community'. But had he lost his touch? Could he still come up with the goods?

It seemed as if he couldn't concentrate on anything properly. I had moved back to New York and Paolo was constantly travelling, but spending most of his time in England. Even there, my sister told me, he was preoccupied and increasingly volatile and short-tempered. She would take calls and urgent messages from suppliers who were awaiting some final decision from Paolo before shipment. Paolo would have promised to get back to them quickly with his answers, but then he would leave the country, having either forgotten the arrangement or lost interest in the project. If these suppliers had not been thinking about the prospect of a large Gucci contract, I am sure they wouldn't have been so persistent.

However, despite Paolo's erratic work schedule, somehow new lines, including a beautiful, china dinner service, were eventually assembled for his new collection. Paolo was keen not to antagonise the main Gucci business and so, sensibly, had decided to stay away from producing anything that could be seen to be in competition with the main Gucci label, like handbags or other potentially contentious items.

These days, he didn't even ask me if I wanted to travel with him. Often now on his 'business trips', it was essential that his English secretary accompany him. Deirdre had acquired a new wardrobe of smart, expensive clothes from somewhere and had also received some styling advice and the skills of a talented hairdresser. She'd always looked neat and clean but, frankly, rather dull. She appeared as she was – a suburban housewife and mother-of-two in her early thirties. She was petite and slim and, with her dark hair cut into a sleek bob and her new sense of style, the improvement was noticeable.

It felt as if Gemma hardly saw her father – he was away so much – and when he was around, he appeared distracted. In New York, we had a new nanny called Ruth who also became a firm friend and, later, would prove her loyalty by standing by Gemma and me when the going got tough.

During this period, we were living in an apartment in Essex House, overlooking Central Park. There, we could enjoy the convenience of hotel service but were still able to make it homey with our own personal possessions. It was comfortable and convenient but not very big. Even with his mind elsewhere, Paolo had noticed it, too.

'Now that the little one is growing up, why don't we look for somewhere larger?' he had suggested. So, once more, we were house hunting, although I sensed that Paolo's mind wasn't completely on the job in hand. Maybe he was looking for more property investments. We still had the other apartments in New York, but I wanted a proper home in my favourite city. Whatever our considerations, eventually we settled on a beautiful, new luxury development called the Metropolitan Tower next to the famous Carnegie Hall. Paolo bought three apartments – one two-bedroom and two one-bedroom – on the 64th floor. The idea was to knock them into one fabulous, three-bedroom home with a wrap-around view of New York. Wow! I was really excited – it was a fabulous project. Paolo was also enthusiastic and was busy getting involved in the architectural details. He insisted that the standard white doors be removed and replaced with the most beautiful, handcrafted, tall, cedar doors he had sourced in Tuscany. They weighed a ton and it was complicated to get them shipped over.

Paolo had also set up an office in the Metropolitan office suite and it was there –and on his travels – that he worked on his first independent collection for the new shop. The premises had already been selected. The store was on the corner of Madison Avenue and 59th Street. With all the refurbishment needed, it cost around $11 million.

When he eventually launched his first solo collection a few years later in the Madison Avenue store, under the label 'Designs by Paolo Gucci', it was a huge success and a complete sell-out in the first ten days of opening. Eventually, when we split up, Paolo closed the business as a way of thwarting me and proving to the authorities that he had no assets. It was amazing the lengths he was prepared to go to avoid paying me any money. He must have lost millions of dollars on the New York shop alone but, more importantly, he also lost his reputation and, I believe, his sanity.

I suppose that in every failed relationship there is one moment when you just realise with frightening clarity that it is never going to be all right again. Up until that time, there is always a glimmer of hope that bridges can be rebuilt and problems solved. Then comes that pivotal moment – a last straw – an event that, even as it happens, you know is going to be unforgettable for the rest of your life. It will always be a landmark moment, dividing your life into a before and an afterwards. Maybe it's the moment when you stop loving, when you realise that you are on your own and not part of a couple any more. A moment when you know that the effort required to keep the marriage afloat is just too much for one person to bear.

In my case, that 'last straw' moment was our twelfth wedding anniversary on 2 December 1989. Things between Paolo and me had been pretty shaky for the past two years – it was as if he had become a different person since his sell-out from Gucci.

I had wondered whether he might have been having an affair, he was away from home so much, and Gemma and I wouldn't see him for weeks on end. Sue and I often talked on the phone about my suspicions. She also knew Paolo very well and possibly, during this period, she and Lucy saw more of him than Gemma and I did. She guessed that there might be something going on, but neither of us had any idea who the other woman could be. Sue told me that she'd never seen anyone stay the night in the main house. We discussed Deirdre – her change of image and even the fact that Paolo had bought her a car – but both of us dismissed the idea as totally implausible. The car was, after all, second-hand and she needed it for her work. Of course, she spent a lot of time with Paolo – they worked together and she was, after all, his PA. Sue had never seen anything untoward, not a special glance or touch…nothing at all.

We agreed that it simply couldn't be Deirdre and the conversation moved on to the fact that, with Deirdre's 'new' car, my father now 'owned' eight vehicles, including a tractor. We laughed at the fact that Paolo never liked to put his name on anything. Even his driving licence (which was Italian) was so worn out to be almost totally illegible, which was just as well because it was also horribly out of date. My father, well into his eighties at this time, had an impeccable driving record, so all the Gucci vehicles were in his name for insurance purposes. The estate itself was registered to some company in Liberia and to get to the bottom of Paolo Gucci's own assets would be a task of Herculean proportions. Sue and I agreed that it would be impossible to ever get to the end of Paolo's paper trail.

Although I didn't love him as I once had, I knew that I would find it impossible to accept his unfaithfulness. Even though it was a Gucci trait – all of the Gucci men had at least one mistress and most of the Gucci wives (with the possible exception of Patrizia) had to accept this as going with the territory of being married to a Gucci.

I had the impression that if Paolo was living a double life, it wasn't giving him much pleasure. With me, he appeared confused, nervous, irritable and unhappy. He still told me that he loved me and that I was the only woman he had ever loved and, when we did get to sleep together, we still had a satisfying sex life. But he was often niggling and critical with me – it was as if he wanted to provoke an argument to justify his behaviour. On one occasion, after he had behaved particularly badly, he gave me the most beautiful mink coat. Although I had a lot of furs, this was a masterpiece, consisting of 99 skins of laced mink. If I wore it along Fifth Avenue, women would stop and ask me where it had come from – it

Trick or treat! Gemma and me in 1988.

was so magnificent that I needed a bodyguard to accompany me when I wore it! It wasn't just presents, though…there would still be times when he would be 'the old Paolo', the man that I had loved.

Before our tenth wedding anniversary, he had asked me what I would like and I had said that I would love a diamond solitaire ring. Paolo always had a great eye for jewellery but had, instead, chosen a ruby ring and matching earrings from Fred of Paris. It was a beautiful present and cost a fortune but it was not what I had really wanted.

So here we were – two years later – having somehow made it to our twelfth wedding anniversary. Gemma and I were in New York and Paolo was in the UK and due to join us for the celebration.

I was really excited, as I had bought him a fabulous present and couldn't wait to see his face when he opened it. It was a bronze of his favourite Arab horse. He had recently bought a world champion called Sheytina from a stud farm in Kentucky. She was exquisite, a perfectly-formed black horse, breathtaking in her beauty and, deservedly, his pride and joy. I was thrilled to have discovered a magnificent bronze statue of her made by a sculptress in Arizona. It measured about 18in in height by 18in, and stood on a wooden plinth. It had cost a small fortune – around $4,000 – but I was happy to pay for it with a commission I had earned on an apartment sale. Ruth the nanny and Gemma had both seen it when it had been delivered and, like me, knew that it would delight Paolo.

Gemma caught the atmosphere of anticipation and was jumping up and down on one leg asking how much longer 'til Daddy would be there. Together, we had bought loads of ribbon and tissue paper and started the complicated job of wrapping the enormous box.

We were all grinning like idiots when we heard the key in the lock, but our smiles were short-lived when we realised that Paolo had returned in a bad mood.

Never mind, I thought, the present was sure to cheer him up. But how wrong I was.

The ribbon was undone and the paper torn off the box, the lid lifted and the look on my husband's face was one of…pure anger. The fact that his reaction was so unexpected made the abuse he shouted at me even more hurtful.

Ruth reacted quickly by guiding a confused Gemma out of the room. Paolo was in the worst rage I had ever seen and he was determined to take it out on me – he called me every name under the sun, particularly liking the sound of 'nouveau rich bitch'. How dare I spend money on something like this?

'But, Paolo, you love that horse,' I protested, 'I am only giving you the bronze because I thought you'd like it.'

There followed much more abuse and name-calling from him as he swept the tabletop with an arm, sending ornaments and papers flying.

'Paolo, what's the matter with you? Why are you behaving like this? I've done nothing to deserve this,' I said levelly.

He didn't reply. His anger seemed to be passing as he sat slumped in a chair.

'You're under so much stress, I think you should see a doctor,' I suggested.

'I think it could be my liver,' he said, suddenly deflated.

I knew that liver disease could cause mental changes. Maybe it was possible that he wasn't keeping it under control as well as we had thought. I went into another room and called the liver specialist who had looked after Paolo for the previous five years.

'He's gone completely mad,' I explained. 'It's no exaggeration, he's behaving like a crazy person,' and I told him what had happened.

An appointment was made straight-away and I coaxed Paolo into a taxi to the medical centre.

Before he returned, I received a call from the specialist. 'Jenny, this is out of my area of expertise – your husband needs psychiatric help. I can recommend someone if that would help…'

'Thanks.' I took down the name and number of the psychiatrist and sat staring at the phone, wondering how I would be able to get Paolo to admit that he had a problem. I had come to realise that my husband was, at the very least, 'disturbed'. His behaviour was becoming increasingly irrational, but would he agree to talk to someone?

Maybe the liver specialist had done it for me, because it was relatively straightforward to get Paolo to meet with the psychiatrist. After three missed appointments, eventually he turned up for an extensive three-hour session. Again, I got a phone call at home. The medical secretary explained to me that the psychiatrist thought it would be helpful to talk to me as well. Apparently, Paolo's counselling would take ten days to 'sink in' and I was to report his behaviour during that time.

I thought maybe I was somehow to blame for Paolo's breakdown, but the psychiatrist put my mind at rest on that one. We had a deeply thought-provoking conversation.

'Mrs Gucci, if I took your husband on as a patient on a regular basis it would take a minimum of seven years before there would be any progress. I've been in practice for 38 years treating couples with a wide range of difficulties and, in all that time, I have never met anyone as manipulative as your husband. I very rarely do this,' he went on, 'but in your case, I must recommend that you get out of this marriage as quickly as possible or take the consequences. I would predict that, if not, he will eventually turn to violence.

'It pains me to say this and, if being Mrs Gucci is important to you, then you'll need medication to help you survive.'

It was explained to me that Paolo had a whole range of problems going back many years. Unless I distanced myself from him, he would take me down with him.

It was chilling to hear these words but I knew – in my heart of hearts – that they were true. I took small comfort in hearing the professional prognosis on my sanity – apparently, I was 'one of the healthiest people ever' to walk over the doctor's threshold. He also told me that I was strong and would be able to cope with the bumpy ride ahead. I am sure that neither of us knew exactly how bumpy this part of my journey would become.

Paolo and I needed to talk. I tried to encourage him to go back to the psychiatrist and ask to be taken on as a regular patient, but he was having none of it.

'Fuck off, you *stronza*! [shit] I don't need a psychiatrist – it's you who has the problems. You think you are so fantastic…well, you're not…all he did was waste three hours of my precious time!'

The conversation was going nowhere. Our marriage was going nowhere. It was as if a curtain came down at that moment. His volatile temperament and all the stress were not worth it any more. After 12 years, I was falling out of love with Paolo.

Recognising that I no longer loved my husband was one thing, but deciding what I should do next was quite another. I suspected that Paolo would not give me my freedom easily and I knew that I would have to be very clever in how I handled the situation. My husband was a proud and powerful man and, as history had proved, exceedingly litigious and stubborn. I would need to tread very carefully and would have to have proof of infidelity at the very least if I were to ask for a divorce. I decided to bide my time.

Christmas 1989 was the usual round of New York society parties with and without my husband. Fortunately, I had built up a great circle of my own friends by this stage and Paolo was quite jealous of my popularity. It was as if all the people we knew were recognising a gentle shift in our relationship. Although I hadn't spoken to anybody about my feelings, people could almost sense something was happening to the Gucci marriage, perhaps because we were more often apart than together. Certainly, on many of the invitations I was the chosen guest and, despite being part of the most famous fashion house in the world, Paolo was relegated almost a 'plus one' status. It was as if lines were being drawn and, subconsciously, the people who knew us were choosing sides. Paolo's erratic mood swings – once considered charmingly Latin – were making even his close colleagues uncomfortable.

As soon as the holidays were over, Paolo couldn't wait to get away and I was relieved to see the back of him. He was in a terrific hurry to return to the Normans and his life as an English country squire, while Gemma and I were settled New Yorkers. I was happy to distance myself from all the Gucci madness.

It was early in January 1990 when Paolo rang to tell me that his father had died. An active and dynamic force almost to the end of his life, few people believed that he was 84 years old.

The previous spring, Aldo had been forced to sell his remaining shares in Gucci America to Investcorp, the consortium that had already bought the shares he had previously ceded to his sons. With Giorgio, Paolo and Roberto out of the business and left with only a very small say in how the company would be run, Aldo had little choice but to follow suit. It must have been a sad moment for him, and must have felt like giving up a part of himself, everything he had worked for his entire life…a true end of an era. It left half of Gucci in the hands of the bankers and the other half with Paolo's cousin Maurizio.

Aldo had retreated to Rome and the home he shared there with his long-term mistress Bruna and their daughter Patrizia. During Christmas, he had become unwell and a strong 'flu virus was diagnosed. His condition worsened over the holidays and, eventually, he had slipped into a coma and died. It was all quite unexpected and, despite all their differences over the years, Paolo was obviously shocked by the news.

'My father died this morning – he had pneumonia but it was all very sudden,' he said, his voice shaky and uncertain.

'I am so, so sorry.' I was genuinely very sad for him. Aldo had been such a force – he had seemed invincible and it was impossible to imagine that he had gone. 'How do you feel?' I asked, but Paolo was stuttering and clearly unable to speak. 'Are you on your own?'

He said that he was and promised to phone back when he was more composed. After putting the phone down, I remembered all my meetings with Aldo over the years and how, at first, he had been shocked at my audacity – as a woman and a foreign one at that – to stand up to him. But I knew that although eventually he respected me for it, he realised that I would ultimately be trouble. He had always said it to Paolo. 'Your Jenneee, she's a lovely girl, she sings beautifully, but she's trouble.' His words echoed in my head. I wondered if he knew how prophetic they were. Aldo had also had the measure of his middle son. 'Paolo is always causing some polemic or other,' was another favourite phrase.

But after all their huge rows, even the ashtray-throwing and Aldo's prison sentence for tax evasion, they had the wonderful ability to embrace and make up afterwards. I wondered if they knew how alike they were and that it was from this similarity in their personalities that all the problems and 'polemics' stemmed.

Later, a calmer Paolo talked to me about the funeral arrangements. Aldo was to be buried with all the pomp and ceremony befitting such an icon in the world of fashion. The man had, after all, been responsible for putting Italy and Italian designers on the map – he was the single person responsible for taking the Gucci brand to the United States and round the world.

I knew that all the Gucci women, weighed down by their sables and diamonds, would be competing in the fashion stakes and to get their pictures in the magazines. It would be hypocritical of me to attend such a jamboree, and I didn't want to be part of it. I didn't want to be seen to be cashing in on the fame thing; in fact, feeling as I did that my marriage was over, I craved peace and quiet and anonymity. I would say my own goodbyes to this remarkable man quietly and talk to Gemma myself about her grandfather. I decided not to go to Rome for the funeral service or the burial that was to take place in the family crypt in Florence.

Paolo didn't try to change my mind but, afterwards, phoned to tell me how it had gone. He and his brothers had apparently given Maurizio a very chilly reception, blaming him for causing Aldo's death due, they argued, to being tricked into selling his final part in the company. I pointed out that this would hardly stand up in a court of law and, if anything, it was Aldo's own sons (not his nephew) who had manipulated the situation by walking away from the Gucci business first.

Even in death, Aldo was causing his own 'polemic'. His Will was also controversial. He left his entire American estate (estimated to be worth some $30 million) to his mistress Bruna (whom he had claimed to have married) and their daughter Patrizia. There was no mention of his now-frail wife Olwen (who claimed never to have granted him a divorce) or his sons. Paolo, who received his father's gold watch, said that he would contest the Will – I think, in the end, it was all sorted out reasonably amicably.

17

Deirdre's Story

Work was continuing on the conversion of the Metropolitan Towers and, when Paolo suggested that we take Gemma and her nanny Ruth on a family holiday to the beautiful island of Anguilla in the British West Indies, it seemed like a good idea.

The island was small and peaceful and surrounded by white, sandy beaches. Gemma's excitement as we flew over the Caribbean on a small connecting plane from Puerto Rico was contagious. We were staying at the magnificent Malliouhana Hotel, and had huge inter-connecting rooms so that she could pop into our room at any time. I noted that the island's motto was 'Strength and Endurance' which seemed quite appropriate.

We'd barely thrown our luggage on the bed before Paolo was checking out the phone system. He had to go through the hotel switchboard and then via some central exchange to book a call to the UK. It took ages to make the connection and, when it came through, I could hear him shouting to be heard over the static on the line.

Here we go again…there were definitely echoes of Gozo as Paolo clearly wanted me out of the way while he battled with the island's archaic phone system. No problem, Gemma, Ruth and I were happy wandering through the stunning tropical gardens, playing on the beach or splashing around in the impossibly clear-blue sea.

One day, I popped back to the room to pick something up and it appeared that Paolo had at last got through to Rusper. But he wasn't shouting this time; in fact, he was whispering what appeared to be sweet nothings. I didn't catch the words he was saying but his tone was unmistakable. This was no 'business' call – he was definitely chatting someone up. As soon as he noticed me, he hung up quickly.

'Who was that?'

'Just the accountant,' he replied.

'I don't think so – you were talking to a woman,' my voice was quiet but certain.

'Don't be ridiculous!'

I knew he was lying and suddenly I was really angry with him – I felt as if I wanted to pick him up and shake him before throwing him off the balcony. Although I didn't love him like before, I was furious that he had managed to destroy our relationship, that he had changed so much, that he had made it impossible for me to go on being with him. I felt tears prick my eyes and wiped them away angrily. I hated it that he could still make me cry and that I wasn't as tough as I had hoped.

'How *could* you? How could you spoil everything?'

He looked shame-faced and, somewhere behind this façade, decided to try and brazen it out. 'Oh come on, Jen, it was nothing. I still love you. You know I'll always love you – you're the only woman for me! This,' he said, gesturing to the phone, 'it was just some silly flirtation with an air hostess…she works with British Airways and I can only phone her at certain times. Really, it's nothing serious.'

We both knew that he was talking nonsense. I stormed out, slamming the door behind me; I knew how I could prove it.

At reception, I explained that I had been cut off from making an important international call and would the operator please be so kind as to reconnect me. I waited only a few minutes in the hotel lobby. Then the phone rang. I picked it up.

'Hello, hello...who's that... Paolo, is that you?' The voice was unmistakable. It was a voice I knew really well, but I could still barely believe the implications.

'Deirdre – what's going on with you and Paolo?' I asked. I wasn't angry with her, more puzzled, I suppose. Of course, all the pieces of the jigsaw fitted – it was just that the final picture it made was of such an unlikely couple.

'Jenny? Is that you? What are you suggesting? There's nothing going on, honestly, nothing at all.'

'Don't lie, Deirdre – we'll talk when I get back,' I said and then I hung up.

I knew it was true, all the signs had been there, but I still couldn't believe it. It really was incredible. But here was the proof that I needed. I folded up the print-out of the phone record and put it in my pocket.

Gemma and Ruth were waiting for me beside the pool. Ruth looked up first and realised that something serious was going on.

'Go and take Gemma for an ice lolly,' I suggested, although it was breakfast time. My priority was then and always that our little girl should be protected from being hurt. I would never speak badly of her father in front of her but I knew that I had to confront Paolo with my discovery.

It was here that my theatrical training would pay off – I needed to muster every ounce of self-control. I was icy-cold.

'You're having an affair with Deirdre, aren't you?'

He was from the 'attack-is-the-best-form-of-defence' school and he went mad. 'How *dare* you accuse me of such a thing?'

'How dare I, *what?*' I was full of righteous indignation, brandishing the phone print-out. 'You've been f*****g her in *my* house...in *my* bed!'

'You think you're so clever,' his favourite attack line was wearing a bit thin. On and on he went, shouting at me, threatening me and calling me every name under the sun. But I had learned my acting lessons well. I remained detached and composed: 'I want a divorce.' There, the words were out. They hung there for a few moments in the still air between us.

'And, in the meantime, I want us to behave as normally as possible in front of Gemma. She must be our priority. These last couple of days of our holiday will continue as planned, so, in a few minutes, we'll meet up on the beach as if nothing has happened.'

And that's what we did. An hour later and we were swimming in the sea just like any other happy family on holiday. But, as the day progressed, Paolo became increasingly remorseful. We chartered a yacht to go to St Martin to do some shopping. He held my hand as we walked through the streets of the neighbouring island. He carefully selected a bikini for me and sat close to me on the return boat journey.

'We can work this out, Jenny,' he whispered. 'You know I still love you – you're so special to me. Don't throw away everything we have,' he was almost begging.

'No, Paolo, it's too late. I really think that a divorce is the only way to go.' He couldn't understand how I could be so calm and friendly, yet so distant at the same time, he had no idea how good an actress I was. He was used to coping with the histrionics of his Italian family. His first wife Yvonne would have been hysterical and called the *Carabinieri* to have him arrested – but the reaction of his English wife was unfathomable.

'This way you can have your Deirdre, or whoever you want, and you'll be able to see Gemma whenever you want. I am sorry, but I want out. I know it's sad, but I really believe it would be for the best,' I reasoned.

In truth, I was tired of him. I was exhausted by his irrational behaviour. It takes a lot to bring me down, but I had come to realise that I wasn't as happy as I should have been. I had been amazingly tolerant for so long, because I had loved him and because, in between the awful moments, he could still be the sweet old Paolo and we had shared some wonderful memories. But, as I looked back, his angry moods had increasingly spoiled the happy times and I found myself dreading his next outburst.

The proof of his affair was not really the issue at all: I would never forget how he had gone berserk when I bought him the bronze horse. I knew that I just couldn't live the rest of my life with this volatile man. I was determined to gain my freedom, barely aware that, apart from his father, I was the only person in his life who had ever stood up to Paolo Gucci.

It was March 1990 and I had no idea of the long and painful journey that lay ahead in my quest for freedom. Sadly, it would be a journey not without its casualties.

The transatlantic phone lines between the Metropolitan Tower in New York and the small village of Rusper in West Sussex were red-hot on our return from Anguilla. I needed almost constant contact with my sister, while Paolo had a lot to discuss with his very personal assistant, Deirdre. From his office suite in the same building, he was also getting busy with the fax machine.

'Hi, Jenny,' – it was Sue – 'I was just about to call you. You won't believe the faxes Paolo's been sending.'

What was all this about? She went on to explain, 'They're all lovey-dovey and from him to him!'

'What?'

'Yes, I know it's all crazy but I think I've worked it out. He's showing Deirdre the kind of love letters he would like to get from her…as if she needs some inspiration. It's quite bizarre!'

She then read out an example she'd just torn off the machine. It was quite innocent and affectionate and written in Paolo's own hand; it spoke of how much he missed himself and how he would love himself for ever and was signed with her name. Apparently, it was one of several in the same vein that had spilled over the desk at the Normans' office.

Deirdre hadn't come in to work that day which gave Sue the opportunity to copy them and send them on to me – just a few floors away from where they had originated.

The builders were busy on the 64th-floor apartment conversion. It was a massive job but, because the area was so large, it was possible to live there alongside the 'building site' without too much disruption. There was even a spare bedroom for Paolo, who didn't want to use it, suggesting instead that we should continue to sleep together. I said an emphatic 'no' to the proposition, which seemed to surprise him. We were sitting at the kitchen table sharing a cup of tea and he explained that he would be leaving the next day for Rusper. I was still determined to get a divorce and hopeful that we could arrange things amicably. Hopeful, but, knowing my husband, doubtful that it would happen. I knew that I would need a good lawyer and my sister's spying eyes and ears in Rusper. However, I was aware that as a widow living in an estate cottage and with a young daughter to look after, Sue was in a delicate position. Although she helped with doing the wages and had use of one of the estate cars, she lived her life independently from Paolo and everything that went on with his business. However, she had copies of all the sets of keys for safekeeping.

Around 6.00pm the next evening, Sue had a visitor. Knowing everything that was going on, she wasn't too surprised to see Paolo and greeted him as if nothing had happened. He remained aloof and rejected her offer to come in for a cup of tea.

'Whatever happens here, you don't tell your sister,' he warned.

'No, of course not… I won't interfere,' she told him. She was not sure if she had detected a threatening tone in his voice or whether he was merely embarrassed by the situation. One thing was certain – things would quickly get much more uncomfortable for everybody concerned. She felt a chill of foreboding as she closed the door.

Back in New York, I knew I had to bide my time. I had withdrawn almost all my savings to pay for legal advice in the form of Peter Bronstein, an eminent, mid-town lawyer specialising in divorce. It cost $15,000 to use his services but, I was assured, he would be worth every penny. From his offices 'next door' in the Carnegie Tower, I was advised to be patient. Before serving any papers on Paolo, I should make sure that all the correct evidence was in place.

Money was going to be tight, but Paolo was at least paying the builders, household bills, the nanny's salary and Gemma's school fees. We continued to be civil with each other. He would phone and let me know when he was coming to New York and ask if he could come over and see Gemma. Of course, I agreed and, after she was in bed, we might go out for a walk and – like in the old days – commenting together on other stores' fashion displays. Often I cooked dinner for him and he would stay the night. He always expected that I would share his bed and acted surprised when I told him I didn't want to. We would have breakfast together like any normal married couple and even discuss his business plans and the progress of the new shop. Did I like the building? What did I think of the merchandise? Sometimes he'd ask my advice on style details for the new collection – I was especially good with the clothes and jewellery lines – and then he'd be gone. Often, we wouldn't hear from him for several weeks at a time. As well as the UK, he was spending a lot of time in Italy where the new designs were being made.

At opportune moments, I would slip into the conversation that I still wanted a divorce.

'Why do you want a divorce? We can stay as we are. You can live here and I'll make Rusper my full-time home. Then we can get together and take the little one on holidays…'

'No way, José!' I thought. I could just see my life spread out in front of me. It would be Paolo living his life like his father Aldo, but there was no way that I was prepared to sacrifice my freedom and end up like his mother, Olwen.

'I'll buy you a lovely new fur coat each year and you can have beautiful jewellery,' he offered.

What would I want with another fur coat – I had five already – and I certainly didn't need any more jewellery!

'No,' I repeated. 'What I want is a divorce.'

What I really wanted was my freedom. I wanted my peace of mind, my dignity and self-respect back. This 'biding my time' was taking its toll. It was exhausting and very stressful. Sometimes, I found it very hard to be 'normal' with him. But, of course, I couldn't let him know about my plans and how I really felt.

'Aa-ah, don't you worry about that. I'll get my Italian lawyer to sort something out. It will all be fine,' said Paolo, patting my hand.

'Well, Paolo, if you are talking to your lawyer, it would only be fair to let me know what's happening so that I can have a say in the arrangement.'

'We'll see if you ever get to have your say…' He had a nasty habit of concluding conversations with a veiled threat.

On the surface, it was all very civilised and I was at least content in the knowledge that my own high-powered lawyer was already well advanced in putting together my case. When things got tough, I would wash my hair, put it in rollers, grab a duster and start cleaning. The apartment was always dusty with all the building work going on and somehow I found dusting very therapeutic.

It was another hot New York morning in June 1990 when the phone rang and Sue told me the latest news. The phone extension in her cottage had buzzed, indicating a call going through to the office in the main house. Paolo was in Italy and she suspected that he would be calling Deirdre about something.

Since Anguilla, Deirdre had been studiously avoiding Sue, so my sister was surprised when, a few minutes later, there was a frantic banging on her door and a desperate-looking Deirdre asked if she might come in.

'She looked terrible,' said Sue, 'and her arms were full of papers. She told me that Paolo had been on the phone and had fired her. He had told her to leave immediately, to pick up her personal things and drop off the keys to her car with me but not to speak to me.

'She was clearly agitated, so I told her to come in for a moment and there – right in the middle of the kitchen – she just collapsed in a dead faint on the floor!'

Sue managed to pick her up and almost carried her through to the living room, fanning her and coaxing her back to consciousness with kind words and little sips of brandy. Deirdre had become hysterical but eventually told Sue the whole story.

Apparently, it had taken four years of concerted effort on Paolo's part to persuade Deirdre to go to bed with him. He had used every ruse and ounce of his Italian charm and persuasion, eventually bullying her into submission. Since I had found out about the affair, he was now demanding that she leave her husband and move into a house he had chosen for her in the village. He had already put a reserve on the detached, double-fronted, thatched home which was to be their love nest.

But Paolo had either over-estimated his appeal, or underestimated Deirdre's commitment to her husband and children. She told him that she couldn't do what he was asking and suggested they cool their relationship. Paolo had gone completely mad at her rejection and had apparently been virtually stalking her ever since, having been spotted several times hiding in bushes outside her house.

Her husband, a remarkably understanding man, had known what was going on and had decided to stand by his wife and do everything he could to keep the family together and to make sure their children wouldn't suffer.

Sue made Deirdre stay quiet as she took a call from Paolo. Her instructions were clear – she was to take away his secretary's car and all her office keys and make sure that she never ventured on to his property again. 'You do not speak to her or listen to anything she tries to tell you.' He was, in Sue's words, 'spitting fur and feathers'.

Deirdre's was a sad story and, knowing Paolo to be incredibly manipulative, I realised that once he had set his sights on her, she had not stood a chance. I also recognised that she could prove an important ally in my divorce. I decided to pay her a visit.

My lawyers had advised me not to leave the country but I needed evidence from Deirdre, so this visit to England was a cloak-and-dagger affair. Having first checked that Paolo was out of the country, I arrived at Heathrow late one evening and spent the night with a friend in Richmond. From there, I phoned Deirdre and told her that I wanted to talk to her. She sounded relieved but apprehensive to hear my voice and quickly agreed to keep the meeting a secret.

My friend drove me to her house near Horsham. I was hiding in the back of the car under a blanket. I knew that Paolo had his spies everywhere and I also dreaded being spotted by the press who were really interested in the story of my marriage break-up.

Deirdre's house was like its owner – neat and tidy – an ordinary, three-bedroom, semi-detached family home. It was exactly 1.00pm, the time we had agreed, when I rang the doorbell. Deirdre answered. Her hands were shaking and I could tell that she had been crying. Her eyes welled up again.

'Oh, Jenny… I am so sorry,' she sobbed.

I put an arm around her shoulders and we went into the living room where her husband, after a polite greeting, tactfully left us alone.

'Don't worry,' I said, 'we'll sort this out – but I need your help.'

'Yes, anything, anything at all I can do, you can count on me,' she promised.

We sat down and I carefully placed my classic Chanel bag on the coffee table between us and listened as she told me everything about her relationship with my husband. I was shocked to learn that he had first attempted to seduce her years before when she began working for him. I smiled wryly to learn that, when he eventually succeeded four years later, he had had problems getting it up on occasions. So, in the days before Viagra, that's where the testosterone had come into it.

'I don't mean to boast,' I said, knowing that it was inappropriate, but I couldn't help myself, 'but in all the years *we* were together, he never once had a problem with me.'

She was too upset to recognise the implications and we both surmised that he must have felt guilty about the affair.

I learned that, indeed, they had used my bedroom, and that he had also taken her to Manchester, of all places, and the motor show in Geneva. He had heartlessly calculated how he would use her without any consideration for her family and the impact that the affair was clearly having on them.

She told me about the house he had planned to buy for her and how furious he had been when she had turned him down. I knew about the stalking from Sue but was horrified to hear that she had had a visit from the police one night saying that they had received a report that she had mental problems and was an unfit mother. They needed to send someone around to check that her children were all right. Deirdre's nightmare got worse and worse. Thank goodness for her husband, who was clearly being supportive and had taken the attitude that we all make mistakes and this was hers.

When she turned Paolo down, he had been furious and told her, 'You'll always regret not coming with me and so will your children. They'll never forgive you for not choosing me.' When he said that, it was, she explained, 'like a skin coming off my eyes – as if someone had thrown a bucket of water over me and, at last, I had woken up and could see clearly the kind of man he was.' She appeared relieved to have got the whole story off her chest.

'Look, Deirdre, I am not angry with you. I think that your and you family should just forget him. Leave it behind you and start again. But don't forget me, because I am going to need your help. In exchange, I promise to do everything in my power to keep you out of this. I know that some people around the estate know what has happened but I promise that the press will never hear about your part in all of this from me. I promise to keep your name out of it.'

And to this day, I have kept my promise. Deirdre is not her real name.

I was very nice to her – I never once accused her of taking my husband, because I knew it hadn't been like that. If he had been an ordinary guy and this had been some fling, it would have been different. But what Paolo had done was just appalling.

Deirdre and I hugged and our pact was sealed. We girls must stick together, we agreed.

I picked up my bag and left. It had been a huge strain but it was mission accomplished. In the back of the car, I checked the small recording device that was in my handbag given to me by my lawyers. Yes, the whole conversation had recorded perfectly.

I didn't feel bad about tricking Deirdre into putting her story on tape. It was my means of survival and was essential for Gemma's and my future. Besides, Deirdre had pledged to help me and, in return, I would keep to my side of the bargain. We were two English women who had joined forces to gang up on one Italian man. Paolo would go ballistic.

In fact, when I finally told him about my meeting with Deirdre some eight months later, I actually thought that he might levitate with anger. He literally changed colour. How like Aldo he had become.

'Never underestimate, number one, a woman scorned; and two, an English woman,' I said with a certain smugness.

He couldn't get his words out he was so angry.

'No one is straighter than English women,' I added calmly. 'You won't get any of those Italian histrionics with us – no snivelling into hankies. We'll just face things and get on with them.'

'You, you…' he stuttered, 'you think you're so clever.'

We were back to that old line again.

'Well, yes. I think I have been quite clever this time,' I said. 'But do you know what, Paolo? All I want is a divorce. Please give me a divorce.'

But he wouldn't.

Back in Rusper, Deirdre was keeping to her side of the bargain. After the ground staff had left at 5.00pm, she and Sue would sneak into the main house and photocopy every document that looked as if it might be in any way helpful to my case. My lawyers had suggested they make copies of any bills and receipts for furniture or antiques, for instance. Paolo had bank accounts everywhere. The photocopier shut down twice through over-heating.

18

There's No Fool...

These were the early days of my bid for freedom and it was like watching the plot of a soap opera unfold. I woke each morning wondering what might happen next, in the firm belief that nothing my husband might do could surprise me any more. In a strange way, I felt detached – it was like reading about myself in the gossip columns – it was almost as if it was all happening to someone else and, in this kind of abstract way, I watched and waited. Little did I know that I'd only reached about Episode 3 and this series was destined to run for nine years.

Camera…lights…action – the set is my home, the building site in Metropolitan Towers. It's very early in the morning. The sound of the phone ringing wakes me.

'Sorry to wake you, Jen,' said Sue, phoning from Rusper. 'You're just not going to believe this…'

'Whatever has he done now?' I asked, groggily coming round.

'He's with Penny. She's in the kitchen with him having breakfast wearing your dressing gown!'

Just when I thought that nothing would surprise me... I was stunned.

'*Penny?* The 18-year-old stable girl?'

'Yes.'

'Penny with the long, red hair?'

'Yes.'

'Are you absolutely sure?'

'Yes, I'm certain. Everyone here is talking about it.'

I had suspected that he was seeing someone else. On my 36-hour undercover visit, Sue had smuggled me into the main house to pick up some personal belongings and I had seen a woman's clothes hanging alongside mine in the wardrobe. I'd wondered who they belonged to, and now I knew. Paolo and I had quite a large age gap – 17 years – but Penny and Paolo? There must have been 40 years separating them! I really couldn't believe it.

'Sue, are you certain they're having an affair or could there be some other explanation?'

'Jen, I'm absolutely positive – he's even given her my old car and I've seen her wearing some of your clothes!'

Sue wasn't sure how I would react. In fact, I suddenly saw the funny side and burst out laughing and, across the miles, Sue joined in. Ruth the nanny came into my room to find out what was going on and she also thought it was hilarious. Gemma came into my bed for a morning cuddle, pleased that we were all happy, but not understanding why.

I explained that Daddy had a new girlfriend and that she was very young. 'Yuck!' was her response and I tended to agree with her.

Gemma was my main concern and I wanted to keep her life and daily routine as normal as possible – she would never hear me saying anything bad about her father, but I would always answer her questions honestly. As an only child she had spent a lot of time in the company of grown-ups and had a mature attitude to all that had happened.

Before I issued Paolo with the divorce papers, Gemma and I would frequently travel back and forth to Italy and England together. We were in the back of a taxi from Kennedy Airport to midtown after a brief visit to the family and to pick up some of my things from Rusper. Gemma must have been 7 years old and she knew that I was upset with her father.

'Why aren't you and Daddy together any more?' she suddenly asked.

'Do you want to know the truth, darling?'

Her little shoulders came up and her head dropped down but, in a quiet but firm voice, she said, 'Yes, I do.'

'Because Daddy went to bed and slept with Deirdre.'

'Eeeeeuw!' Her expression seemed to sum it up quite well.

'And Daddy is my husband so I didn't like it,' I went on, managing to keep a smile in my voice.

'How icky!' She had learned all about the facts of life and she obviously didn't like the picture conjured up in her mind. Gemma had been brought up around fashion and beauty. 'Deirdre doesn't look anything like Claudia Schiffer,' she pointed out. Maybe if Paolo had chosen to stray with Gemma's favourite top model, he might have been forgiven.

'No, she doesn't,' I agreed. 'Anyway, Daddy's having a silly childhood-thing at the moment and that's why we're here,' I explained.

'I'm getting hungry now – can I watch TV when we get home?'

I knew that Gemma would be all right as long as I was always honest with her and answered her questions truthfully.

The gap between Deirdre's rejection of Paolo and Penny's replacement was very short – just a matter of weeks. I couldn't help but wind him up about his new girlfriend. She would often call ahead of his visit to New York and I would always pass on the message.

'Penny's been on the phone for you.'

'What's she calling here for?' he sounded very uncomfortable.

'Maybe she wants to have a chat with me about your habits.'

'Don't be ridiculous.' Coming from him, that was rich. 'Don't you worry about me – there's plenty more where she came from!'

'Good for you! You just go off and shag yourself stupid – I am so happy that you've got the stamina. Enjoy!' It always made him mad when I took that tone – so level and matter-of-fact. He couldn't bear it that I didn't get jealous. I was never jealous; sad and unhappy that our marriage had failed, but never jealous.

'Oh…and, darling,' I added sarcastically, 'just a word of advice… you've got this kindergarten problem. Do you want any information about modern music – maybe I can teach you some topics to talk about that will interest a teenager…something about pop groups perhaps?'

'You think you're so funny.'

'No, not at all…just trying to help.'

He would invariably lose his temper at that point.

On this particular occasion, I knew that I had the upper hand because I also looked sensational. I was wearing a short, chiffon Chanel skirt with a Swarovski crystal jacket and high Manolo Blahnik shoes. I had made a tremendous effort for a cocktail party at Donald Trump's. Paolo had not been invited and was planning to spend the evening with Gemma, who was out at after-school class at the time. I had left him dinner in a pot on the stove.

'Your skirt is too short,' he said.

'Since when? You always liked it when I wore this outfit. Nothing's changed – I am the same weight as when we got married.'

He wanted to know where I was going, and was obviously unhappy about not being included in the invitation.

'Why are you going there?'

I would have thought it was obvious. 'Because I don't want to talk to you. You'll be on the phone to Penny all evening. Obviously, you are in love with her – I am going out. Isn't that logical?' I said reasonably.

He'd start shouting and screaming at me and swearing in Italian.

'Good luck to you! I just hope that she has a good sexual appetite – obviously, I never did – and that you're able to keep up with someone so young.' I knew how to hurt, too.

'You don't understand, Jenny, I am a very lonely man,' and then he burst into tears.

I stroked his face tenderly and, for a moment, I felt sorry for him. He appeared pathetic to me. 'You brought everything on yourself,' I said quietly. 'I did everything I could to be a good wife to you – I stayed up at night and paced the floor with you when you had problems with your family, I cooked for you, I was a good lover, I ran our homes, there was nothing else I could have done – but an 18-year-old I cannot be. Enjoy your dinner!' And on that note, I left him feeling sorry for himself and went off to my society New York party. He was asleep when I got home.

Almost a year after the fateful Anguilla holiday, and my lawyers finally phoned with the news I'd been waiting for. 'Jenny, we've got enough to act on. Paolo's in New York and we are going to serve him with the divorce papers today.'

The 'server' visited the office annex at the Metropolitan Towers. 'Mr Gucci?'

'Yes – who wants to know?'

The envelope was thrust into his hands.

'What's this?' he asked, genuinely puzzled.

My friend Joe Olivieri, Paolo's assistant, told me that when Paolo opened the envelope and discovered the divorce papers, he was literally speechless. Apparently, he nearly collapsed and had to be helped to a chair. He was silent for the rest of the day – he didn't even make or receive a single phone call. I don't think that, up until that moment, he had believed that I was serious. I think he thought it was just a phase and that we would get back together some time. He was literally in shock.

The next day, he was full of righteous indignation. 'You won't believe what Jenny has done,' he said to Joe. 'She's filed for a divorce. Look here, [brandishing the legal documents] it quotes "irreconcilable differences" and adultery…she even names Penny Armstrong. How dare she behave like this?' he stammered.

Joe told me later that he came up with a wonderful retort. 'I hardly think it's Jenny's fault,' he said, 'she wasn't there putting your dick into Deirdre, or Penny for that matter, was she?'

When he got over the initial shock, Paolo quickly sprang into action. From the beginning, it was clear he was going to play dirty. Not only was the building work on the apartment stopped immediately, but the builders were also instructed to disconnect some of the plumbing and electrics. I came home to find the toilets and bathroom fittings lying in the middle of the floor and electrical wires hanging dangerously out of open sockets. It was only by calling in some favours that I managed to organise some basic damage repair – apparently, one of the builders was a relative of a friend of a friend. He took pity on me and reconnected some essentials before packing up his toolbox and leaving for the last time.

Paolo was flexing his muscles. He was furious that I had crossed him. Perhaps, up until then, he hadn't believed that I was serious but the legal documents told a different story. My lawyers advised me on no account to leave my home. We all feared Paolo might change the locks and would have no scruples about making his wife and daughter homeless. We were also concerned for Gemma's safety. I believed that, in his current state of mind, Paolo was capable of anything and there was a strong possibility that he might be planning to kidnap her.

He was also determined that my sister would suffer. Running the Rusper estate was like running a small company – the maintenance work never stopped and, as well as outside contractors there were five or six full-time staff for the house, gardens and pool, excluding the people working with the horses. Sue never knew whom she could trust because Paolo would always find someone else to do his dirty work. The atmosphere was horrid and he would shout abuse at her across the yard.

During the depths of winter 1990, Sue often found that she had no hot water or heating in her house. It had been fitted with oil-fired central heating with the main tank situated in Paolo's garage. Someone had been instructed to turn off the tap, which supplied her home.

'What should I do, Jen? It's freezing in here,' Her teeth were chattering on the phone and I could hear a puzzled Lucy in the background. The poor child couldn't understand why her beloved uncle should have turned against them.

I advised Sue to contact her lawyer who, in turn, would contact Paolo's lawyer and, eventually, the heating would be turned on again. It happened four or five times that winter. I felt dreadful that my sister and niece should be targeted just because I had crossed Paolo. I was very glad that my parents had had the foresight to leave and weren't around to witness this.

Paolo found lots of ways to make Sue suffer. After he had taken away her car, she was in a terrible position; in an isolated village with only a twice-weekly bus service there was no way for her to get to work at a nearby boarding school or for Lucy to get to school. Having always insisted, 'It's your car…your car…a gift…' he changed his tune the moment the divorce papers were served. He took away her keys, although the car remained in the underground car park at Normans gathering dust.

I told her to use my car – it was even registered in my name and Sue had the log book. But somehow he had lied and managed to get another log book and it just disappeared. Fortunately, friends came to Sue's aid and lent her a Mini Metro. She parked it in her usual spot in the garage and was surprised the following morning to see it had a flat tyre. The mechanic who came to fix it discovered a nail embedded in the tyre – I suppose it's just possible that she had driven over a nail – possible, but in the current climate of revenge, unlikely.

A few days later, she was driving to school in the morning when the engine kept cutting out. It turned out that the radiator hose had been cut through.

'The bastards are out to get me,' she told me on the phone.

This time, the mechanic advised her that it had been slashed with a Stanley knife and that she should go to the police who would have prosecuted, but the lawyers advised caution. So although she kept the evidence, we didn't act, although, looking back, we should have as there could have been a terrible accident.

Needless to say, Paolo himself was out of the country at the time.

In the weeks following the divorce papers being served, it became obvious that Paolo was not going to co-operate. On the instructions of the lawyers, I returned his credit cards. I had only used them for the bare necessities which, with hindsight, was pretty stupid. I could have even bought a car with his American Express but I hadn't abused them at all.

Until a settlement was agreed, the court ruled that Paolo was to pay Gemma and my expenses and household bills. Our standard of living was to remain the same as before and he would be obliged to pay the nanny's salary and Gemma's school fees. I would submit the bills to our lawyers, who, in turn, would pass them over to Paolo's legal team. I suppose they then instructed Paolo to pay the bills – but he never did.

Within six months, the court had barred him access to the Metropolitan Towers and from seeing his daughter. But still he wouldn't pay anything to us and refused to give me a divorce.

Over the next four years, we would find ourselves in the New York State Supreme Court in Manhattan before Justice Phyllis B. Gangel-Jacob on average two or three times every month – some weeks it was as often as every day. Even the lawyers had never seen anything like it before.

Peter Bronstein told me that in his entire 25-year career as a divorce lawyer and his father's before him, he had only seen one other case where there simply was no other side to the story. 'Clearly, you have been a good and loyal wife,' he said. 'Your husband is a menace and we'll get what we can for you. It's very rare to have such a one-sided divorce case – you are only the second I have ever seen.'

It was nice to know because sometimes I wondered if it was my fault. It was all such a mess and getting messier by the day. The lawyers all underestimated what Paolo would be capable of and, in turn, he himself underestimated my strength and resilience. It was stalemate. He had a team of four top US attorneys and they certainly had their work cut out. It would have cost him a fortune and I wondered if he was paying them. I knew that, early on, the head of his legal team recommended that Paolo pay me $5 million and give me one of the properties. 'Mr Gucci, then you will have a peaceful life and your daughter won't be affected,' he advised.

'No,' Paolo retorted, 'I am not going to give her a penny – ever!'

The lawyer was nonplussed. He had never come across such defiant stubbornness. He'd never met a Gucci before. 'This is New York. Your divorce is in New York's jurisdiction,' he explained. 'You are going to have to give her something.'

But Paolo refused point-blank and fired the lawyer. He then challenged our marriage in Haiti, claiming that it had not been legal and so was null and void. It took months and mountains of paperwork to prove that we were indeed married. It was eventually recognised by the New York justice system and that was why our divorce case would be heard in the New York Supreme Court.

Over the years, I would get to explore every square inch of the civil court building off Foley Square, Manhattan. I spent so much time there I even knew where the best toilets were to be found.

I became friendly with two other lawyers in Paolo's team. At the Supreme Court one day, one took me aside. 'Mrs Gucci, I just wanted you to know that I am quitting your husband's case. I don't think I have ever come across such bizarre behaviour in my life. I hope that you get everything that Peter Bronstein is asking for you,' and with that he kissed me on the cheek. 'You are a lovely woman and I am so sorry for what we are putting you through,' he added.

I wondered what specifically he was referring to.

A couple of days later, I would find out when a large brown envelope was delivered to the apartment. With a dreadful sinking feeling, I signed for it. Paolo's team had shopped me to the immigration department: I was going to be deported. I felt my knees buckle and realised that I was about to faint.

I had known that my B2 visa had run out, but could do nothing about it as my lawyers pointed out that there was no way that I could leave the country to reapply. It was ironic that Paolo had never allowed me to try for a Green Card because he had feared that I would then get a job and leave him. Now I was in this impossible position of facing deportation and being split up from my daughter who had an American passport. This was one of several 'lowest moments' I would be forced to face.

I have somehow managed to survive all the awful things that happened through the amazing support of my friends. Paolo's behaviour was so dreadful that everyone we knew – including all those who worked for him – was on my side. If he had been discreet and behaved properly, no doubt many wouldn't have got involved but, as it was, his behaviour was quite appalling. Friends loaned me the money to hire the services of a major immigration lawyer. They knew that I was in danger of having a nervous breakdown. I would wake up screaming, as my recurring nightmare was Gemma being snatched from me. I had just four days to prepare my case.

The appointment was made and, together with my immigration lawyer, I went to Number 1 Police Plaza, New York, where, alongside all the other illegal immigrants who had been rounded up, I had my fingerprints taken and posed for a mugshot.

'Do you want to go home?' I was asked by a surly official.

'Of course, but there's nothing I can do at the moment.'

My lawyer explained my case and, later, Justice Gangel-Jacob would also file a report. After another week of sleepless nights, it was decided that I could stay in the US until the court case was resolved and Gemma's schooling was not to be disrupted in any way.

None of us knew that it would be six years before I would be allowed to leave the country and that, when I eventually did return to the UK, Paolo would play his final, unbeatable trump card.

19

All that Glitters...

December is a wonderful month in New York and December 1992 was no exception. The city had come alive with sparkling lights and the atmosphere literally tingled with excitement as traditional Christmas songs were belted out from all the shops and restaurants and staff wearing fixed grins and Santa costumes wished everyone 'Happy Holidays'. It really is a magical time, especially for children, and although Gemma wasn't a spoiled New York brat, she did go to a good school – Trinity School (founded in 1709, making it the oldest continually operational school in New York) – and her friends came from very wealthy families.

Paolo had tried to argue that Gemma be transferred into a normal state school but the judge had thrown out that request, insisting our daughter's education should be a priority and her life should be disrupted as little as possible by her parents' acrimonious divorce. Her Christmas present list was quite long that year and, yet again, I just couldn't believe how Paolo – with all his wealth – could be so cruel to ignore his little girl at this time. He was still defying the court orders and flatly refusing to pay us anything. Even more worryingly, he was, I had heard through the lawyers, trying to evict us from the Metropolitan Towers. He was more determined than ever to make me suffer – and if his daughter was hurt in the process, so be it. He just didn't care.

I knew that – despite all the problems – I would do everything I could to ensure that Gemma enjoyed the holidays. Alongside the tedious extra maths tuition and the energetic Irish dancing classes, she had also learned to ice skate and it was wonderful to watch her swirling round the Rockefeller Center rink with the other skaters, looking every bit as if they were featuring in a Christmas card scene. I wondered if Paolo had any idea how much he was missing out on watching his daughter grow up. She had lots of party invitations and, somehow, I would make sure that she had the right outfits to wear and gifts to take to her hosts. My sister Sue and her daughter Lucy would be joining us and a small tree was already decorated in the apartment.

I seemed to manage to hold it together through Christmas but, as the New Year approached, with all its thoughts of fresh hopes and new beginnings, I could feel myself crumbling under the weight of all my problems. For how long would this battle continue? I was no nearer

New Year's Eve 1992 – despite everything, I was still able to sing.

reaching a settlement or getting divorced from Paolo than when we had first split up. Paolo was now living in Rusper with Penny…and all my possessions. To add insult to injury, I knew that I was not looking my best; in fact, to put it bluntly, I looked a mess.

It was in this state – duster and head in hand – that the two Joes found me one morning before New Year's Eve. Joe Olivieri was a wonderful friend. He had been Paolo's personal assistant for many years and was Gemma's godfather but, like so many people who worked closely with Paolo at this time, he had lost respect for his 'boss'. Another friend, Joe DeLeo, was what was called a 'raw space designer' who specialised in decorating shops and commercial properties. Both had obviously decided that I needed an overhaul, too.

They didn't pull any punches. 'Look at you… Jenny, you look terrible…awful…a complete mess!' Joe Olivieri touched my greasy hair with disdain. 'I can't believe how you've let yourself go. For heaven's sake, book an appointment and get your roots done!' He pulled out a wad of money from his pocket and started peeling off notes.

'… And your nails…and…ugh, get a pedicure, too,' added the other Joe, who was looking at my bare feet as he also brandished his cash at me.

There really was no arguing with them – they were right; but it did cost money to look well groomed in New York City. I protested about taking their money but Joe was already on the phone making the appointment for me. They sorted out the practicalities, too, like arranging to pick up Gemma from school, and took over my home for the day. 'We don't want to see you back here until 4.30 at the earliest,' said Paolo's former assistant.

'We've got a party to organise,' added his friend, already with tape measure in hand. 'You look like a witchy tramp! Just go,' as they unceremoniously pushed me out the door.

It was about 5.00pm when I returned home gasping for a cup of tea. My blonde hair was back to its former, gleaming glory, fingers and toes were pristine and pink and all the bits in between had been buffed and polished. I was positively glowing from the transformation…and so was my home.

The whole apartment had become golden. At first, I couldn't quite take it in and then I realised that they had covered all the walls with yards and yards of gold lamé material. Joe DeLeo explained that it had been left over from some theatre job and he thought it would work well in my apartment – which it did. Swathed across the walls and part of the ceiling the material succeed in covering the depressing metal girders, tumbling electrical cables and rough plaster work, making the room feel like the inside of a pale, golden mine. They had also brought lots of baby tables, each covered with linen cloths and decorated with a golden pot of flowers. It was all set out for a party.

'This is your Christmas present,' they said. 'The food and drink is all organised – invite who you want. We're going to have a party!'

Gemma came running out echoing their words, 'We're going to have a party...we're going to have a party!'

I burst into tears.

We had a wonderful celebration. Gemma wore a new party dress and I ended up playing the piano (I still had a grand piano) until 4.00am. Maybe 1993 would be a better year. Although the tables with their special cloths and decorations had to be returned, the golden wall hangings stayed in place for the next six-and-a-half years.

It never fails to amaze me how adaptable we all can be when put into strange and different situations. It wasn't long before the daily calls to my lawyers, the regular court appearances in front of Justice Phyllis B. Gangel-Jacob in the Manhattan Supreme Court and having no money in my purse all became as normal as brushing my teeth.

Everyone around me had been sucked into the maelstrom that my life had become. The whirlpool not only encroached on my family and friends, but also acquaintances. Even the teachers at Gemma's school had been warned to report any suspicious behaviour as there was a genuine fear that Paolo might try and kidnap her, especially since the judge had now forbidden him to come anywhere near the Metropolitan Towers or to see his daughter at least until he started to pay what he owed us. Even our doormen had become collaborators in keeping Paolo away and, when necessary, shuffling me out of the building's rear exit away from any unwanted press attention.

'Mrs Gucci doesn't want any visitors,' they'd tell Paolo, tactfully blocking his path.

'But *I* own the building!' he would shout.

'I'm sorry, Mr Gucci…'

And in the midst of all this madness, I was adamant Gemma's life would be as normal and untouched as possible by everything that was happening. This was why, however tight money became, I insisted on keeping a nanny and, later, au pairs for her. Sometimes, I would feel mentally exhausted by all the legal stuff and Paolo's uncompromising attitude and then having a young 'playmate' for Gemma was a wonderful antidote. When things became fraught at home, they would be on hand to take her roller-skating in Central Park, out shopping or for an ice cream. The au pairs came from wealthy families and had allowances from their parents and only needed their board and pocket money. It was a good deal all round as they were happy to stay at a safe and prestigious address in New York and learn English.

On the nanny front, Ruth had fallen in love with, and then married a New York cop. Michelle, our last full-time nanny, stayed for 18 months. She was a very clever girl, who later got a degree in forensic science and went into crime investigation before moving to Spokane in Washington State. Gemma loved all her nannies and Michelle had encouraged her academically and made her work hard at her schoolwork.

It was now time to move into the world of au pairs. I had been advised to try the Mormon Church and, a few days later, a 19-year-old member of the Church of Jesus Christ of Latter Day Saints moved into our 64th-floor apartment. I'll call her Marie.

I had my reservations during the interview but I was desperate to find someone to be with Gemma and ignored the warning signs that she might not fit in. Gemma hated her on sight – not a good start. She had a sort of 'edge' to her. 'I am an opera singer,' she announced early on.

'Oh, are you?' I was surprised – at least here was some common ground. I explained that I was a performing soprano. 'I must hear you sing,' I said encouragingly.

'No, I must hear *you*.' It was almost thrown down as a challenge.

Eventually, I did listen to her and it was horribly obvious that she didn't have the voice to achieve her ambition to be a dramatic soprano. It turned out that she suffered from depression and I felt sorry for her and decided to take her under my wing, but she turned out to be quite a liability.

The doormen at the Metropolitan Towers normally greeted me warmly but, on this particular occasion, it was clear that they felt awkward and embarrassed as I returned, somewhat preoccupied from yet another court appearance. They had always been friendly towards the nannies, too, but this time I could hear mutterings that Marie would have to go and that she had clearly done something pretty unforgivable. I headed for the usual lift, but was steered towards another bank of elevators – the usual one was 'Out of Order'.

I wasn't sure what would await me when I opened the door. Gemma rushed up, hugging me and gabbling, 'Mummy, Mummy, Marie brought a pony here!'

Although highly improbable, it was true. This strange, troubled girl had borrowed a small pony from a friend and walked it six or seven blocks from the Mormon Church at Columbus Circle and straight into one of the poshest buildings in Manhattan. Before the doormen could stop her, she had taken the poor creature into the lift where it was so terrified that it had proceeded to poop everywhere. It had freaked out completely but, somehow, they had eventually managed to coax it down again and out of the building.

The superintendent, a very kindly and understanding man, called round to explain the damage. Apparently, the carpet in the lift had been ruined and would need to be replaced. I was almost in tears when he said that I would have to pay for a new carpet.

'This really can't go on… I am afraid you'll have to get rid of her,' he advised, 'she's nutty as a fruit cake.' It would appear that there had been previous confrontations between Marie and the lobby staff and she was not a favourite downstairs. I needed this like a hole in the head. But the people working in the Metropolitan Towers all knew of my precarious financial state and the superintendent took pity on me and eventually found the money from some other budget to replace the damaged carpet.

Wearing the famous butterfly necklace made by Piccini of Florence.
It had strands of gold balls and pink pearls attached to a butterfly made
of diamond and ruby roulades.

I wasn't going to go back to the Mormon Church and was looking
for another au pair source when a friend recommended that I try the
Austrian embassy. I'd always loved Austrian girls and they, in turn, would

be keen to perfect their English. What I hadn't bargained for was two for the price of one.

Anna and Lena were identical twins who refused to be separated and were prepared to work for me for one wage. They stayed nearly a year and were a real joy to have around. They covered for each other and, if one felt unwell, the other would always fill in. Both were artistic and Anna especially was a really good artist who taught Gemma to draw.

Life was a continual juggling act of trying to make ends meet. I was late with the school fees and the Tower's superintendent had given me yet another extension on paying the building maintenance bills when, one evening, I was sitting gazing at the gold lamé walls searching for inspiration. Since Paolo had halted all the building work, our New York home that should have been so beautiful remained unfinished and raw. Although Joe's golden wall hangings concealed some of the building work, a mass of wiring and piping still protruded from the ceilings and unfinished timber framework was visible in every room. I had used the magnificent huge doors we had ordered from Italy as room dividers, while some electricity cables still spilled dangerously out of open sockets.

'I must remember to warn the twins to be careful with their hairdryers,' I thought. Anna and Lena, sensing I needed some quiet time, had taken Gemma out for a chocolate floating ice-cream soda treat. I turned my attention to the magnificent view above the New York skyline. Suddenly, a casual remark made by a friend popped into my head. Like me, she knew and got on well with lots of gay people and had mentioned two – not a couple – who were desperately looking for somewhere to live. My home – which had been originally built as three apartments – covered half of the entire floor. Space was one thing I had plenty of.

Steven was an antique restorer specialising in Georgian silver, who was trying to get over the break-up of a 25-year relationship and prone to drowning his sorrows in vodka; and Peter, a theatre producer, also moved in.

They both fitted in perfectly. Each paid $600 a month rent and it was a great arrangement all round. As well as the Austrian au pair community, we now had regular soirées with all these good-looking, artistic, creative people. My old friend Edward Gold, a chief purser on American Airlines, had set up his easels in the triangular wedge of the apartment. He loved to paint there on his days off. Paolo and I had first met Ed some years before when he looked after us on a long-haul flight. He was very witty and we had all got along so well together that, after landing, we exchanged phone numbers. I think he was quite surprised when, some weeks later, I phoned him. We got together to do some Christmas shopping and a firm, lifelong friendship was born.

Steven had been brought up under the Raj with an old colonial type of education with governesses and his section of the apartment was half the main living room that also doubled as his antique workshop where he restored mostly old lamps and silver items.

These were my daily companions who helped me through the dark times and brought humour, fun and laughter back into my life.

If I am ever asked to recount the funniest thing I have ever seen – the single event that has made me laugh until it hurts – it would have to be something that happened around this time. It was a reasonably normal kind of a day – Gemma was at school and Ed, whose wedge-shaped art studio was adjacent to Steven's room, was painting at his easel. Suddenly, and completely unannounced, Steven burst out of his room to the strains of Tchaikovsky's *Swan Lake*, wearing a tutu, a load of jewellery and a large grin. It was immediately obvious that he had fallen, rather spectacularly, off the wagon. In fact, he was so drunk that with each pirouette he would lose his balance and crash into the walls. Somehow, the sight of him with his beard and pink tutu, and his garbled explanation in his upper-class, aristocratic accent that he thought a little ballet might cheer everyone up, was hysterically funny. Ed and I literally collapsed with laughter.

It really seemed as if we lived in some sort of mad house – what with a neurotic Jewish artist in one corner and an aristocratic, tutu-wearing, bearded ballet dancer in another, and eccentric Austrian au pair twins in the middle! How lucky I was, though, despite all the awful things that were happening with Paolo, to have such a wonderful network of people around me. We all supported each other – there was a terrific bond between us. I am also sure that, growing up surrounded by such an interesting and creative group of people, Gemma benefited enormously, too. Even today, I notice how 'normal' people quickly bore her.

The rent money certainly helped with the day-to-day expenses of living in New York, but it didn't begin to cover the large bills – like Gemma's school and the lawyers' fees – which continued to mount up. Whenever I had serious money worries, I would go into cleaning mode. I don't know why, but washing my hair, putting it in rollers and tackling every surface with a duster always helps keep me calm.

This was how Steven found me one day as he guided me to a chair and completed the ritual by putting the kettle on. Steven had his own problems and battles with depression, but he swept them aside to help me. 'What's the matter, Jen?' he asked kindly.

'I don't know. I just feel as if I can't go on.' I could feel tears welling up. 'I haven't got any money left – there's nothing at all and I don't know what to do.' I felt very low and desperate. 'I haven't even got money for groceries,' I sobbed.

He put a kindly arm around my shoulders. 'I've got some money saved up and I want you to have it,' he said.

'I couldn't possibly take your money,' I protested.

'Look, I don't need it and you've been so good to me. It will pay Gemma's school fees for a year...'

'No,' I interrupted, but he was insistent.

'It's only money and it really doesn't mean anything,' now he was crying, too. 'Please take it, I am begging you.'

What a wonderful, kind gesture. He gave me around $6,000 dollars and, I am happy to say, I did manage eventually to pay it back.

During those dark years, there were many friends who were kind and generous in lots of different ways. Although there was no money for treats or special things, we never actually starved. Something or someone would always come to our rescue – like my lovely friend Kay, who was married to a very wealthy Wall Street banker.

'Jen, you're in such a state, please call Glen. I know he would love to help you,' she suggested one day.

But how could I? How could I ask someone for money? It kept me awake at night and made me feel physically sick. But I was desperate and so, with a shaking hand, I took the phone.

'Hello, my dear,' said this lovely, gentle man. 'Jenny, how can I help you?'

I told him about my predicament.

'How much would you like?' He asked the question so sweetly and with such consideration that it didn't sound like I was asking for a handout.

I started to explain my needs. 'I have to pay the phone bill, the lawyers, utilities and Gemma needs...' Actually, the list went on and on and I realised I was babbling.

'I'll give you $10,000,' he put me out of my agony. 'I'll send my secretary around with it straight away,' he offered.

'I'll pay you back as soon as Paolo gives me what he owes,' I stammered.

'It really doesn't matter, Jenny. Kay and I love you very much and we just want to help.'

I am happy to say that I did pay them back, too.

Gemma wasn't the only one with the active social life – together, we were invited for weekends as houseguests in Rhode Island and I would always manage to find enough money for petrol and to take a bunch of flowers as a gift. I also received invitations to smart social occasions and dinner parties. Fortunately, I still had a wardrobe full of expensive clothes that would have to last me a long time. Sometimes, I suspected the other guests knew or had read about my predicament and, on other occasions, I think they were ignorant of it. I wasn't happy talking about all my legal battles with Paolo and preferred to switch off from all my problems when I went out. It was nice to listen to other people chattering about inconsequential things or to explore life outside the confines of my golden apartment.

At one such dinner party, hosted by some wealthy Italians, I found myself sitting opposite a friendly woman who worked for Sotheby's, specialising in African and Naïve art. We got along really well and, when she gave me her card, I tucked it away in my handbag, hoping we might meet up again.

A few months later and, of course, the situation with Paolo remained unresolved. Despite all the court orders, he still steadfastly refused to pay me any money, either as part of a settlement or for Gemma's needs. In March 1993, he had been arrested by police in Bridgeport, Connecticut, for failing to pay £250,000 he owed in back maintenance. It happened in the town of Darien, Connecticut, when he was leaving the offices of some business associates. Peter Bronstein was with me as I watched in horror as the police car had driven up, and three plain-clothes officers handcuffed him and took him off to jail. He remained behind bars for one night before his lawyers managed to get him released on bail. I imagine that he had had to give assurances that he would pay me what he owed, but he never did. He would then escape the country and we wouldn't hear anything from him for a while. And so it dragged on.

Paolo obviously believed he was above the law and – as the weeks turned into months and then years – I began to wonder if he was right. The divorce case dragged on and on, and in the meantime, I was in desperate need of money.

It was Ed's idea. Painting away at his easel one day, he pointed out that I had several thousand dollars' worth of art hanging on my golden walls. Many were valuable examples of Haitian art that has its own, quite exclusive niche market. Some of the pieces I didn't even like, especially a painting of a lunatic asylum in Cape Haitian, Haiti's second-largest town. It was quite a clever painting, with lots of crazy faces and a black-and-white tiled floor, but I found it rather disturbing, especially knowing that the artist who had painted it had himself been committed. When I moved into the apartment, I found just the spot for it – in the guest toilet over the cats' litter tray! Let Bouncer and Bonzo and any visitors appreciate this work of art. I felt I had enough problems of my own.

Incidentally, Bouncer and Bonzo were blonde tabbies who had come from the Yorktown farm (more of which later) and Gemma especially loved Bouncer who was huge, weighing in at about 26lb. Bonzo was mad as a hatter, possibly as a result of too much Haitian art appreciation in the loo.

There were two other Haitian paintings – one a brightly-coloured landscape by Dorleans, and the other by another well-known painter, Bazile. I decided to get in touch with my contact at Sotheby's.

She remembered me, but had bad news. 'You've just missed our large Haitian art sale and we've not got another one scheduled for two years,' she said.

'Oh, no!'

She must have heard the desperation in my voice because she then came up with an idea. 'I think one of the big collectors is here in New York at the moment. I'll give you her number.'

Half an hour later, this Haitian art expert is visiting the guest toilet and ooh-ing and ahh-ing appreciatively over the mad expressions in the lunatic asylum with Bouncer scratching in his tray and Bonzo waiting to sharpen his claws with a demented look in his eyes. She walked out a few minutes later with the three paintings under her arms and I had her guaranteed cheque for $7,000 in my hand.

Over the years, I became quite good at selling things. I learned to let go of anything that didn't have a sentimental value, but things that did, like my wedding rings with the baguette diamonds, I kept and gave to Gemma on her 21st birthday. I sold lots of jewellery, including a 16-carat amethyst ring surrounded by diamonds that ended up on the finger of Anthony Quinn's wife.

Friends would approach me discreetly if they knew of someone who wanted to buy exquisite pieces and clandestine meetings were set up at which I received a fair price for items. Rings and necklaces of different-coloured sapphires, diamonds and rubies all disappeared from my jewellery box and were converted into much-needed cash. Even my solid-pink diamond butterfly pin – made by S.J. Philips of Bond Street and re-worked as a necklace – had to be sold to pay the lawyers. It was an unusual piece and a favourite as the wings moved and glinted in the light as I walked.

I hardly dared think about what I would do when I ran out of things to sell. How long could I hang on? How long would Paolo fight before some sort of justice prevailed?

20

Dark, Destructive Days

It seemed a lifetime ago that the divorce papers had been served to Paolo. During those early days, we had all been optimistic that maybe my journey to freedom would be a smooth one. My lawyers knew his legal representatives and I was assured that, as they were such a professional team, it would be relatively easy to reach an amicable settlement. How wrong they all were.

Early on in the proceedings, Judge Phyllis took the lawyers aside and asked both teams if there was any chance of reconciliation. Apparently, she told them that Mr Gucci was behaving as if he was still in love with his wife and that this was why he was acting with such venom.

I don't think that this was the case, but I believe that, by then, he had lost his grip on reality. I know he had a tremendously soft spot for me and, in a way, a grudging respect for the fact that I wouldn't back down. It was similar to his relationship with his father – we both refused to back down. Aldo had been right – I was 'trouble' but Paolo had another 'polemic' up his sleeve…he declared himself bankrupt.

It was something my lawyers had discussed as a possibility, but with a fortune of at least $40 million and numerous properties, they had ruled it out as being too far-fetched and impossible to pull off. Once again, they had underestimated Paolo's determination to destroy me by any means possible. I cannot begin to imagine how complicated it must have been for him to hide his money and make sure that the deeds for Normans, Metropolitan Towers, Yorktown Heights and other properties would be virtually untraceable, held as they were by obscure companies in Lichtenstein and Liberia. He even closed the New York shop on 59th and Madison, despite the fact that in its first and only five or six weeks of trading it had been hugely successful, having done 38 per cent more business than predicted. It had taken three years to build and create the new lines and had represented his lifetime ambition to establish an independent Paolo Gucci business. I knew that he had spent at least $11 million on this project so far. It was quite terrifying the lengths he was prepared to go to 'prove' his bankruptcy and to make me suffer. And much worse was to come.

The Yorktown Heights estate, which included Millfield Stables in Westchester County, was about a 45-minute drive from New York city. We had chosen this magnificent home together in 1989 as a weekend and holiday retreat from the city. The main house was dominated by the enormous living area where we had two Steinway pianos. The estate also included a four-car garage and separate guest house that was beautifully decorated throughout with Ralph Lauren designs. There were 32 acres of land including 7 acres of manicured gardens, complete with a white picket fence.

The stable block was a quarter of a mile walk from the main house and this was the home of Paolo's 80-odd Arab thoroughbreds and Gemma's pony, Beatrice. In addition to the eight full-time grooms and stable staff, there were several part-time employees. During our legal wrangles, we also kept the local locksmith in work as Paolo continually changed the locks in an attempt to keep me out; and then I would call the locksmith to change them back again. But, as part of my strategy to keep Gemma's routine unchanged, I was equally determined not to be thwarted. She had a special friend, Patrick, in the area and his company, together with the attraction of riding her beloved Beatrice, made it a popular weekend destination.

The main house, as with all our homes, was decorated with fabulous antiques and paintings. Antique shopping had always been one of Paolo's and my favourite Saturday afternoon activities. When we were in the UK, we'd visit Petworth in West Sussex where I am sure the dealers would tip each other off that we were in the neighbourhood. After negotiating reductions on the asking prices, Paolo would typically spend £5,000–£6,000 during those expeditions. Throughout those outings, I rarely felt the need to assert myself. Sometimes, he'd hold up two paintings for me to choose and usually we were in agreement – only very occasionally might I disagree with his decision. After making our selection, the dealers would be given their shipping instructions as we discussed where each piece would look its best. All the details would be forwarded to Deirdre, who would make the necessary payments and finalise the transport details.

It would be the same scenario wherever we were – Milan, Bologna or Florence. I especially remember the cellar of a shop in Florence that turned out to be a treasure trove of antique delights. There, we bought a side table that had belonged to Enrico Caruso and selected an 11th-century, hand-painted organ decorated with images of the disciples. It was in a pretty poor state of repair and Paolo found a specialist restorer in New York who charged $10,000 to bring it back to its former glory. It was then shipped to Rusper.

Paolo had a special fondness for tables and furniture and we had lots of valuable pieces, from a Regency table to farmhouse dressers. Some of our possessions were almost as well-travelled as we were. We always laughed about one favourite table made from silver beech wood that had been across the Atlantic several times.

But laughter and travelling tables were a distant memory as I drove my Jeep Cherokee up to the Yorktown Heights stables one Saturday morning. Gemma and I had popped in to see Patrick and his mother, Peace Sullivan, and had learned that Paolo was in residence. Even without this information, I could sense his presence on the estate. All the staff appeared nervous and on edge and I was aware that most were actually frightened of Mr Gucci. It must have been catching, as I also felt a sense of foreboding. The sooner Gemma had her ride and we got home, the better.

We jumped out of the car quickly and Gemma ran across the yard to give Beatrice some carrots and a hug. A stable girl was helping her saddle up when we all turned to see my car being driven away by one of the grooms. Oh no! I had left the keys in the Jeep, thinking it would be safe.

Paolo came striding over and I quickly helped Gemma mount and trot away on Beatrice. She mustn't hear this conversation.

'Now you can see who is powerful,' said Paolo.

'Oh come on,' I begged, 'I *have* to have a car, please bring it back.'

'*Never*! I am going to take everything away from you – you will be left with nothing at all!' I could tell that he felt fantastic and was really enjoying himself. I also knew that he meant every word.

'How will we get home?' I felt tearful. How could he be so cruel?

'I don't care,' he said through clenched teeth. And he turned and walked away.

Some of the stable girls had the good grace to look uncomfortable as they carried on with their chores. I walked down the hill to the Sullivans, who were horrified about what had happened, and we collected a sobbing Gemma. I phoned my lawyers, who reiterated that what Paolo had done was completely unacceptable. I had always had a car; I needed a car if Gemma was to continue with her riding lessons and, to add insult to injury, Paolo had at least five cars at the estate.

During our next appearance before Judge Phyllis, Paolo was once again held in contempt of court, given a serious warning and ordered to give me a car – a black Ford Taurus was to be transferred into my name. I knew the car but it had disappeared and, of course, Paolo once again refused to co-operate.

For the next eight months or so, I was faced with the additional expense of renting a car for the weekends, or Gemma and I would sometimes go up to Yorktown Heights by train and Peace would meet us at the station. I always took a bundle of keys with me as the locks were constantly changed. We never knew what we'd find there and sometimes we even had to have a police escort on to the estate – we became quite notorious among the local police force. It would, of course, have been considerably easier to give up on Yorktown Heights, but I was stubborn and determined not to allow Paolo to beat me. I didn't want to let him win and why shouldn't Gemma be allowed to ride her pony, albeit in a horrible atmosphere?

The latest staff recruited for the estate looked more like thugs hired to do Paolo's bidding, and there was a feeling of total mistrust and fear. By this stage, I believed that Paolo was, at best, unbalanced and, at worst, completely crazy. It was clear that he would do anything to hurt me and I was convinced that my life might be in danger. I was constantly on my guard, believing that he might hire a hit-man who would, for instance, stab me in what would look like a street mugging incident. My lawyers considered that he didn't have the 'psychological profile' to arrange a murder. I actually felt that he was capable of anything.

'Mrs Gucci... Jenny... Jenny... Mrs Gucci...'

'Mummy... Mummy!'

Patrick and Gemma tumbled into the kitchen at the Sullivans' home, all red-faced and shiny from running down the hill.

'We've found it...we've found your car...' They were so excited that they were falling over each other as well as their words, telling me of their adventure. I had left them in the stable yard about an hour earlier and Alex, one of the more friendly stable girls, was especially attentive. While she was talking to us and saddling up Beatrice, she kept pointing to one of the larger stables at the end of the block. I hadn't really registered the gesture, but the children had, and they decided to embark on an adventure worthy of any Enid Blyton *Secret Seven* book. After their ride, they had taken Patrick's bicycle and, once the coast was clear, used it to climb up, trying to reach the high window of the shed. They weren't quite tall enough but they managed to get a ladder and, with that, had reached their goal. Using their hands to cup their faces against the glass and shielding their eyes from the reflection, they managed to see inside and there it was...our treasure – the black Taurus.

I didn't hesitate for a moment and called my friend the locksmith.

It was agreed that a reluctant Patrick and Gemma should stay behind for safety and, a few minutes later, the locksmith and I went to the shed that was doubling as a garage and I instructed him to break the lock. Immediately, a couple of heavies appeared and attempted to stop us.

'You can't go in there,' they challenged.

'Watch me,' I said, bold as brass, barging through the now-open door.

As usual, I had a pocket full of keys, and found the right one and put it in the ignition. It started on the third attempt and I drove off, leaving a cloud of dust in my wake.

Back at the Sullivans, we worked out what to do next. We decided to hide the car at the home of a girlfriend in nearby Chappaqua (where Bill and Hillary Clinton now live) and then Gemma and I would go back to New York before deciding on the next step.

Gemma – who was still on a high from the whole adventure – and I had barely got in the door of the Metropolitan Towers when the phone rang.

'Mrs Gucci?'

'This is the NYPD. We've got a vehicle reported stolen.'

I swallowed. 'And what vehicle would that be then?'

'A black Ford Taurus…did you take it?'

'Yes, I did.' There was no point in lying, but I wondered if I shouldn't have spoken to my lawyers first. I went on to explain, 'I've got a court order saying that I should have one of the cars on the estate.'

'Are you Mrs Gucci?'

'Yes…let me guess. You have had a call from Mr Gucci in Italy reporting the car stolen and telling you that I took it. I am married to him and we are in the middle of a divorce.'

'Mrs Gucci, it sounds as if you have had an exciting day. Why don't you cook yourself a nice dinner and put your feet up with a glass of wine. Congratulations!' And with that the NYPD hung up.

I called Peter Bronstein the next morning to tell him what had happened and he was thrilled for me and told me to bring the car back to New York and use it as normal –which I did.

After months of frustrating legal manoeuvres that hadn't changed anything, there was something immensely satisfying about taking the law into my own hands. I was on a roll. Next, I decided that I'd remove a few items from the main house to decorate the apartment. Although I had a court order to go into the house, on my next visit two burly estate managers barred my way. 'We can't let you inside,' they said.

I decided to use the authoritarian approach. 'How *dare* you tell me what I can and can't do!' I blustered, assuming more forcefulness than I actually felt.

'Well, if we can't stop you going into the house, we are going to watch you every minute you are there.' They had obviously been given their instructions.

'If you do that, I'll call the police,' I threatened.

Suddenly their attitude changed. 'We don't want to do this, Jenny... we're only doing what we've been told.'

'Well, if anyone asks, tell them you saw me and I refused to obey your orders,' I suggested.

I raced up to the house and, once inside, made a speedy selection of things I could take before all hell broke loose. The car was parked outside and its cavernous boot glinted its invitation. I lifted paintings from the walls, all that I could carry, thinking that each one might pay a term of schooling or at least improve our Metropolitan Towers home. Almost as an afterthought, I dashed back inside to grab a huge copper pot that I thought might look great with a plant inside in the corner of the living room. I threw it on the back seat beside Gemma and set off for home.

Paolo went berserk. I heard about his reaction through his lawyers and also, a long time later, Penny would confess that my minor rebellion caused him to pace the floor for several nights and made him unable to eat.

The first I knew of his response was a call from my lawyers saying that he had called in the police and was taking a criminal action against me. Apparently, it was the Charles I copper pot – valued at around £200 – that had struck the nerve. There had been five transatlantic phone calls to someone from his lawyers' office about this copper pot. He couldn't eat, he couldn't sleep...he *had* to have his copper pot back. His lawyer called Peter Bronstein and allegedly said, 'I think we've got a problem with this guy – he's not normal!'

Since I had started divorce proceedings from Paolo Gucci, I had run the entire gamut of emotions – anger, frustration, hatred, pity and, perhaps in the early days, even sympathy. This strange man was the person I had once loved, who was the father of my child. He had been kind, loving and supportive to my parents and my widowed sister and niece, but now he was behaving like a monster. With the clear-sightedness of childhood, Gemma put it all into perspective. 'He's not like my daddy any more,' she would say and, when Paolo phoned up to speak to her, she frequently made an excuse: 'Tell Daddy I'm busy. I'll talk to him again when he's back to being like my daddy.'

Some mornings, I found it difficult to get out of bed, wondering how I could face another day of confrontations, broken assurances and disappointment. On those days, all I wanted to do was curl up under the duvet and become invisible. It was at those times that it was especially helpful to have an au pair on hand to make things normal for Gemma. 'Come on, Gems, let's go for a run in the park,' they'd say. I just needed a little time to pull myself together to fight another day. And the darkest part of this journey was yawning on the horizon; it beckoned to me enticingly. And now there is no way forward in my story without sharing it. This next part is as painful and unpleasant as it gets. It is an experience I have tried to erase from my memory and one that I found impossible to speak about before. To this day, it remains painful for me to recall, and may be similarly painful for you to share.

It was the smell that first alerted me to the fact that something was seriously wrong. The atmosphere was poisonous enough at Yorktown Heights, as well as back in Rusper, where, among the staff, no one knew who they could trust and confide in; but as I breathed in what should have been the usual sweet, early-morning air of the rolling Westchester County countryside, I just knew something was horribly wrong.

I felt sick with fear and dread. It had first hit me when Sue had phoned the previous evening. Her message had been garbled and unclear.

Since she had moved out of the Normans estate, her information was at best second-hand. She had received a call from someone who reported seeing one of the horses collapsed in a field and the witness asked whether Sue could help. My sister had suggested calling the RSPCA to investigate, especially as there was talk in the village that the other Gucci horses were also being neglected. Paolo was apparently setting out to 'prove' his bankruptcy by showing that he couldn't afford to care for his animals.

It couldn't be true. I had, almost crossly, accused Sue of exaggeration and rumour-mongering. Of all the dreadful things that had happened so far, this simply was incomprehensible. Paolo would never allow his precious horses to starve. No sane person would go this far to prove a point, to make it clear to the court that he had no money for his wife and child, or to buy these beautiful, innocent animals the food and basic care they needed to survive.

It was early 1994, and it had been a few months since my last visit to Yorktown Heights. My nerves had been in pieces and I had felt unable to face the inevitable confrontations that were always waiting for us there. By now, we needed a police escort to get on to the estate and this was also very upsetting for Gemma. I had also noticed (with a degree of relief) that although Beatrice was still a much-loved part of the family, other hobbies and interests were stealing my 11-year-old daughter's free time.

When Peace Sullivan called from the farm suggesting I come up straight away, my heart sank further. An ABC news helicopter hovered over the main stable block. I spotted their TV cameras protruding from the sides, and I could see ASPCA (American Society for the Protection of Cruelty to Animals) workers in their bright jackets bustling around on the ground. The scene that greeted me began to unfold almost in slow motion. It felt like minutes, but was probably only seconds before I could fully grasp what was going on. There was no way to avoid the truth – these once-magnificent Arabian thoroughbreds – some world champions – and all worth hundreds of thousands of dollars, were being allowed to starve to death. Those that could still walk were being rounded up in a corral – a kind of triage unit – to asses their state.

I will never forget that smell. It was of pungent ammonia, not in any way like the normal, healthy, horsey smell. This was a dark smell – a smell of fear, suffering, despair and death.

In the wild and left to nature, horses will happily graze almost all day. They have delicate digestion systems though and, when stabled, need well-balanced feeds twice a day. No one seemed able to tell me when these 80-odd horses had last been fed or watered. There were no fine heads with bright eyes and warm, wet muzzles looking out over the rows of stable doors, no welcoming 'whinneys' to be heard. In fact, the yard was eerily quiet below the drone of the news helicopter. The animal rescue team efficiently carried on mixing life-saving vitamins with water and tempting some of the seriously malnourished to drink a little before offering them food.

For some, the rescue had come too late and I watched in horror as the bodies of two young fillies and a colt – their bellies distended – were carried away. Someone told me they were waiting for a crane to lift a few of the horses that couldn't walk to the transporter for treatment at a large animal hospital nearby. But could those poor creatures hang on long enough for the legal red tape to be cut through? Despite their dreadful condition, legally they were still valuable horses and a court order would be needed before any could be removed from the estate.

I started to talk to Kate, a stable girl, and one of the few faces I recognised. She told me that none of the staff had been paid for weeks and most had gone away. There was no feed left for the horses and she and a couple of friends had continued to come in and do what they could but when she realised she simply couldn't cope, she had called in the ASPCA, who, in turn, had tipped off the press.

Together, we looked into the stables until I couldn't take any more. Some horses were lying down listlessly on rancid straw, their leg joints looking swollen and too sore to hold them up; some were frighteningly skinny, while others had painfully distended bellies. Coats that normally gleamed and shone were dull and mangy with bald patches alongside shaggy tufts. Some, in the final stages of starvation, were losing their manes and tails, probably having been chewed at by desperate stable mates.

Even with my untrained eye, I could see that many clearly had signs of laminitis, their untreated hooves curled and split. The knees of those that were still able to stand were bent at odd and deformed angles. Most were covered with sores and open wounds, and even in the cool winter temperature, large black flies hovered round like vultures. It was a sickening sight that I have never been able to erase from my memory and, in the nights that followed the grim discovery, I would wake up screaming, seeing their empty, dull eyes staring back at me – not so much with accusation, more puzzled miscomprehension. These poor creatures appeared to be asking the same questions as the rest of us – '*Why?*'

And one question persistently fixed itself in my mind – 'What sort of monster could do this to innocent animals?'

I called on friends, including the Fishers, who had sold us the estate, and people rallied round bringing vets, medicines, food and supplies to the stables. We also tried to help the 50-odd champions Paolo had at our other upstate farm in Spencer Town. I found myself in an impossible situation – I had barely enough money to feed myself and my child, let alone enough to care for hundreds of thoroughbred horses in the States and UK. Later, I learned that Paolo had also abandoned his horses at Rusper, where the final death toll was seven.

In England, an investigation would follow and Penny was eventually charged and found guilty of cruelty to eleven horses. In the USA, the ASPCA issued a citation against Paolo but he was out of the country at the time and died before he could be traced and brought to justice. The RSPCA brought the prosecution against Penny, and, initially, she was fined £23,000 and banned from working with horses for ten years. The prosecution had asked for a lifetime ban, but bearing in mind that she had two young children by then and this was her only source of income, it was reduced to ten years. Those in court at the time considered she had only narrowly missed a jail sentence.

A year later, magistrates at Chichester Crown Court rejected her appeal against the sentence and increased the suspended sentence on each cruelty charge by four months. Again, the court listened to the inspectors' evidence of discovering starving and emaciated horses, some so weak they could hardly walk. The prosecutor said that the animals were suffering from 'diarrhoea and listlessness'. One filly had to be put down immediately and the vet estimated she had not eaten for two weeks. Eleven others were removed and taken to an animal welfare centre for intensive care, but six of them failed to recover.

I am not sure of the exact final death toll at Yorktown Heights, but I do know that at least six horses died of starvation and several others perished afterwards from various diseases.

I decided to stay up at the Yorktown Heights house for a while to try and sort out the problem. A few days after the original, grim discovery, young Patrick came rushing in with the latest news from the stable yard. Several huge horse transporters had arrived under an armed escort. I went to have a look. The horse boxes all carried a name I recognised – 'Gainey: Arizona'. Gainey was an important Arab breeder and I knew that some of Paolo's horses had come from his stud. Now he had come to take them back as his stablehands, each carrying a shotgun, stood guard. Clearly, they were not going to be stopped by any court ruling.

I stood by and watched with relief and admiration as some forty or more sick and weak thoroughbreds were slowly guided into the transporters and set off for a better life. I suppose technically it was stealing, but no one could possibly object. I wanted to see them all go and, shortly afterwards, the judge sensibly lifted the restrictions and the remaining horses were either adopted by private individuals or cared for by animal charities and vets. It was almost the end of a tragic episode.

Those were my darkest days and I have found it very difficult to relive the memory of what happened. Even after all these years, I cannot begin to understand how anyone could be so cruel to innocent, defenceless animals. Those horses were supposed to be Paolo's pride and joy and he professed to love them. It was as if he had swung manically from loving to hating. Maybe he had tried to starve his wife and daughter into submission – although, in reality, someone would always help us – but poor animals had nowhere to go for help. It was impossible to get inside such a sick and twisted mind.

I wondered at the time if Paolo was mentally ill, but now I think that to call him 'insane' is an insult to people who really struggle with their mental health. I don't think that he was 'mad', but 'bad'. Possibly he had a streak of pure evil in him, especially in the light of the end he had ordained for Beatrice… Gemma's pony had somehow escaped the horrors of the stable yard and was grazing happily in a paddock close to the house.

I was cooking a pasta sauce in the kitchen and my old friend, English journalist Vicki Mackenzie, was staying with me along with some other houseguests while Gemma was sleeping over at the Sullivans'. We were enjoying a glass of wine around the kitchen table and I could feel myself beginning to relax for the first time in weeks. The last horses were due to be dispatched in the morning and, when I saw Lesley and Kate, the stable girls, at the door, I assumed they'd come for the sack of carrots I'd just picked up from the greengrocer.

They were big, strong girls and they had both been incredibly supportive and helpful recently, making it quite clear where their allegiance lay. It was obvious they had something difficult to tell me and, after a couple of false starts, Lesley, who appeared to have lost a lot of weight through the stress of the previous weeks, blurted it out. 'Jenny, you have to know something,' she began. 'Paolo phoned and gave Kate the order to take Beatrice out back and shoot her!'

The room started to swim in front of my eyes. Was there no end to the horror? My knees buckled and the next thing I knew was that I was on the floor, pounding it with my fists. 'The man is mad – I am going to kill him – I'll kill him!' I was aware that I was screaming hysterically, but somehow I couldn't stop. 'Not Gemma, too? Isn't it enough that he should hurt me, but not be so cruel to her…if he as much as touches her, or makes her unhappy, I'll kill him!' I was incoherent and hysterical but, at that moment, I believe I meant it.

Over the years, people had offered to beat Paolo up on my behalf. But although desperate and broken, I don't think I would ever have resorted to violence; I like to think that I would never have sunk that low. I always felt that, eventually, I would get away permanently or something else would happen…which it did.

Of course, Kate refused to carry out the order to destroy the perfectly healthy pony and was keeping a close eye on her to make sure that no one else would do Paolo's bidding.

Gemma never knew that her pony's life was in danger and we quickly arranged for Beatrice to go to another family. She was very understanding, however, as she had virtually outgrown her and realised that it was time for Beatrice to have another little girl. We said a lovely goodbye to this dear friend with carrots and kisses.

January 2020 – West London

The email pinged into my inbox.

I recognised the sender – it was from Will who is a percussionist with the Boston Symphony Orchestra. He had been a regular visitor to Yorktown Heights and had played a big part in the few happy memories I have from those days.

'Check out the link below', Will suggested.

The ABC news story was accompanied by an aerial view of the estate taken from their helicopter…a huge fire was clearly destroying the main house. The date was three months earlier – November 8, 2019 and the headline said it all "Yorktown fire destroys former Gucci estate."

I watched in numb fascination as the roof then upper storeys were devoured by the flames. Luckily the current owners had been away and no one was hurt. The blaze had started in the early hours of that Friday morning and quickly engulfed the whole house. It had taken fifty firefighters seven hours and water from the estate lake to bring it under control.

Other news reporters hadn't far to dig to reveal the recent sordid history of the estate: that Paolo had once owned the same 34 acres on Baptist Church Road, including his farm known as Millfield Stables where, I read, "more than 100 Arabian horses suffered malnutrition and neglect while he dealt with a divorce".

What an odd choice of words, as if the two events – the cruelty to innocent animals and the divorce from me – which was never 'dealt' with – were inter-linked.

The scene from the news report was shocking and somehow surreal – more fitting for a gothic novel (think Jane Eyre's Thornfield Hall) rather than Upstate New York and a house that I had once called home.

As a couple it had been our retreat – a place in the countryside to relax from the heat of the city. It was meant to be part of my divorce settlement but when it eventually passed to me, I found myself liable to pay an outstanding tax bill of quarter of a million dollars. Lawyers' fees had eaten up nearly all the rest of the money from its sale.

Although the house held no happy memories with Paolo, there had been some from other occasions… Gemma riding Beatrice, playing drunken and hilarious croquet games with friends in the beautiful gardens, house parties and amazing Christmases with more than twenty people sitting round the enormous table in the dining room and me singing duets with guests from the opera world.

Yes, there were some happy memories but – with the exception of the kitchen and the library – I had never liked the house. In the family we had referred to it as "The Swamp" because it was horribly sticky there in the summer. The humidity was over-bearing and the vast lake that we had on the estate would literally steam.

Unpleasant memories were much more prolific…like the dreadful row with Paolo's daughter Patrizia. She had arrived unannounced one weekend to demand that I leave the premises saying that I had no right to be there. She refused to calm down and the situation quickly escalated. When she started screaming threats at me, the police were called and explained quite rationally to her that the law was on my side and she was escorted off the premises. It was a ghastly scene and the thought of it, even after all this time, makes me very angry because it was so unjust. I find myself thinking about her sometimes and I only hope that she has found some sort of happiness. I have read that she is now a successful designer (she must have inherited her father's flare), artist and writer.

Now, all those memories from Yorktown Heights – the good and the horrible – had literally gone up in smoke. Fire is said to have cleansing properties – we can only hope that this is true.

Watching the news footage of the blaze again, was very strange. It was not particularly cathartic, but any whiff of nostalgia was gone. The house meant nothing to me any more.

21

Prison, Patrizia and the Press

The Gucci family has always been fodder for gossip columnists throughout the world. I still had contacts with UK journalists from my first husband's Fleet Street days and I counted a couple of leading New York freelance writers among my friends. Sometimes, if I wanted to put my side of the story, I'd call Nigel Dempster. He was always interested in hearing from me and running a piece about my ongoing battles with Paolo.

The Guccis were newsworthy and, with Aldo's carefully contrived PR machine no longer around, and Paolo's careless attitude towards his public image, there was plenty to write about. British and American journalists, together with their global counterparts, especially in Italy, continued to have a field day. To date, there was the juicy scandal of our divorce, the cruel starvation of the horses, Paolo's relationship with his stable girl…and many other side issues and dramatic exposés that kept the columns filled with Gucci-mania.

As the *Gucci-Dallas* style soap opera rumbled on, the stories became ever more preposterous leading ultimately to the arrival on the scene of the 'Black Widow' formerly known as Lady Gucci, Patrizia Reggiani, and her headline grabbing comments following her husband Maurizio's murder and her conviction. The execution style killing in elegant Milan and the subsequent murder trial captivated a global audience in the late 1990's right through to the present day, especially with the two Patrizia's comments regarding the production of the *House of Gucci* film. Who can forget Paolo's daughter, Patrizia, causing the *Guardian* headline in April 2021: SHORT, FAT, AND UGLY: GUCCI FAMILY LASHES OUT AT CAST APPEARANCE IN NEW FILM Or the column inches of outrageous comments provided by the Black Widow, Patrizia Regianni...from the "mere bowl of lentils" description of a very generous divorce settlement, to giving 'poor eyesight' as the reason she hadn't undertaken the shooting of Maurizio herself.

But earlier, it was the tiresome legal wrangles involving Paolo's bid to use his name to launch a fashion line in Britain that were deemed newsworthy. A headline in the Daily Mail in 1990 read: JUDGE BRANDS GUCCI GRANDSON A LIAR as the High Court blocked Paolo's bid to 'cash in' on his family name. Vice-chancellor Sir Nicolas Browne-Wilkinson stunned the court by finding my husband to be 'an extremely unsatisfactory witness in general'. The story went on, 'The 59-year-old, who is balding but sports a greying pony-tail, had told "deliberate lies" according to the judge.'

His decision had added Britain to the list of Italy, France, Belgium, Switzerland and Liechtenstein where Paolo was not allowed to use his name. In fact, it would appear that it was only in the United States where he had succeeded.

Paolo's cousin Maurizio, who then headed the company, had attended the ten-day hearing and was presumably satisfied with its outcome. When I read the story, I wondered if the two men had ignored each other, or, as in the old days like their fathers before them, embraced warmly and had lunch together when the court adjourned.

In the past, Paolo had often spoken to me about his lack of respect for Maurizio's decision-making at the Gucci helm. At the time he took over the company in the mid-1980s, it had capital assets estimated to be worth $800 million and, as if keen to shrug off his soft and inexperienced image, he quickly instigated a raft of changes. Following an extensive audit, he fired 150 employees, got rid of many of the cheaper Gucci items and took the ready-to-wear lines out of general stores so that the few remaining clothes items could only be sold exclusively in Gucci shops or franchises. All these changes at once were possibly too many and too drastic to succeed and Paolo, his father and brothers had real concerns that Maurizio would run it into the ground.

But it was his cousin's extravagant spending, specifically a luxury yacht, that turned out to be Maurizio's Achilles heel. Paolo had never been a sea-faring man and maybe he was jealous of Maurizio's lifestyle. When we were together, he would go on and on about the *Creole*, especially when Maurizio had both the yacht and the crew all decked out in Gucci colours for the Admiral's Cup. I just thought, good luck to him. At least he was enjoying spending his money, but Paolo was convinced that the $7 million used to restore the yacht had been found illegally. The 70m sail boat had once belonged to the shipping magnate Stavros Niarchos and the original $1 million price tag – which included gold taps, a screening room and reportedly even impressionist paintings hanging on the walls – had paled into insignificance as the bills for its restoration started to come in. In his typically litigious manner, Paolo set about trying to prove the 'irregularities' in his cousin's finances and, once he found some papers referring to a Panamanian company set up by Rodolfo, he sent copies of his finds to all the Italian authorities and some sort of raid on Maurizio's home and office followed.

In those days in Italy, it was illegal to move money from overseas. It appears, however, that Maurizio had been tipped off and set sail for Switzerland, where he took up residence for several years until he was able to clear his name from the various accusations levelled at him by his relatives at home. The Italian press loved the story, running headlines such as Maurizio Gucci Flees Arrest and The *Creole* Betrayed Maurizio Gucci.

Then there were the Gucci, Coochie, Coo headlines of 1992, when the UK newspapers discovered that 'the pretty stable girl who had captured the heart of the millionaire fashion tycoon was expecting a baby in the New Year'.

Penny had two children with Paolo – her little girl Alyssa was born in 1993 and her son, Gabrielle – Paolo's only male child – was born two years later. By this stage, Paolo had ceased to acknowledge his responsibilities for Gemma, so I could hardly feel warm and fuzzy about his new babies. Gemma herself was distraught when I told her the news – 'But I thought I was Daddy's baby,' she cried. As a little girl, she had been devoted to her father, but later insisted that 'Daddy wasn't Daddy any more'. In the early days of Paolo's affair with Penny, I had stopped Gemma from staying with them. It felt wrong and uncomfortable.

In August 1991, Paolo asked the judge for permission to take Gemma on holiday in Greece. I was very concerned, but the court came up with a solution in the form of several conditions. These included that I would see Gemma directly on to the plane and that her nanny Ruth would accompany her throughout the holiday.

Gemma and Ruth packed their bags while I tried to hide my concerns. The day of their planned departure came and went without a word from Paolo. Understandably, Gemma was upset at being abandoned, but not nearly as much as when we saw in the paper a double-page spread of pictures of Paolo frolicking with a topless Penny on a Greek beach under the headline WHERE IS YOUR DAUGHTER, MR GUCCI? Apparently, Paolo had been too mean to pay for Ruth to join them.

Another newspaper took the angle that Paolo was enjoying 'cut-price paradise', having opted for a 'romantic break, tourist-class'. The article went on to say that although the 60-year-old Italian fashion tycoon could probably have bought the Greek island of Zakynthos, he

I have always enjoyed afternoon tea.

had instead chosen a cheap package holiday at a young people's destination with his 21-year-old girlfriend.

I called some press contacts and made sure that Paolo and Penny were photographed at every turn – even shopping in a Greek supermarket. The UK papers arrived in the afternoon in New York and I had quite a laugh over them. 'Silly old bugger,' I thought, 'look at him making a fool of himself!' Judge Phyllis B. Gangel-Jacob – who had a reputation for being especially tough with men – didn't see the funny side of his behaviour and the Greek holiday disaster certainly counted against him.

'You are contemptuous,' she said to Paolo on his next court appearance. He had turned his back on her.

'What's that?' he laughed derisively.

During the early days of their relationship, the press hounded Paolo and Penny and, on at least one occasion, Paolo lost it with a photographer who was camped out at Rusper with a long-distance lens. It was incredible that my husband honestly thought that he could hide his affair from me. He genuinely believed it would be enough to instruct Sue and my other friends not to tell me anything. Maybe his family didn't talk to each other, but mine certainly did. And, in turn, I got pleasure from passing on the juicy bits to my gossip-columnist friends.

And so it went on as column inches on the acrimonious break-up of my marriage became column feet and yards. In retrospect, I think the media were generally quite kind to me over the years. They seemed to paint me as a determined and strong woman, and not a gold-digger. I suppose they saw me as I was – quite a normal person, the daughter of a north London bookmaker, and a former dental nurse who had been married to a millionaire fashion tycoon. It could have happened to anybody.

Hello! magazine carried a feature on me 'speaking out' in July 1993. The pictures in my home in the Metropolitan Towers with my mother and daughter show the gold wall hangings from the previous New Year celebrations. I look carefree and happy, sharing a cup of tea with my mother and holding Gemma's hand as she skates in Central Park. I am quoted as saying, 'I just want him to be fair to me and I don't think he is. I desperately want a divorce.' And I did.

Just when I thought it couldn't get any worse, I was 'quoted' in another headline in the *Daily Mail* from April 1994: I LOVED HIM ONCE, BUT NOW HE'LL STAY IN PRISON UNTIL HE PAYS ME WHAT HE OWES.

It was a dark, wet day a few weeks earlier when I had found myself yet again – I had absolutely lost count of the number of appearances at the Manhattan Supreme Court – in front of Judge Phyllis. This was the first time I had seen or heard from Paolo since the traumatic loss of the horses over the winter. As usual, I explained to Gemma that I was going to court and that I might be upset when I came home, but not to be worried because everything was fine and she'd be going to her dance class as usual at 6.30pm.

I was not really surprised to note that, although officially bankrupt, Paolo was still immaculately turned out. He made his usual disparaging comment to me along the lines of 'You think you're so clever…' followed by 'bloody lawyers'.

He appeared to have a new legal team. I found it ironic that, although throughout his business life he was constantly surrounded by advisers, he always ignored their advice.

Paolo's lawyers told the judge that their client's assets were controlled by the Federal Bankruptcy court, but Judge Phyllis noted that it had been a 'voluntary bankruptcy' filing and therefore Paolo could withdraw the petition at any time to pay me the estimated $479,825.30 that he owed.

Judge Gangel-Jacob asked him, 'If you have no money, Mr Gucci, could you please tell the court how you managed to fly here for this hearing?'

Paolo turned round to speak to his lawyers and ignored the question. Even from where I was sitting at the back of the court, I heard him refer to the judge as 'that stupid Jewish bitch'. She must have heard it, too, but calmly repeated her question.

Eventually facing the wrong way, Paolo muttered something about borrowing money from his brother for the flight.

'Can I see the tickets?' asked Judge Phyllis.

'No,' said Paolo, swearing at her in Italian under his breath.

And suddenly she lost it. 'You have lied and lied to this court, Mr

Gucci. You haven't obeyed a single court order and I am sick and tired of your behaviour,' she said. 'Mr Gucci – you are going to jail!' She slammed the papers down on her desk.

Two burly sheriff's deputies appeared as if from nowhere and frogmarched him out of the room and down to the cells.

I couldn't believe it. I sank down into my seat and, head in hands, began to cry uncontrollably. Sobs wracked through my body. How could we have sunk to such a depth? This man I had once loved, the father of my child, was prepared to do almost anything to prevent us reaching a divorce agreement. He had already spent one night in the cells in Connecticut and the horse starvation saga was terrible, but now he was even prepared to serve a jail sentence to hurt me.

Paolo Gucci served seven weeks in the Bronx Penitentiary for contempt of court. Would a time in jail make a difference to his attitude? Not really. In the future, it just made him more reluctant than ever to return to the States, correctly fearing that another prison sentence awaited him.

In the meantime, it was important that I should tell Gemma the news that her father had gone to prison before she heard it on the TV or from a school friend.

She was at home when I arrived. 'Why are you crying, Mummy?' she asked, seeing my red eyes.

'I am just very tired, darling. And Daddy went to jail this afternoon – I wanted to tell you before you heard it on the 6.00 o'clock news.'

'Humph,' she muttered, as if she was considering all the implications. 'He must deserve it or the judge wouldn't have sent him there,' she said logically, adding, 'What's for tea?'

Gemma always managed to stay grounded throughout the ordeal. Later, Paolo phoned her from prison but she refused to speak to him. 'It's ridiculous,' she said, repeating her mantra. 'I don't want to talk to him any more. When Daddy gets back to being Daddy, I'll talk to him then!' She was right on the money.

To the press, it was another great Gucci story. Some papers got a picture of Paolo through the bars of his cell and the *New York Post* had

Paolo in his prison uniform of bright-orange jumpsuit with some reference to it not carrying a designer label, and quotes from his cellmate Joey who was in for stealing cars. Where would it all end?

I was so caught up in keeping my head above water that I had given barely a consideration as to what impact the media stories would have among my Gucci relatives…until I received a phone call in January 1995.

'Jeeeeniferr?' purred a female voice with the distinctive Italian accent. 'Ees Patrizia.' Of course it was. I should have recognised the voice of Maurizio's estranged wife. 'I am in New York…let's get together for lunch one day,' she suggested.

I said I was very busy and so we settled on tea the following afternoon instead. I wondered why she had chosen to contact me. Perhaps she wanted to compare notes on unhappy marriages and the strange Gucci psyche.

She explained that she was staying at a friend's apartment on Central Park South and, from that, I assumed that, since her split with Maurizio, she was no longer allowed to use their apartment in the prestigious Olympic Tower. Although she had been successful in getting the New York address she wanted all those years ago, Rodolfo had not put the apartment in her name. It seemed that both our husbands were adept at registering their properties through Liechtenstein-based companies, but the main difference between the two Gucci cousins was that Patrizia's husband was at least meeting his financial obligations to his wife and daughters. In fact, he was being very generous to her and she remained an extremely wealthy woman after their separation.

She greeted me warmly with a hug and kisses, as if it had been a matter of weeks rather than years since our last meeting. As always, I was struck by how tiny she was; somehow, I felt gawky and ungainly in her presence. Even in her extremely high heels, she was barely 5ft. Her short, dark hair was immaculately groomed and her heavy make-up had been meticulously applied. She was wearing a beautifully-tailored Chanel suit and a clatter of gold bracelets slipped down her wrist as she beckoned me to sit down. I was reminded how the society pages had often likened her to Joan Collins.

At first we caught up on family news and I learned that her mother

Silvana was remarkably well and being very supportive and that her teenage daughters Alessandra and Allegra were a comfort and a delight. Both were accompanying their mother on this shopping trip to New York.

We also spoke about Patrizia's health. I knew that after years of suffering from crippling headaches, she had been diagnosed with a non-malignant brain tumour in 1992. The family had all thought that she had been behaving like a drama queen and was exaggerating her condition in the wake of Maurizio's desertion. But, apparently, we had all misjudged the poor woman who was, in fact, seriously ill, and the outcome of the operation had been touch and go.

'No, I am fine now,' she explained, touching the side of her head with her scarlet fingernails in an involuntary gesture. 'You know, the bastard did not even visit me in hospital. I nearly died, and he never came to my bedside.'

I expressed surprise.

'My mother persuaded him to come and see me when I was recuperating at home and you know what he said?'

I shook my head.

'He said to me, "Why didn't you die?" Can you believe a husband would say such a thing to his wife? He wanted me dead and out of the way so that he can be with that *puttana*. You know, he actually thinks that he's in love with her!'

'Well, perhaps he is,' I suggested.

'No, he is incapable of love,' she retorted, dismissing him totally. 'Why do these Gucci men change when they get money and power? They are pathetic! Mau was different after he got his inheritance...he changed completely, he became a monster. He was a child [in fact, he had been 34], inexperienced and immature.'

I had to agree with Patrizia. Paolo, although older, had also transformed completely after he sold out to Investcorp.

'I think it was the fault of their fathers,' I suggested. 'Both Rodolfo and Aldo were dreadful parents.' Rodolfo had suffocated and over-protected Maurizio, while Aldo had been a tyrannical bully with his sons.

'Yes and, in turn, they had been treated badly by the old man

Guccio. But it is still inexcusable,' she said. 'I can never forgive Rodolfo for the damage he did to my marriage. He wouldn't even let us breathe. He wouldn't let Mau do anything, not take any decisions, nothing. I never want even to say his name again. He never thought that I was good enough for his precious son but, in fact, without me, Maurizio would have been nothing. He was always weak and he needed my strength behind him.'

We spoke more about the husbands we had once loved; and Patrizia asked me if I was prepared to put up with the other women. She was surprised when I told her that I didn't care.

'The person I married is not the man who is shagging all these girls – to me, he is completely pathetic.' I went on to explain my views quite graphically.

She said that she had been following in the press the story of my break-up and Paolo's voluntary filing for bankruptcy and all the associated scandals. 'But he is the father of your child,' she protested. I think that she had thought that we would somehow gang up together to plot revenge against them both.

'Look, Patrizia, to me Paolo's not even worth the energy,' I explained. 'He's betrayed me and I hadn't done anything wrong.'

'Neither did I.' I could tell that she was disappointed by my reaction.

'I am sure you didn't,' I agreed, not wanting to go down that road.

'I really admire you, Jenny…you are very brave and strong to fight him as you do. I think they are all crazy – they need therapy,' she said.

I agreed; here, I was on familiar territory as I explained the visit to the psychiatrist who had predicted that Paolo would need intensive help for a minimum of seven years and that it would be only a matter of time before he would turn violent against me. We paused as a maid served tea and 14-year-old Allegra, in jeans, a T-shirt and tumbling hair, burst into the room and greeted me with a friendly smile.

I noticed a magazine open on the horoscope page and a pack of tarot cards on the coffee table. 'Do you still believe all that?' I asked Patrizia. 'Do you believe in cards telling the future?'

'Oh yes,' she said emphatically. 'I have taken a lot of comfort and direction from the cards since Mau left us.'

'I wouldn't give you two pennies for a card reading although I do believe in some spiritualists,' I argued.

'Many people consult psychics and astrologers, even Princess Diana.' Patrizia was obviously in good company. It was clear that she was not prepared to sacrifice any part of her lifestyle, and her spending appeared to be as lavish as ever. 'Why should I? Why should my children suffer because he now has a stupid girlfriend?'

It had been widely reported in the press that Dr (an honorary title) Maurizio Gucci was in love with a 40-something blonde decorator from Milan, Paola Franchi. They had been together for some time and it was reported that Maurizio wanted to marry her.

'I will never, *never* give him a divorce! You see, I still care. He will always be my husband and the father of my children.'

'But don't you want your freedom?' I knew that I craved mine.

'No, never! He's my husband and he has obligations to me and to the girls.'

We agreed that Paolo had become a monster and I was adamant that I would not put up with it.

'But what will you be left with?' she asked.

'I don't know – maybe enough to have a house, a car...'

'It really is ridiculous...they all have so much money,' Patrizia observed, and she vowed to help me find where Paolo had hidden his assets. She said that she had contacts in Switzerland who would help. It was a good job that I didn't hold my breath for the information she promised, because she never came up with it.

The phone rang and, while Patrizia chatted to her caller in Italian, I glanced around her friend's apartment and my eye stopped on a chunky cigarette box on an occasional table. It was made from gold, imprinted with crocodile skin and encrusted with precious stones. It was hard to believe that it was 'real', it looked flashy and the equivalent of costume jewellery rather than the real thing. I recognised it immediately as part of Gucci's *Orocrocodillo* line that she – Patrizia Reggiani – had designed. Some years before, she had persuaded her husband to allow her to design her own jewellery line. With its crocodile theme, it had certainly been distinctive and, even by Gucci standards, very expensive.

'Is that one of your pieces?' I asked when she hung up the phone.

'Yes, did you like the line I did for Gucci?'

'It was beautiful,' I said. In fact, it was beautiful in an obvious, big, shoulder-padded, 1980s kind of way. It certainly wasn't my style and I knew that, at around $15,000 per piece, the experiment had not been a commercial success and that Patrizia would not be allowed to design for the company again.

She led me to the guest bedroom to admire a pair of earrings from the *Orocrocodillo* collection – they seemed to swamp her as she held them up to her lobes.

The room was full of shopping bags from all the top New York stores and Patrizia explained how much she missed the city but had decided to make Milan her home. With my experienced eye, I counted at least ten Manolo Blahnik boxes. She and her daughters had been on quite a shopping spree and I hoped that Maurizio would continue to prosper so that he could support his high-maintenance family. On the bed was an exquisite sable coat that I learned was a recent acquisition and had been made in Italy.

'Try it on,' she urged. My sable was fabulous but this one was even better. I did and, of course, it looked ridiculous. Full-length on Patrizia, it was barely a jacket on me – we both laughed at the sight.

I was getting ready to make my exit and glanced at my watch thinking about picking up Gemma from school. Just before I left, Patrizia asked casually for the phone number of Cindy Adams, a high-powered journalist with the *New York Post*. Somehow, I felt that getting the number might have been the main reason for my invitation. I phoned it through to her later and we promised to get together the next time she visited New York. I don't know whether Cindy ever did a story on Patrizia or whether she was 'yesterday's' news, but I do know that two short months later, every journalist in the world would want to talk to her.

In the light of what happened next, I have run over every detail of my last meeting with Patrizia hundreds of times, wondering if there were any clues as to her state of mind. I would sum up her personality during our last meeting as charming, maybe slightly preoccupied and certainly very angry with her husband, but she never said to me anything like, 'I am so furious with him I could kill him...' – nothing like that at all. In fact, if our conversation had been recorded, I probably sounded more furious with Paolo than she had been with Maurizio. Undoubtedly, she was disappointed that he was living with Paola Franchi and horrified at the implications for her daughters if they ever had a child together. But whatever the future held, she made it abundantly clear that she would never willingly grant Maurizio a divorce.

If I think back to the ostentatious *Orocrocodillo* line that Patrizia designed, I can understand how she might have felt comfortable working as a 'design consultant' at Bozart, a costume jewellery firm in Milan, after her release from jail in 2014. Three years earlier she had turned down an offer of early release because it had been on the condition that she take a job. The very idea of working had horrified her. Rejecting the condition of her parole she had told her lawyer: "I've never worked a day in my life and I don't intend to start now". But Bozart was clearly a good fit for the recently released Black Widow. The upmarket firm specialises in large, ornate, dazzling pieces – a flashback to the glitzy, *Dynasty* era of the 1980's. Although petite, Patrizia would have been able to identify with the large, flashy pieces – neither could ever be described as low-profile or under-stated. The first collection she collaborated with for Bozart was inspired by the colours of her pet macaw, Bo, who famously accompanied her on one of her first acts of freedom – a shopping jaunt in the city's fashionable *Via Monte Napoleone*.

The members of the paparazzi who spotted her couldn't believe their luck. There she was, the Black Widow, dressed up to the nines, dripping jewellery, and wearing huge sunglasses with a parrot on her shoulder – Lady Gucci was back.

But, chronologically, the crime had to be committed first...

22

Murder in Milan and a Death in Tooting

It happened at 8.30 on the morning of 27 March 1995.

Paolo's cousin, Maurizio Gucci, the last of the Guccis to run the family firm before selling out two years earlier, had been shot dead in the street near his office on the Via Palestro, one of the most elegant suburbs of Milan. Two shots in the back of the head and a third to the temple had killed the 46-year-old instantly. It looked like an execution.

Paolo phoned with the news. 'Hello, Jenny...' I knew instantly that something was very wrong. His voice was trembling and weak.

'How are you?' I asked formally.

'Not so good. Maurizio is dead...murdered!'

I collapsed on to a chair. 'Good God in heaven, when is it going to stop? All you Guccis...you're all such a mess. Those poor girls...' I was thinking of his daughters – Alessandra, then 19, and her 14-year-old sister Allegra.

Then I asked about Patrizia and Paolo told me he hadn't been able to get hold of her yet. In fact, she had been staying at the family holiday villa in Saint Moritz at the time. Paolo had phoned me almost as soon as he'd heard. Although he was with Penny, he obviously thought of me as family and I was, after all, still his wife.

'Let me know if there's anything I can do,' I offered. 'And watch your back, because there's someone out there who's out to get you all.' I really believed that he might be next.

'I am a bit nervous,' Paolo admitted. 'Something isn't right…maybe it was the bloody lawyers.'

After the call, I made a cup of tea and sat down in front of the television to learn more details. All the Guccis had enemies and Maurizio had been the last to sell out to the Bahrain-based investment bank, Investcorp, for $120 million. Undoubtedly, he had managed to offend a lot of people, family as well as colleagues, through his extravagance and lack of consistency. Born out of a deep-seated insecurity, he had a reputation for changing his mind and upsetting people in the process.

But murder? Who would want him dead? I think I was in shock.

The evening news was full of gruesome pictures of the bloodstained steps where he'd fallen, diagrams showing the direction of the bullets and the getaway car, and Maurizio's body covered with a white sheet being taken away. Inevitably, there were hastily assembled montages of archive shots of Maurizio in his Gucci colours on board the *Creole* taking part in the Admiral's Cup race, his father Rodolfo during his Hollywood days, Patrizia and the girls, as well as recent footage of the more reclusive Maurizio with his girlfriend Paola Franchi. The whole Gucci story – complete with all the bitter in-fighting and family rivalries – was condensed into a few seconds. Someone was quoted as saying, 'It wasn't one of the Guccis who did this. If it had been a Gucci, he'd have buggered-up the job. They bugger-up everything…' which struck me as quite amusing in a sick sort of way.

The Milan chief prosecutor speculated that a paid assassin had carried out the murder, but that it had not been a very professional job as the killer had fired one shot too many. Apparently, two would have done the job just as efficiently.

As Maurizio hadn't felt the need for a bodyguard, he surmised that the victim had not been threatened in the past and hadn't felt that his life was in danger.

I barely had time to take it all in before the phone started ringing. Journalists around the world were obviously exchanging phone numbers and somebody told a colleague that they knew a Gucci who could provide an insider's view.

I was quoted in the papers, magazines and on TV, telling them all the same thing – I was terribly sad and that, whatever differences my husband might have had with his cousin, I had always liked and got on well with Maurizio. And no, I couldn't imagine who might have wanted to harm him.

In the early days, suspicion had naturally fallen on Patrizia. I was asked if I thought she would have been capable of murder and I answered that I really didn't know her well enough to speculate.

Off the record, I had wondered that question, too. She had never been particularly nice to me and, undoubtedly, she was angry and disappointed that her husband had rejected her and now had a new woman in his life. She had shamelessly courted the Italian media, appearing on television chat shows done up to the nines claiming – not very convincingly – how hard done by she was. When she had referred to her very generous divorce settlement as 'a mere plate of lentils'. I wondered how she would have coped if faced with my non-existent portion of lentils, and Paolo's total lack of co-operation. Under the circumstances, I had little sympathy for her.

She was also furious that her ex-husband had let the Gucci business slip through his fingers. Being a Gucci (although she had to abandon the name once her protracted divorce was finalised) and a member of a worldwide fashion dynasty was crucially important to her. I could well imagine that she would not have been able to cope with another woman taking her place as Mrs Maurizio Gucci together with the power, status and money that went with the title. As I had learned during our time together in New York, being a Gucci was her whole identity. Years later, in 2014, after serving her prison sentence, unbelievably she had told *La Republica* newspaper that she hoped to be taken back into the Gucci business. "They need me," she said. "I still feel like a Gucci – in fact the most Gucci of them all."

Patrizia was also fiercely protective of her daughters and, as a Swiss resident, Maurizio would have been able to leave his money to whomsoever he wanted. As the prosecutor had spotted, all the possible motives for a crime of passion were in place.

She was also being uncooperative with the investigators, refusing to answer questions about Maurizio's financial affairs and bank accounts. Within hours of learning that her ex-husband had been killed, Patrizia had taken legal advice on behalf of 'the heirs of Maurizio Gucci', his daughters. She intended to have Paola thrown out of her home, the apartment she had shared with Maurizio for five years.

The following day, a court official sealed off the apartment in Milan's exclusive *Corso Venezia* area and Paola was given only a few hours to pack and remove her possessions and find somewhere else to stay with her eleven-year-old son. Patrizia had returned to Milan to oversee the takeover in person, insisting that Paola would have to prove any large items – such as antiques and furniture -belonged to her. She was, she insisted, protecting her daughters' inheritance. Although Maurizio's divorce from Patrizia had finally come through a few months before, at the time of his death he had not yet made any provision for his girlfriend who he planned to marry. His ex-wife and their daughters moved into to the apartment and stayed there, very comfortably, for the following two years until one of Patrizia's accomplices boasted about Maurizio's murder to the wrong person.

Maurizio's funeral was held on 3 April and there was no doubt that Patrizia was the principal player. Wearing a dark suit, black leather gloves, a dark veil and dark glasses, she sat in the front pew with Alessandra and Allegra, also in dark glasses, on either side. Before the service, she told the hordes of waiting TV cameras and journalists, 'On a human level, I'm sorry. On a personal level, I can't say the same thing.'

The press had been full of the story of Maurizio's murder, drawing comparisons with mafia-style executions. Even the fashion magazines with their longer lead times would have a field day, ensuring the story would run and run. Three months later, *Vanity Fair* carried a 13-page spread under the headline A GUCCI KNOCKOFF.

Paolo told me that Maurizio's death had turned into a media circus and so he had decided to stay away from the funeral. His daughter, Patrizia, whom I had helped get a job in the family business with her uncle years before, represented the family.

It would take two years of investigation before a case was put together against Patrizia Reggiani Martinelli (her full name), and her four accomplices, including her friend and clairvoyant, Pina Auriemma, who, she claimed, had arranged the killing without her knowledge. The case went to trial in March 1998 which was when the media dubbed Patrizia 'The Black Widow' and Pina 'The Black Witch'. Patrizia's one-time friend turned informer two months before the trial started claiming that she had been offered $1.5 million to take the blame for the murder but was in no way prepared to be the scapegoat. What good would the money be if I was in jail, she argued.

She told the court how she had contacted an old friend, Ivano Savioni, who had lined up the killers – Orazio Cicala, a Sicilian who ran a pizzeria, who had been tasked with driving the getaway car. He'd also come up with the actual hitman, Benedetto Ceraulo.

In court Patrizia admitted paying her psychic friend the equivalent of around £250,000 but insisted that it had not been for murder; claiming that Auriemma had planned the hit independently and then threatened to frame Patrizia if she didn't pay. But then, with typical inconsistency she had added: 'It was worth every lira."

Over the weeks and months of the trial, the Italian public salivated gluttonously over every little morsel of the case. It had all the ingredients – jealousy, obsessive hatred and betrayal – of a great drama, with the added advantage that it was true. The characters were also compelling to watch as they clearly highlighted the differences in Italian society, with the wealthy Guccis represented by the arrogant and pampered Patrizia on one side, contrasting with the poverty of Pina and her trio of killers on the other. Patrizia had also kept a diary in which she poured out her feelings of hatred and bitterness towards her ex-husband. On the day of his death, she had tellingly written one word – 'Paradise' – in a black border. The week before, she had rather enigmatically written, 'There is no crime that cannot be bought.' But maybe Patrizia hadn't spent enough on this one. Pina only got a monthly stipend of $1,600 from her former friend and the conspirators were caught when they had been recorded plotting a way of putting pressure on Patrizia for more money.

On each day of the hearing, a new bombshell was dropped. One of the most shocking was when Pina alleged that Patrizia's mother Silvana had also been involved in the conspiracy and had herself attempted another method of doing away with her son-in-law, but that plot had fallen through because of the cost involved. Silvana vigorously denied the accusations and quite correctly nothing came of them.

When she took the stand, Silvana freely admitted that Patrizia talked openly about finding a killer for her husband, but that no one had taken her seriously. She also claimed that Pina was the strong force in the friendship and that the fortune-teller was able to manipulate her daughter into doing anything she wanted.

At the end of the six-month trial, Patrizia and all four accomplices were found guilty of murdering Maurizio. Patrizia was sentenced to 29 years' imprisonment (later commuted to 26 years), as was Cicala. Savioni received 26 years and Pina Auriemma 25. Only the actual killer, Ceraulo, was sentenced to life. It was unusual that the person who had ordered the killing received a shorter sentence than the man who had actually done the deed.

In 2004, after years of campaigning on their mother's behalf, Alessandra and Allegra won a retrial for Patrizia. Allegra had gone on to study law at university in an attempt to understand the case better and to clear her mother's name. She, her sister and grandmother have tirelessly campaigned for Patrizia's release, even taking the case to the European Court of Human Rights in Strasbourg. They have always insisted that she was innocent and eventually convinced the judge in Venice that the operation Patrizia underwent to remove a brain tumour in 1992 had fatally affected her judgement.

The Venetian court had been chosen to hear the appeal as it was considered to be neutral territory, whereas Milan, Florence or Rome all had too many connections with the Gucci family. There was no argument that Patrizia had wanted to kill her husband or that she had hired people to do the job. 'The only issue,' said the prosecutor, 'is whether the woman was in full possession of her mental faculties when she planned the killing of her husband.' A brain scan had apparently shown a cerebral lesion.

The Black Widow's time in prison is reasonably well documented. Although she was not allowed her jewellery, fur coats or designer clothes, her daughters and mother visited regularly, taking her gifts of luxurious face creams, cosmetics, magazines, underwear and silk nightclothes. I also heard that towards the end of her sentence she was allowed outside for day release and the occasional shopping expedition. Other concessions negotiated by her lawyer included keeping pot plants and, bizarrely, a pet ferret called Bambi, who sadly came to a sticky end when another inmate accidentally sat on it. It is reported that Patrizia doesn't like talking about her time in jail and that it 'feels like a bad dream'. She served 16 years of her sentence. Her early release in 2014 was due to 'good conduct' and health reasons. 'Remorse' has never been mentioned.

When we first learned of Maurizio's death, it seemed as if the dreadful killing was just one more tragic twist to the ongoing Gucci family saga.

Paolo was very shaken by his cousin's murder and feared for his own safety. Although he had never employed bodyguards as such, at his West Sussex home he certainly surrounded himself with some suspicious-looking 'estate workers' who wore tough expressions and appeared as if they would be prepared to carry out any order. Undoubtedly, he, too, had many enemies and, knowing how he treated Gemma and me after I dared to cross him, I can only surmise how he must have behaved in his business life.

When we were both actively involved in Gucci, I was still very much in love with my husband and always saw any of the family rifts and rivalries from his perspective. It seemed then as if all the family were against him, but I know now how difficult and irrational he could be. I think I was the only person who had ever challenged either Paolo's or his father's behaviour. No one else had ever dared to. Paolo could never believe how I was prepared to stand up to him, how I refused to be bullied by him, or how, when I chose my battles, I could be cold, clever and calculating. He had been totally shocked to learn that Deirdre and I were working as a team against him; he never got over it.

During our marriage, Paolo had been fabulous to my family and especially kind to my parents, but that was in another period. Whatever virtues he might have had, he lost them all when he hurt those helpless horses. It was as if his brutal, spiteful side had completely taken over.

Despite everything, it was clear to me that he could still be charming and almost mesmerise people if he chose to turn it on. Deirdre had fallen under his spell and probably that is what had happened to Penny, too. How else can you explain how someone who was a professional horsewoman could have become caught up in something as despicable as that which had occurred at the Rusper stud? These were horses she had known and cared for. I believe that some of the stable girls, both on the upstate farms and in England, were also in some way swept away by his charisma. But, my goodness, when they saw the light, they turned on him with a vengeance. I thought some of the American stable girls might rip him apart! Many at Yorktown Heights later apologised to me and came round to my side.

At Normans, too, I also had a pocket of support, which prompted a tirade of abuse from Paolo. 'Look, what you've done now, you *stronza*!' He was literally screaming down the transatlantic phone line.

Often, when he called these days, I would hang up, but today, I tried the rational approach. 'What are you talking about, Paolo?' I asked tiredly. 'All I've ever tried to do is get you to pay for your daughter and give me what you owe me…'

But he wasn't listening. 'You've burgled the place. You've stolen all Penny's jewellery and you've taken my father's gold watch!'

'Me? Don't be ridiculous!'

'Yes, it was you…you set it up.'

'You're an idiot! Why would I do that?'

'Because you need the money.'

'Well, you've got money,' I pointed out.

He didn't deny it.

'Paolo, if you've been burgled, call the police and get them to take fingerprints.' It seemed the sensible approach. 'You really are an idiot…but at least you make me laugh,' I added as an afterthought.

'You will see who will have the last laugh.' As usual, he couldn't resist resorting to a threat as a conversation-stopper.

The police were called and it turned out to be one of the decorators who had always had a soft spot for Gemma and me. The West Sussex estate, being so large, needed a care-taking team permanently employed for its upkeep. Apparently, the decorator had climbed a drainpipe and stolen only personal items as a way of making Paolo and Penny suffer for what they had done to us.

After that outburst from Paolo and a few more conversations about Maurizio's murder, things went quiet. I wasn't especially concerned because these long silences had happened before. Usually, they were his way of avoiding Judge Phyllis who, on this occasion, ordered him to appear in the Manhattan court to make a deposition. A message came back from Paolo's legal team saying that their client was too ill to travel. To be honest, I didn't believe it – I thought it was once again just another ploy to get out of paying me what he owed. It was highly likely that he would face another spell behind bars for further contempt. I was mentally exhausted by the years of psychological warfare and I just wanted some peace and quiet.

Gemma and I took advantage of Paolo's absence to spend more time at Yorktown Heights. By avoiding the adjacent farm and stable yard that was now empty and abandoned, we were able to relax there and enjoy the company of the friends who came to stay. Could it be that Paolo was also finally tired of it all and that, after seven years, we might at last be close to reaching a settlement? It had, after all, been several months since I had needed the services of my friend the locksmith.

I had been advised to change my New York lawyers. Apparently, this often happens in protracted cases. Lenny Spielberg and Kevin Harrington, my new legal team, found it difficult to believe everything that had happened, but they appeared cautiously optimistic that the end might be in sight. Meanwhile, Paolo's US bankruptcy lawyers continued to hover in the distance.

Whenever the suggested share-out of properties had been mentioned, I had previously staked my claim on the Metropolitan Towers apartment, but recently a business friend had advised me that Yorktown Heights would be a better bet. I was also hoping for $5 million dollars in cash from Paolo's $40 million fortune. This didn't seem unreasonable.

It felt like the right time to approach Paolo directly and to speak to him face to face. I felt sure that by now, and with Penny and two young children in his life, he might be more amenable. I decided to go to Rusper unannounced and confront him. It would also be an ideal opportunity to pick up a few possessions from the house and to see my parents again after about eighteen months.

It felt strange as the plane touched down at Heathrow on 10 October 1995 to know that I would be setting foot on English soil for the first time in six years. For all that time, I had never dared to travel outside the States, terrified that if Paolo heard that I had left New York, he would seize the Metropolitan Towers apartment and once more get me banned from Yorktown Heights. I doubted whether I had enough strength left to continue that struggle. I couldn't bear the thought of again resorting to getting a police escort each weekend to visit the farm. I shuddered – not from the chilly, early-morning English autumn wind – but at the prospect of being homeless.

In the taxi to the hotel, I was running over in my head the conversation I would have with Paolo and wondering whether it would be an advantage if Penny was also around for the discussion. I knew, from my sister's network of friends in the village, that both were in residence at Normans. I had also heard disturbing rumours that Paolo was unwell and even that he was on a waiting list for a liver transplant. Someone had spotted him a few days before wandering aimlessly through the country lanes, looking lost and dishevelled and talking nonsense to himself. It might sound callous, but I really didn't feel sympathy for him. I reminded myself of the 14 years I had looked after him and reckoned that it was Penny's turn now.

I just felt terribly tired. Once in my hotel room, I threw my suitcase on the bed and started to run a bath. When the phone rang seconds later, I felt a now-familiar sick sensation of premonition. Only my lawyer, my sister Sue, Gemma and Angelina the au pair, had the number of the hotel. Warily, I picked up the receiver, dreading another bombshell. It was my lawyer, Lenny Spielberg, who broke the news.

'Jenny,' he said gently, 'Paolo died an hour ago.'

What? It wasn't possible. How could this happen now, when we were on the point of resolving everything? What had he died from? I wanted details and Lenny said he'd call back as soon as he had more information.

I dropped the phone and collapsed on the floor and cried and cried until there were no more tears left. I cried from exasperation, frustration, anger, sadness – from every emotion. I sobbed as the whole of our life together flashed before my eyes. I remembered the happy times we had shared and, most of all, I cried for everything that had gone so bitterly wrong and all the suffering he had caused. He had thought that I would fold, but I hadn't – I had stayed the course and fought and fought to the end. I had built a wonderful support team of friends around me, but in a moment of clarity, I realised that, although I had survived, neither of us would turn out to be the winner.

I curled up and continued to cry inconsolably. How extraordinary, I thought, that Paolo had died just as I was setting foot in England to see him, both of us losing that final opportunity to make our peace.

And then it was over and I never cried for Paolo again. I poured myself a large vodka and tonic from the mini-bar and took a gulp of the refreshing drink. It tasted wonderful and I felt an overwhelming sensation of relief flooding through me.

My next thought was for Gemma. Once again, I had to tell her the news before she saw it on the television. I called her godfather, my old friend Ed Gold, and asked him to collect her from school and sit with her. But Angelina had already told her about Paolo's death. She been a little tearful but, on seeing her uncle Ed, she'd suggested going for a burger at Planet Hollywood.

'It's very sad, I feel a little sad,' she said, 'but I'm OK. I didn't really know Daddy very well,' she explained to her godfather, who later told me that she had been very cool and composed. In fact, it had been two years since Gemma had last seen her father and had always insisted that he had not been like her daddy for a long time.

'I want to say one thing about Daddy,' she later told her godfather through a mouthful of burger. 'I know I must speak to Mummy about it, but I don't want to go to his funeral. Please don't make me go.'

When I heard this, I resolved that there was no way that I would put her through that. For years, Paolo had done nothing for his daughter – friends had paid for her education and even her medical bills, not that she knew that. Damn right she wouldn't have to experience what would undoubtedly turn out to be yet another mega-media circus!

The funeral was held in Horsham's Roman Catholic Church and Paolo's body was later taken to Florence where it was interred in the Gucci family crypt. He was to lie next to his mother, Olwen, who had died just two months earlier.

Clive Limpkin, an old friend from my ex-husband's Fleet Street days, came to the rescue and when he told me that seven different press centres had been set up throughout the village waiting for my arrival, I knew I had made the right decision to stay away. The situation was especially bizarre when I discovered that, three weeks before his death, Paolo had travelled to Italy and stayed with his ex-wife Yvonne and daughters Lisabetta and Patrizia. He had apparently wanted to make his peace with them and I was saddened that, if he had known that he was dying, he hadn't offered the same closure to Gemma and me.

I was also sorry that I wouldn't be able to talk to Paolo's daughters. I still feel a great deal of affection for them both and I suspect that they never knew how often I intervened with their father on their behalf. There were cars and holidays that neither would have had if I hadn't screamed at Paolo to be more generous with them. The last time I had been to Rusper, before my exile, Lisabetta was broke and had also been staying with her two children. The weather had been cold and they hadn't any warm clothes. One of my last shopping expeditions with Paolo's credit card had been to buy winter clothes – coats and boots – for Olympia and little Cosimo.

Yvonne, Lisabetta and Patrizia had chosen to come to England for the funeral. Amazingly, they had decided to stay with Penny and her children (two-year-old Alyssa and Gabrielle, their three-month-old baby) at Normans. *The Sun, News of the World, Express* and *Telegraph*, as well as various news agencies, were all there to cover the story and I could only imagine how much extra spice would have been added to their stories – of the WIFE VERSUS MISTRESS variety – had I turned up as well. The mourners' line-up of ex-wife, mistress and various children – from adults to babies – was quite unusual enough without Gemma and me. When journalists asked me why I had chosen not to pay my last respects to my husband, I said that I felt it would have been hypocritical to do so.

'My marriage is finished,' I was quoted as saying. 'Paolo Gucci is out of my life. There will be no "last respects" because he clearly didn't respect me,' I pointed out. I was later told that the turn-out at the funeral had been tragically small – less than a dozen, apparently. The mourners were well outnumbered by the press corps.

Gemma had been amazingly brave and sensible about it all but had refused to meet up with her father's other 'babies' and clearly wanted to remember Paolo as he had been during happier times.

Even in death, Paolo left an exceedingly complicated mess behind him – he died intestate.

I remember some years previously discussing his legal affairs and being amazed to discover that he had never made a Will. 'You really should make a Will,' I had gently suggested.

'F**k off,' he told me ungraciously. 'Nobody gets nothing when I'm gone. I don't care what happens after I'm dead!'

But, of course, a lot of other people did care. Paolo Gucci had been worth an estimated £30 million when he died – despite claiming to be bankrupt and not having enough money even to buy a pint of milk, according to a feature on Penny in *Hello!* magazine a few months later. Most of his money was hidden away in secret Swiss bank accounts and his properties were in the names of obscure offshore companies.

Meanwhile, the American bankruptcy lawyers were edging ever closer to getting hold of whatever they could salvage from Paolo's estate.

23

The Gucci Wars

Paolo had died of liver failure at St George's Hospital in Tooting.

After going to Brixton to pick up his death certificate, I stayed on for a few days to see my parents. It was something of a cloak-and-dagger affair as the press were looking for me. Clive Limpkin reported that they were camped out with their telescopic lenses under hedgerows near Normans and some had already called my mother asking where I was. I had chosen to make my base in a small hotel just a few miles away and decided to lie low and not give any interviews before heading back to New York.

On the return flight, my thoughts and concerns were very different from the outward journey. Then I had had hopes of being able to persuade Paolo to see reason. My situation might have been precarious, but heaven alone knew what I would have to face now.

I wasn't sure where the bankruptcy lawyers would hit first, but strongly suspected that I would be forced out of the Metropolitan Towers apartment. Paolo dying intestate while still technically 'bankrupt' was the worst possible scenario. I knew that the future would be hellish but there wasn't much more that I could do but sit back and wait and see what would happen next.

I decided there was one course of action I could take on my own: two months after Paolo died, I returned unannounced to Normans to collect some things. I couldn't help but notice that the place was looking decidedly shabby. Without a full-time staff, the splendid Tudor manor house and surroundings were quickly falling into disrepair. The outdoor swimming pool was filled with green, brackish water and was far more inviting to the millions of insects that had made it their home than to any would-be swimmer. The garden furniture looked dirty and the sparkling pool parties we had held there seemed a lifetime ago. The once immaculate garden where we had hosted Gemma's christening party when she was four years old was now overgrown and weeds were sprouting along the drive to the main house.

Penny was inside, reading a newspaper in the kitchen. She didn't look up when I went in. I noticed that she'd cut her hair.

'Stop reading the paper and burying your head in the sand – you've got to listen to me! Look what he's done to you.'

Still no response…she barely moved. The short, red curls remained in place and I could see the back of her pale neck.

I tried again. 'You've got two lovely children, Penny, but look what he's done to you!'

She appeared broken and I saw that her hands were shaking. I realised she was afraid of me.

'Look what's happening,' I said firmly.

In fact, we didn't really know what was happening. It was all such a mess and I imagine Penny had no idea when or if she would

Relaxing in Marbella – life was more settled in Spain, but there was still one more battle to face.

275

be thrown out of the house. Other plans for selling or developing the stable yard had been voiced.

'I've come here to get some stuff,' I explained to the back of her head.

She looked up and I noticed the dark rings under her eyes. She looked older than 26.

'Yes, take what you want,' she said in a small voice.

I went over to the safe and opened it – all the silver inside had gone. I went back to the kitchen.

'Penny, I am very tired and very angry. You are lucky I haven't thrown you out on your ear.' I was reminded how swiftly Patrizia had moved against Paola after Maurizio's murder. One of the New York bankruptcy lawyers had felt sorry for Penny, homeless with two small children, and facing criminal charges of animal cruelty. 'I think I've been very patient and now you are going to help me. Then I, in turn, can help you.'

Something seemed to click and her demeanour changed. 'How can I help?'

We started by retrieving some of Gemma's precious toys. Little Alyssa went running off to help – she knew where they were all kept and volunteered to bring them. She was very sweet and later came down in her tutu and danced for me.

When Penny could see that I wasn't a threat, I asked her how she had got herself in this predicament. 'You really are a stupid girl,' I told her.

She couldn't say anything.

'Let's be honest, he's left you without a penny, Penny!'

She agreed. 'Um, I know,' she said.

'Stick with me,' I suggested, 'and you might get something – on your own, you won't.'

My British lawyer who had come with me thought I'd handled things particularly well. 'Well done, Jen – you were marvellous,' he told me later.

We had a large van parked in the yard and the removal men – who all knew the story – were great, encouraging me to take certain things. I wasn't sure what I was allowed to remove and what had to be held back for auction by the bankruptcy lawyers. My New York lawyers, who ruled my life, recommended caution. I should only take what I could prove was rightfully mine, they said. I listened to them. Many of the valuable antiques had already gone and others – like the collection of 12th-century religious paintings Paolo had had lovingly restored in Italy – had been allocated for the Sotheby's auction to pay off Paolo's debts. If I had had my time again, I would have kicked the door down and cleared the house and then faced the consequences.

I took some paintings, china and silver and then looked around Normans one last time. In Gemma's bedroom I had felt slightly chocked but for the rest... I hated it. I had no sentimentality for the place and thought that if the lawyers could ever prove ownership, let them have it! I just wanted to get out and away from there as quickly as possible.

I don't know whether or not the deeds were ever found – if the property was in the name of a Liberian company, you would have had to have gone to Liberia to track them down. Or perhaps they were in a safety deposit box in Lugano... I don't know. One way or another, the bankruptcy lawyers found a way and the estate was sold. I believe it made £2.5 million. The contents were auctioned by Sotheby's for a reported £11 million.

As expected, the Metropolitan Towers was also grabbed by the bankruptcy lawyers. I was given $7,000 to help pay for my move. Gemma was still at school and we had to stay in New York, at least until she finished her education there. I found a lovely, two-bedroom apartment across the road. With a rent of $4,000 a month, I knew it would be tight, but I had very little choice. The move itself cost a staggering $8,000. As always, money was a constant worry.

In 1996, I was finally allowed to sell the Yorktown Heights estate. It was costing me almost $4,000 a month just to run it, and I had begged unsuccessfully to be allowed to put it on the market sooner. I had been excited to hear that some people from the CIA had been round, examining the place with a fine tooth-comb. Rumour had it that Bill and Hillary Clinton had been interested in buying it but, unfortunately, it had failed to come up to their high-security requirements.

Once the sale had gone through, I had to pay $235,000 in back taxes and over $400,000 for the lawyers. When all my debts had been paid off, I was left with $350,000 in the bank.

In November 1996, my late husband's battles with the Gucci business were finally put to rest when the bankruptcy court approved the sale of the rights to use the name 'Paolo Gucci' to the main Guccio Gucci company for $3.7 million. It still seemed amazing that this was the end of a fight my husband had fought all his life. When he had won one of the battles in the war – by at last opening his own New York store in his name – he had closed the successful business a few short weeks later as a way of 'proving' he had no assets to back up his bankruptcy claim. It was a horribly sad tribute.

Over the years, I had spent approximately $1.3 million on lawyers' fees. It was an astronomical amount and it has to be asked: were they worth it? How would I have managed without any lawyers at all?

I believe that, even with Judge Phyllis and right on my side, I would have been left destitute. I am confident that Paolo would have had me thrown out on the streets as he had frequently threatened. I am not certain if the same fate would have awaited Gemma – probably, he would have

Through it all, I have always had my love of music.

taken her to live with him. Of course, I would never have allowed that to happen.

I had no choice but to fight him and I needed lawyers for the war. I believe that, in New York, I had chosen the best battleground. My daughter is an American citizen and I was happy there. Surely I was entitled to some happiness?

It was strangely liberating to be in charge of my life again. For the past seven years, my every move and decision had been governed by the lawyers; and here I was, at last, an independent woman. I might have only had a couple of hundred thousand in the bank, but what was there was mine. It was a heady feeling to know that, at last, I had won back my freedom. Although it was a huge relief, I also recognised that I was totally exhausted.

On the outside, I was still 'good old Jen', always up for a laugh and ready with a smile and a joke, but inside I felt pummelled, battered and bruised. It would take until around 2001 for me to feel human again.

In the meantime, life moved on. I continued to have a good social life with a loyal and supportive circle of friends and plenty of admirers, too. I had an eight-year relationship with a musician who I met when I got a part in the New Jersey State Opera. He was very good with Gemma, but we were great friends rather than compatible lovers and, eventually, decided to go our separate ways. Maybe it has been my fault, as I haven't really managed to be in love with anyone since Paolo. For a long time, I felt as if I had nothing left to give to a new relationship and would turn down offers of dates.

Being mistress of my own destiny might have been a new and heady experience, but it didn't pay the bills. I had to take a long, hard look at my options. Without a Green Card, I could never get a salaried job in the United States. So where did that leave me? I had a big decision to make. Reluctantly, I acknowledged that I could no longer afford to live in my beloved New York. Facing this harsh reality was softened somewhat when I happened upon Marbella in the South of Spain. I had spent a lovely holiday staying there with friends, and when they contacted me later to let me know that some new houses were being built in a nearby luxury development with views of the iconic La Concha mountain – I knew I'd found my next home. I moved into the house in 2002, and two months later all my possessions from the New York apartment arrived via an enormous 18-wheel truck. This was just what I needed – a fresh beginning.

Alongside giving singing classes, I had lots of business ideas bubbling away. According to my friends, I had enviable good taste and an eye for glamour. All the years working alongside Paolo had taught me a lot about designing and PR and I was approached to put together a line of silver jewellery with semi-precious stones. I trod carefully around the delicate area of using my name and disclaimers were printed on the labels of the finished items. I veered away from including watches or anything that could be confused with the Gucci brand. The line was beautiful and sold well throughout Europe via the Home Shopping Network.

But that was as far as I got…all the planned projects were stopped in their tracks when Gucci Incorporated succeeded in an action against me. Apparently their lawyers were able to convince a judge that I was not a proper designer, but merely cashing in on the Gucci name – despite the fact that all my products carried the caveat that they were not in anyway associated with Gucci Incorporated. It was devastating news. I had so enjoyed working alongside an American home furnishing company to produce a beautiful Renaissance/Florentine style line of bed linen and bathroom accessories; and I had been looking forward to launching a skincare range which was to be made in Israel. But everything was finally stopped in 2007 when I was accused of 'diluting the Gucci brand' and was made the subject of a Temporary Restraining Order which prohibited me from using my name on any merchandise in the U.S. It was a bitter pill to swallow and, although I tried to contest the ruling, it was always going to be a David versus Goliath struggle but with a non-biblical outcome. I will never forget the phrase that was used by their legal team in the LA courtroom: 'however long it takes, we will outspend and bankrupt her.'

Paolo had always used the epithet 'bloody' when referring to lawyers and I couldn't help but agree with him. I had to acknowledge that it wouldn't take long to either outspend or bankrupt me. By this stage, I only had a few hundred euros to my name and as for bankruptcy… Paolo had clearly shown how easily that state can be achieved.

Sometime before I had given up on the dream of unearthing my husband's missing millions. Having previously convinced myself that at least some of Paolo's vast fortune must be hidden away somewhere, I had hired (on a contingency basis) a private investigator to search for it. However, we were both advised that, even if the cache was discovered and despite the time lapse, any money found would have to be spent paying off creditors and Paolo's bankruptcy. So the thrill of discovering a possible treasure trove in some faraway vault was thwarted. Paolo had taken the secret of the hiding place to his grave, and that's where it will have to stay.

The new legal struggles about using my name and their financial implications cast a shadow over what was, otherwise, a happy period of my life. I made new friends and also enjoyed my home and simply breathing in the clean Mediterranean air as well as working in my garden. As always I found solace in my music – it really is the best therapy – and I enjoyed performing at several Costa del Sol concerts. You can't be modest and perform opera in front of an audience. You have to have an ego and I believe that it has always been the strength of my inner *diva* that has kept me going through difficult times. I have also surprised myself by discovering that I am a good and patient teacher. I was fortunate enough to learn from some of the best voice coaches in the world and I enjoy passing their methods on to my students.

But as the legal arguments across the Atlantic dragged on, I was overwhelmed by a sense of *déjà vu* as I was constantly reminded of Paolo's endless fights with Aldo to be able to use his name and produce his own 'Paolo Gucci' line. There was a definite sense of history repeating itself. From the moment I met Paolo until a considerable time after his death, I don't think a single day passed without some intrusion from a lawyer.

With hindsight, and now knowing how much the lawyers would cost and how it would drag on and on for years, I should have re-thought the whole divorce process. In the early days, the lawyers had suggested that he pay me a one-off settlement of $7 million. No property, just a financial settlement. If we had been able to negotiate from there, everything might have been so different. But, apparently, he tore up the papers and threw them into the air, swearing at me in disgust.

I don't ever regret marrying Paolo. It was absolutely marvellous being Mrs Gucci! There were no drawbacks at all. I enjoyed every moment of it – the travel, the servants, the parties, everything. I loved my husband deeply and, for ten years or so, I was blissfully happy. At the beginning he had been a wonderful, warm and kind man. Our relationship only started to change soon after Gemma was born. It was as if, as 'mother of his child' – rather than his 'mistress' – he lost interest in me. He needed the excitement of an affair and maybe, if he had been discreet and continued to be caring towards me, I would have been able to turn a blind eye, but instead he flaunted his girlfriends. Then, after he sold out, his personality further changed as he became unbearably callous and cruel.

Paolo might have been the key player in bringing down the Gucci family dynasty by causing mayhem and then being the first of the family to sell out, but I am made of sterner stuff. Perhaps he thought that by declaring himself bankrupt and then dying without making provision for his wife and children, he was having the last laugh. But clearly that wasn't so. Paolo Gucci was the ultimate loser. He died at the age of 64 a confused, bitter and unhappy man, poisoned not only by his liver, but also from his twisted mind. Meanwhile, I – Jenny Gucci – have survived to fight another day, and I still had one more battle to face...

24

Full Circle

It was the last thing I had expected to find when I returned to my Marbella home on a cool December afternoon in 2013. I had been to the inland village of Benahavis for a light *tapas* lunch with my friend Penny and was looking forward to putting my feet up for a *siesta* as I wasn't feeling 100% – I was recovering from a cold which had developed into bronchitis. I parked my car in the street outside the gated community, walking in through my little garden and put the key in my front door lock…but it wouldn't turn.

Memories of the locksmiths' visits to Yorktown Heights were accompanied by a dreadful cold, sinking sensation. I noticed a barely legible notice pinned to the door. My stomach turned over and my knees buckled beneath me as the implications of the words sank in. It said that I was not allowed into the property under any circumstances and there was a number to call for further details. A couple of deep breaths later I rang the number and discovered it belonged to a legal practice – more bloody lawyers – and I was told, in English, the same message as on the door. I was forbidden from entering the property.

Yes, it was a dreadful shock but as I began to absorb the facts of what had happened a sensation of calm enveloped me. This could be my route out, this could be my escape, it might enable me to go home – my real home – back to London. Although I had been content in Marbella, there had always been the vulnerability that comes from not having a regular income.

The moment of calm acceptance was short-lived as the reality of my situation truly sank in: I was homeless and very angry. How dare they lock me out of my house not even allowing entry to pick up some basic necessities like my asthma inhaler, a toothbrush or even my passport. How dare they? I was furious and decided then and there that I had the strength for one more battle… I would break in.

The technicalities of the operation were actually very simple. A builder neighbour lent me a long ladder and I smashed an upstairs window with a brick and climbed through into my bedroom. Sitting on the edge of the bed, I used the inhaler and caught my breath before attempting to gather my thoughts. Yes, of course I was in shock but, to be completely honest, my house being seized by the bank hadn't come as a total surprise. I had, however, expected to receive some sort of warning letter following the delay of my mortgage repayments. But this was at the height of the financial crisis and many banks – including mine – were in trouble. Also, as I would later discover, someone wanted my house. I suspected that this was why I hadn't heard from the bank for 18 months – there had been no contact at all. Ironically, I had the money in the bank ready to pay the mortgage, but had been advised by a lawyer not to transfer it until the bank had reached their 'conclusion'. That 'conclusion', it would seem, was to take my house.

At 6.30 that evening I had an unannounced visitor. The tall and extremely good looking lawyer had a blunt message for me: "*Señora* Gucci you are not meant to be here."

He had made a big mistake if he thought that I would meekly obey.

"Don't you dare tell me what I can and can't do," I hadn't raised my voice – the threatening tone was enough.

"You are very lucky that I haven't called the police. My passport is here, and all my possessions *and* my medication… I feel I can't breathe…"

The implications were left hanging in the air between us.

He backed down first – as I knew he would. "Well you can't sleep here," was his parting shot. I packed a small suitcase and my friends who live nearby came to pick me up. Their spare room was my sanctuary for the next three weeks.

If there is one thing I have learned in life, it is that you should pick your battles and this one was definitely not worth the effort. Mentally, I had already drawn a line under my Marbella life – lovely as it had been. Let them take my house, I was not going to fight for it. I was still, and always would be, a city girl at heart and London was calling. It was time to go home.

Each day I would re-visit the house to pack up all my belongings. I had worked out a more convenient route to access the building by re-connecting the electricity to the underground garage door. When the house was cleared and the removal van had left, my dear friend Francis Butler came to pick me up for Christmas at his home in Cádiz.

As we drove off he said: "Don't look back, Jen. Forget it, you're never coming back here again".

In the New Year we all headed to London where I was to be a guest in Fran's Brook Green flat for the next four months. It was never intended to be such a long stay, but I was gazumped on my first choice of apartment, and it took a long time to settle on a second choice in Fulham. During this time especially, I will never forget Fran's kindness and generosity. Those who recall the magical Spanish evenings at his *Finca Besaya* restaurant will know Francis Butler as not only a consummate host, but also as a gifted singer with a theatrical presence and vast knowledge of classical music. We share a love of opera and I never tire of his company and his irrepressible sense of humour. Honestly, I don't know what I would have done without him.

I signed the lease on the Fulham flat on April 17th 2014. Although I have lived at some of the most prestigious addresses in New York – not to mention the the magnificent villa in Florence, vast Rusper estate and Yorktown Heights – I can report that I don't think I've ever been happier than in my small Fulham flat. This was a welcome healing period when

I could quietly relish my independence. A few singing students slightly augment my pension income and, I am able to live within my means, enjoying the relief that comes from not having any debts. Crucially, for the first time, there are *no* lawyers in my life.

Am I scarred by the past? Physically, possibly.

Recently a painful right knee led me to an appointment at the Chelsea and Westminster Hospital. I was told that I have osteoarthritis. This wasn't genetic so, what could have caused it?

"I suppose this means, no more high heels," I asked.

"Yes, that would do it."

"What about walking for eight years on the cobbled streets of Florence in stilettos?"

"Yes that would 100% do it," I was told.

Unfortunately, a nasty bout of COVID at the start of the pandemic has also left its unwelcome legacy in the form of lasting damage to my lungs. I am still struggling to come to terms with the fact that, without the necessary breath control, my singing days are now over. Throughout

With my dear friend, Francis Butler.

my life, music has been the one constant – it has kept me grounded and it has always been my loyal therapist. These days, I cannot listen to certain operas – my favourite arias which were once in my repertoire – without feeling incredibly sad. It's just too painful to hear them sung, however beautifully, by someone else. At the moment the loss of my singing voice is very raw, but maybe with time...

Although I might be physically scarred by what has happened, I am not scared of it, or of whatever the future holds. Having faced and overcome so many challenges in my life, nothing really frightens me any more: not even COVID.

In May this year I took the big step of moving from Fulham. Strangely enough this move – I hope my last – has brought me back to Maida Vale where my journey, as a newly married girl in the Swinging Sixties, began.

Packing up boxes for a house move always rekindles memories. In the old days, with Paolo, we rarely stayed anywhere for more than three weeks at a time – we were constantly commuting between London, New York and Florence – our Gucci luggage was always in use and I knew exactly what to pack for each trip. But house moves are very different – more visceral – you are forced to go right to the back of your wardrobe and have a thorough clear out.

I am often asked what happened to all my beautiful designer clothes. Most were given away over the years – like all the belts that I gave to the nanny when my shape changed after Gemma was born, and the scores of fabulous bags in every colour imaginable that I no longer have occasion to use. I have only kept one or two treasured items like a beautiful silk scarf with twenty or more colours in it that Paolo designed in the 1970s and a favourite, gorgeous handbag from the 1978 collection. I have a few classic silk shirts and one or two matching cashmere cardigans and that's about it.

For several years now, I have felt very differently about fur coats. When Paolo was buying them for me, it was before the days of People for the Ethical Treatment of Animals (PETA) and I – like so many people – wasn't aware of the cruelty involved in their production. Currently two of my furs are in a 'consignment store' (a second hand designer shop) in New

York, still waiting to be sold, another was made into the lining of a rain coat, while the full length mink was re-designed into a swing-style car coat. Would I ever wear them again? I don't know…possibly in New York or if I were to go skiing.

At the time of writing, I am busy unpacking boxes and settling into my new home. I know that I will be content here. There is a wonderful sense of familiarity about this area of Little Venice. It is just a five minute walk from where I lived all those years ago. On Maida Avenue, beside the canal with its barges and house boats, the memories of taking Wellington and Boots for their walks are as vivid as if it were yesterday. I can even point out all the trees where they would cock their little legs. It is as if my life has come full circle…back to where it all started. If I were searching for closure, then I have found it.

Epilogue

It began when I read (in the New York Times) that Sir Ridley Scott was going to make a film called *House of Gucci*. I found it unsettling as for years I hadn't thought about the past, and here I was being catapulted back in time. As I allowed the waves of nostalgia to wash over me, I became aware of his presence... Paolo was with me. There he was – so clearly – by my side in the kitchen of my Fulham flat, as I prepared a salad supper; and he stayed through the evening – on the sofa – as I watched television. I couldn't stop thinking about him, so it wasn't surprising that I should dream about him that night. I have had very few vivid dreams in my life and this was to be one of them. Such dreams are also known as lucid dreams – when all your senses are heightened to beyond reality levels. Whatever it was called, the memory and every tiny detail remained with me for days afterwards...

I walked in to my favourite restaurant in the world – Il Cigno, (the swan) in Mantua, Italy. I wasn't young but carried the confidence of someone who knows they're looking their best. My make up was perfectly applied, my hair well-groomed, I was carrying a Hermès bag, and wearing a beautiful beige-grey, full length fur coat because it was very cold outside.

Paolo was sitting at the end of a long table with a group of about ten young Italians who, my subconscious dismissed, as 'unimportant' and blurred them out of focus.

My companion turned to me, "Oh my goodness, look who's sitting over there."

I felt easy and comfortable seeing him again. "Oh well," I said, "It's been so many years, I will go over and speak to him."

He looked healthy and very handsome.

"Well, hello," he said, in a warm and welcoming manner.

"Hello, Paolo."

"What are you doing here?"

"I'm with my friends for lunch," I explained. He nodded acknowledgement in their direction.

"Look Paolo," I continued, "so much could be said…" here I put my hand on his, which he lifted from the table to return my grasp. His skin felt warm and dry.

I looked into his familiar eyes, "Look, I forgive you".

He had tears running down his face as he whispered, "Thank you, thank you".

The moment passed, I realised that I was hungry, and so I turned and left.

I remember draping my coat over the back of a chair and sitting down before saying to my friends: "Get me a drink!"

It had all felt so real that when I woke up I had to shake myself out of it.

In reality, I had forgiven him years ago – he was and always would be the father of my wonderful Gemma.

The sensation of the dream had left me with the comforting feeling that, although it had been really nice to see him, I was also relieved to walk away.

I was in a good place. I had peace and tranquility and I don't need much else these days. All I want is to be able to spend time with my daughter, son-in-law and gorgeous grandson.

I am, at last, content.

London, June 2021

Lightning Source UK Ltd.
Milton Keynes UK
UKHW010119031121
393296UK00001B/115